THE NEW COMPLETE

KEESHOND

by Carol and Ron Cash

Illustrated by Mary Alice Smiley

First Edition

BOOK HOUSE
New York

Howell Book House
Macmillan Publishing Company
866 Third Avenue, New York, NY 10022

Collier Macmillan Canada, Inc.
1200 Eglinton Avenue East, Suite 200
Don Mills, Ontario M3C 3N1

Library of Congress Cataloging-in-Publication Data

Cash, Carol.
   The new complete Keeshond.

   Bibliography: p. 304.
   1. Keeshonds.   I. Cash, Ron.   II. Title.
SF429.K4C37   1987   636.7′2   87-3881
ISBN 0-87605-199-9

Macmillan books are available at special discounts for bulk purchases for sales promotions, premiums, fund-raising, or educational use. For details, contact:

> Special Sales Director
> Macmillan Publishing Company
> 866 Third Avenue
> New York, NY 10022

10   9   8   7   6

Printed in the United States of America

To the Memory of Eloise Geiger —
Our mentor and our friend.

Contents

Foreword

THIS BOOK is an absolute mandatory purchase if you are considering buying a Keeshond, own a Keeshond as a pet, are an established Keeshond breeder, or if you are a serious student of the dog fancy in general. In my opinion, this book is THE definitive book on the Keeshond.

The Keeshond world desperately needed an accurate, up-to-date book on our breed. It has been 17 years since Mrs. J. Whitney (Clementine) Peterson's classic *The Complete Keeshond* was published by Howell Book House. Mrs. Peterson's research on the history of the Keeshond and very thorough knowledge of Keeshond *objets d'art* still cannot be topped.

Carol and Ron Cash have managed to pick up where Mrs. Peterson left off and then some! Here is a factual, responsible, information-packed book on the Keeshond—at last! Best of all, it's fun to read and not at all pedantic and plodding. These two books should be on every Keeshond lover's bookshelves cheek-by-jowl as companion pieces—the breed as it was nearly 20 years ago; the breed as it has evolved today.

Just who are the Cashs? Ron is a Police Captain with Cleveland State University Police, Carol is an Administrative Assistant/Sales with the General Electric Company. They also own their own phototypesetting business. Carol and Ron built their first home and they wanted just the right dog to share that special home. They found that special dog in the form of a Keeshond named *Car-Ron's Akela Frost Bear*. He was perfect for them as a pet and THEN one fateful day the Cashs discovered dog shows. Akela won a ribbon and the rest, as "they" say, is history.

Akela soon became a champion and the Cashs were hooked on Keeshonds, dog shows, and the camaraderie that makes up the dog show world. Knowing that Akela's show quality was a lucky accident, the Cashs decided their next Keeshond should come from a more illustrious background. *Wistonia Warbonnet* was shipped to them from the famous Wistonia Kennels of Nan Greenwood in California.

Ron and Carol joined the Buckeye Keeshond Club and became instantly active. Since 1975, one or both of them has served until recently as an officer, including several terms as president. They also joined the Keeshond Club of America in 1975. In the meantime, they added a few more furry friends to their household: Two more male Keeshonds and their foundation bitch, Ch. Fearless FanciFree of Car-Ron. The Cashs were now up to five Keeshonds. Fanci quickly became a champion and ended up being ranked the #2 Keeshond Show Bitch in the nation in 1978. That same year, Fanci's litter brother, Am. and Can. Ch. Fearless Focalpoint came for a visit and never left— the original "dog who came to dinner . . . "

In 1977, Ron and Carol (with the help of Debbie Dorony-Lynch) began publication of Keezette International as a forum for communication and education. Carol serves as Editor, Ron as Associate Editor and together they do the editing, typesetting, layout and publishing of Keezette. It is the breed's only magazine. I can only assume Ron and Carol must have been bored as at that point in time they had merely six dogs and four cats lolling around their home, were extremely active in their regional club, and both had full-time jobs.

In 1979 Ron and Carol became breeders of record when they bred their Fanci to Ch. Denwood's Gurney Halleck. Typically illogically, Ron and Carol kept four of Fanci's six puppies. (I am hoping for your sake by now, that your next door neighbors are nothing like Ron and Carol.) With the "pupulation explosion" bringing their household total to 11 dogs, you'd think that Ron and Carol might grow slightly disenchanted with the dog world.

Not so! In 1979 Ron served as Chairman and Carol as Show Secretary for the Keeshond Club of America National Specialty. Because this show was centrally located in Ohio and because Ron and Carol did such a bang-up job the Keeshond entry broke all records that year. There is so much work involved to chairing and managing a national specialty that we all began to think the Cashs had taken leave of what few senses they had left when they actually volunteered to have Carol again serve as Show Secretary for the 50th Anniversary National Specialty in 1985. Records are made to be broken so this gala event topped 650 Keeshonden! Ron, Carol and John Sawicki were responsible for 90% of the show's tremendous success.

While all of this was going on, somehow the Car-Ron Keeshond clan totaled 18 Keeshonden, most show dogs, all house pets! (Surely these folks bear no resemblance to your next door neighbors!)

In 1983 Ron Cash was nominated for a Dog Writer's Association of America award for his wonderful poem "The Slaven (with apologies to Edgar Allan Poe)." In this poem, Ron wistfully was attempting to remember what life was like pre dogs and pre dog-show activities. With the publication of this poem we all thought that Ron, at least, had found his wits. This thought proved to be a myth when it was RON who brought Rocky home—a stray Keeshond found wandering the streets of Cleveland.

7

Rocky brought the Keeshond head count to a bizarre 19 but received his niche in permanent doggy history when he was immortalized by Ron Cash and Ron was once again honored by DWAA for "The Stray," his story about Rocky.

In their "spare time" Ron and Carol have both judged all-breed matches, specialty matches and Sweepstakes classes held in conjunction with Specialty Shows. Every now and then they actually get a chance to get away and ride around in their leisure boat—don't ask me how or when because it's totally incomprehensible to me how the Cashs have time to sleep much less relax.

Why would Carol and Ron choose to undertake writing this book? It's quite evident by now that it's because they're crazy. Crazy, compulsive and dedicated. Atypical behavior in the "real" world, not so atypical behavior in the wacky, wonderful world of dogs. Who else is better qualified to write the excellent chapter on "Living With Your Keeshond" than a couple who have 19 house dogs? Who else is as acquainted with *all* the breeders in the country (if not the world!) as to be able to coordinate and edit the reams of pages and the hundreds of photos sent to them? Who else is insane enough to take on such a challenge?

All kidding aside, I am very proud to be able to present to the fancy the finest book yet written on the breed. I'm also very honored to have had the Cashs ask me to write this Foreword. I'm well-known for poking fun at dog shows dog people and the dog fancy in various published articles. However, there are a couple of things I do get serious about when it comes to doggy activities: One is the responsibility involved when it comes to breeding purebred dogs; the other is the responsibility of the printed word. Ron and Carol Cash have always been clever, gifted and *responsible* writers and editors. This latest effort on their part is a doozy and literally will be easy to recommend to anyone as a tome on "anything and everything you need to know about the Keeshond." Congratulations, Carol and Ron—again—on a job well done.

Now then, put a pot of coffee on the stove, sit down, take the phone off the hook, and read about the world's Keeshonds. Enjoy!

Robin Stark
Star-Kees' Keeshonden

Can. Ch. Shamrock's Finnian was bred by Shannon Kelly of California and is owned by Ross and Shirley Henderson of Keewinds Kennel in Canada.

Preface

THE BOOK you are holding is the culmination of two years of hard work — not only by these authors, but by the many people who helped us gather the information.

When we were asked by Mrs. Clementine Peterson and Howell Book House to author a sequel to the original classic, we knew it wouldn't be easy. We asked for help and we got it.

We thank the Keeshond fanciers around the world who sent us their priceless photos and who took the time to write about their lives and dogs.

Special thanks are also due Mary Alice Smiley, whose illustrations capture the true spirit of the Keeshond.

Our sincere thanks also extends to: Ellen Crewe for so capably presenting the chapters, Training Your Keeshond and The Keeshond in Obedience; to Jeanne Buente-Young for her easy-to-understand instructions on care and grooming which provide an excellent source of information for both novice and experienced owners; and to Rae LaPotin for sharing her thoughts and experiences on Pet Facilitated Therapy.

We also greatly appreciate the assistance of the following people in compiling data and photographs for their respective geographical areas: Gina Weedon—England, Mai Holmberg and Annika Perrson—Scandinavia (and Rondi Tyler for translating), Gwen Clark—New Zealand, and Karen Findlow-Australia. We would also like to thank Anthea deForest for her help and encouragement in the formulative stages of this book; Sandy Krueger for her suggestions and guidance; and Robin Stark for introducing this book with such a flourish.

Our most profound thanks, though, belong to Mrs. Clementine Peterson for having faith in our abilities, and to Howell Book House for giving us the honor of authoring this book.

Carol and Ron Cash

Please note that photographs of American-owned Keeshonds included in this book have generally met the following criteria, set by the authors, and based on American Kennel Club records:

Dogs having won multiple Groups or one or more Bests in Show
Bitches having won one or more Groups or Bests in Show
ROM or ROMX dogs
ROM or ROMX bitches
Hall of Fame dogs or bitches
Best in Show braces
Winners of Keeshond Club of America Specialties
Top ranking obedience performers
Other dogs of particular importance to the breed

In citing the show and producing records of noteworthy Keeshonds, we have employed the abbreviations in common usage by the dog fancy. For the uninitiated, we offer this glossary:

AKC	American Kennel Club
KCA	Keeshond Club of America
CC	Challenge Certificate
Ch.	Champion
BIS	Best in Show
BBIS	Best Brace in Show
GR1	First in Group. (The word Group is also used alone to indicate a First in Group.)
GR2, GR3, GR4	2nd in Group, 3rd in Group, 4th in Group. (The term Group placement as used in this book indicates a Group win other than First place.)
BOB	Best of Breed
BOS	Best of Opposite Sex to Best of Breed
WD	Winners Dog
WB	Winners Bitch
BOW	Best of Winners
RWD	Reserve Winners Dog
RWB	Reserve Winners Bitch
BIF	Best in Futurity Stakes
BOSIF	Best of Opposite Sex in Futurity
CD	Companion Dog Degree
CDX	Companion Dog Excellent Degree
UD	Utility Dog Degree
TD	Tracking Dog Degree
TDX	Tracking Dog Excellent Degree
OT Ch.	Obedience Trial Champion
ROM	Register of Merit (see Chapter 16 for details)
ROMX	Register of Merit Excellent (see Chapter 16)
HOF	Hall of Fame (see Chapter 16)

Youngsters should be encouraged to interact with their Kees. Here Jon Pierce and Keewicke Nero Wolf receive the trophy for Double Bests in Match at a benefit held in 1982. Jon was the youngest handler that day and, in succeeding years, has grown into an accomplished Junior Handler both in conformation and obedience. Presenter of the trophy is Zsa Zsa Gabor.

(Rich Bergman)

1

The Keeshond: Versatile Companion

***

BEFORE WE BEGIN this book on the Keeshond, everyone must learn to pronounce the two syllables of its name correctly. The first syllable, *Kees*, is a Dutch nickname for Cornelis or Cornelius. The story that ties the Keeshond's name to that of the Patriot Rebellion leader, Cornelius de Gyselaar, will be explored in Chapter 2. The second syllable, *hond*, means "dog" in Dutch and has no relationship to a hound. The suffix *en* (as in Keeshond*en*) is the Dutch plural and has generally been adopted; however, the Americanized "s" is also acceptable. For purposes of this book, we will generally utilize the more modern "s."

Keeshond is pronounced *caze-hawnd*. The easiest way to approximate the correct pronunciation is to remember the lyrics "and the *caissons* go rolling along . . . " Simply add a "d" at the end of "caisson" and you have it. The Americanized version of *keys-hawnd* is also generally accepted, provided you do not commit the cardinal sin of pronouncing the second syllable as "hound."

Now that you have learned how to correctly pronounce Keeshond, you are ready to learn about this versatile companion.

The Keeshond has long been known for its qualities as a family companion and watchdog. While most pet owners are justifiably proud of their animals, Keeshond owners exceed the norm in their enthusiasm for the breed. A well-groomed, happy Keeshond never fails to draw comments from strangers, and small children seem to sense that this is a dog they can approach without fear.

The American Kennel Club-approved Standard describes the Keeshond as a handsome dog of well-balanced, short-coupled body, attracting attention by his alert carriage and intelligent expression, luxurious coat and

The Keeshond is a long-lived dog and some never seem to age. Judge Bob-John Ellieff is shown presenting Ch. Car-Ron's Akela Frost Bear and owner, Carol Cash, with the rosette for oldest veteran (12½ years) in competition at the 1985 Keeshond Club of Canada National Specialty.

Congressman Whitehurst presents the trophy for BOB at the 1972 KCA National Specialty to Ch. Victory's the Patriot and Erik Williamson. Notice that it is Erik that receives the thanks and not the Congressman!

richly plumed tail well curled over his back. His head is a pleasing one with small, pointed ears, mounted high and carried erect, and distinctive spectacles surrounding small, dark eyes. His coat is thick around the neck, forepart of the shoulders and chest and resembles a lion-like mane. His rump and hindlegs are also thickly coated down to the hocks and form the characteristic "trousers" or "Dutchman's breeches." A Keeshond's silver to gray to black color and markings are added eye-catchers.

The Keeshond is a hardy dog that needs little trimming and minimal grooming. His coat is actually "fur," an attribute mainly found in breeds of northern origin. This type of coat consists of harsh, straight guard hairs, standing well out from a thick, downy undercoat. It is odorless, sheds water, seldom mats and is easily cared for. The coat also contributes to the breed's adaptability to various climates. (Incidentally, the soft undercoat is often hand-spun into knitting yarn and makes lovely hats, scarves, sweaters and blankets. Edith Smith of Heavenly Hondspun, Costa Mesa, California, herself a Keeshond owner, has created gorgeous items by combining Kees hair with other dyed yarns and ribbon.)

The officially approved coat color in England, Canada and the United States is a mixture of shadings of gray to black. In each dog, the coloration should range from palest gray or cream (not white) in the undercoat and on the legs, trousers and tail plume, to black on the tips of the guard hairs. The subtleties of these shadings create each dog's distinctive coloration.

In addition to the various shadings, the Keeshond can be found in a variety of colors abroad, including white, red, brown and black. However, in most of the world, the Standard specifically dictates that "any pronounced deviation from the gray color is not permissible."

The Standard states: "the ideal height of fully matured dogs (over two years), measured from top of withers to the ground, is: for males, 18 inches; bitches, 17 inches. Length of back from withers to rump should equal height." In other words, the Keeshond is a compact, medium-sized dog whose shoulder height is approximately an inch below that of the seat of the average straight chair. His size, coupled with his beauty, make him appealing to both men and women and particularly to children. He is also quite adaptable to modern living in either an apartment or home.

Affectionate and intelligent, the Keeshond has been bred for centuries as the ideal family companion and as a sensible watchdog. A Keeshond is not inclined to stray far from home and has no instincts as a hunter or guard dog. The Keeshond personality and temperament are unique and it is a credit to our breeders that, above all else, they have strived to maintain this in their breeding programs.

Kees give their love and devotion to all in the family and are eager to please. Although keenly alert and excellent alarm-givers, Kees are not attackers or "yappers." Once assured that the caller is welcome at their home, they quickly offer their friendship — sometimes a bit too overwhelmingly!

15

Maureen Clements of New Brunswick demonstrates the versatility of the Keeshond: her dogs are housepets, conformation and obedience champions, producers of champions and, as shown here, members of her sled team.

Since there are few barges to be found in the United States, today's Keeshond must look elsewhere. These two Keeshonds, owned by Jim and Judy Kamman of California, seem to have found the perfect solution.

16

Because of their even temperament, Keeshonds also have a reputation of amiability with other dogs. It is possible to add new dogs to your home or to bring a Keeshond in with existing pets with little or no adjustment period. Contrary to old wives' tales, Keeshonds and cats mix quite well and many Keeshond owners share their homes with both.

The Keeshond's instinctively clean personal habits also make him an ideal pet. They are easily housebroken, generally do not like to soil their living quarters, and keep themselves well groomed, licking their own paws and faces of their housemates much as a cat would. Their heredity as Dutch barge dogs carries through to the modern Keeshond. Owners who take their Kees on boats find that their dogs automatically go to the lee side to lift a leg by the railing and will leave their droppings in a sandbox placed on deck for this purpose.

Because of their intelligence, Keeshonds are not for everyone. Although eager to please and easily trainable, they do think for themselves. They must be given proper guidance early in life and not be allowed to become bored. If they have nothing to do, they will devise their own entertainment — and usually it will not be something to your liking. Discipline should never be harsh as the Keeshond has a gentle spirit. A humiliating scolding is a catastrophe to a Keeshond. For a severe infraction of the rules, we grasp the mane on either side and shake (obviously, not enough to rattle his teeth!), while emphasizing the words, "*No*, we don't *do* that!" This is a sufficiently harsh correction for most Keeshonds.

Because of his intelligence and striking appearance, the Keeshond has made his mark in both conformation and obedience competition. Unlike other show dogs, Keeshonds are generally both show dogs and housepets, sharing their lives in and out of the ring with their owner-trainer-handlers.

Because they lack many of the hereditary maladies that affect other breeds, Keeshonds are long-lived dogs. It is not unusual to see a show dog still actively competing at age seven or eight, and there are many instances of dogs living to 16 or 17 years of age. We share our household with quite a few veterans. Our first dog, Ch. Car-Ron's Akela Frost Bear, is now approaching 14 and still thinks he's a puppy. Our 12-year-old Ch. Wistonia Warbonnet races around the yard like a youngster. Am. and Can. Ch. Paladin's My-Oh-My Passionella, owned by Jack and Madeleine Nugent, still loves to show in Veteran competition at the amazing age of 17. Good care and lots of love will guarantee you a devoted companion for many years.

In addition to his obvious prowess as a housepet and show dog, the Keeshond is proving his worth on other fronts. In New England and California, Keeshonds are being used in Hearing Ear programs for the deaf. Because of their intelligence and great devotion, they are ideal companions for the deaf and are often solicited from Keeshond breeders. They are trained in basic obedience and sound response work. According to the

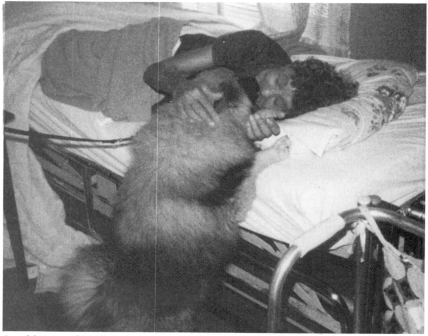

In addition to his obvious prowess as a housepet, the Keeshond is proving his worth as a companion to the ill and elderly. Doris Meadowcroft of Vermont takes her Keeshonds to visit area nursing homes where the dogs bring joy to the residents.

In her work at an outpatient psychiatric clinic, Rae LaPotin makes good use of her Keeshond, Lief.

director of the Hearing Ear Dog Program in Massachusetts, the Keeshond has just that "little bit of rascal . . . that makes a good Hearing Ear dog."

Keeshonds also make wonderful therapy dogs, whether it be giving love to residents of a nursing home who miss the warmth and devotion of a pet, or as a catalyst for communication in a psychologist's practice.

Many kennel clubs and individuals have established regular visits to local nursing homes with their pets. These visits can be rewarding for all concerned: they bring joy to the nursing home residents who often feel unwanted and unloved, they tug at the heart of the pet owner, and are excellent socialization for the dog. Keeshonds are particularly good therapists as they seem to sense when to play, and when to be gentle and loving. Doris Meadowcroft of Vermont regularly takes her Keeshonds — both adults and puppies — to the Linden Lodge Nursing Home nearby; their visits are a delight to the home's residents and staff.

Rae LaPotin of Oneonta, New York, takes her Keeshond, Lief, with her daily to her work in an outpatient psychiatric clinic. His upbeat, happy disposition is infectious and has raised the spirits of both staff and patients. The easy-going, extroverted, stable Keeshond temperament is vital for a working dog, whose adaptability enables him to adjust to many different people and situations. What Lief does at Rae's clinic — just by being there and being himself — is called Pet Facilitated Therapy (PFT). There are numerous types of programs utilizing many different animals. These PFT programs are reaching the emotionally disturbed, the developmentally and physically handicapped and the elderly. Rae has used Lief in many ways in the therapy program: as an obedience dog to demonstrate to one patient that he can control his own life and have something respond to him; to encourage an otherwise unresponsive man to communicate through Lief's constant attention and acceptance. Dogs never judge or criticize; a dog's love is constant, can be counted on to be there and is unconditional. A dog's perpetual child-like innocence and dependence can touch the ever-present "child" in all of us.

Eight characteristics — greeting behavior, ability to give undivided attention, nonjudgmental acceptance, consistency of unconditional positive regard, sensitivity and response to our feelings, emotional safety, easy relationship and ability to meet our emotional needs — make our canine friends the most powerful therapists in the animal kingdom. The Keeshond easily fits these descriptions.

The Keeshond's historical role in eighteenth-century Holland inspired the name, and the activities of English breeders in the twentieth century provided the impetus that led to the breed's being known and exhibited in its silver-to-gray-to-black shaded form as the Dutch Keeshond in much of the world, including Australia, Bermuda, Canada, Japan, Mexico, New Zealand, South Africa, South America, United States, Zimbawbwe and the Scandinavian countries.

Some of Colonel and Mrs. Wingfield Digby's Keeshonds. Sherborne Castle, Dorset.

Typical Wolfsspitz, Aus. & Germ. Ch. Max I, wh. 1896.

2

Early History of the Keeshond

THE STORY OF THE KEESHOND, as it comes down through the ages, is fascinating. He is an ancient breed, well known in some parts of the world, a newcomer in others and completely unheard of in still others. He has been a dog of the people and a dog of the nobility. His popularity made him famous as the national emblem of an eighteenth-century rebellious political party in Holland and, in turn, caused his near demise and relegation to semiobscurity.

Through the recorded findings of paleontologists, the history of the Keeshond has gradually emerged. The Keeshond has been traced back to fossil remains of *Canis Familiaris Palustris* of the Neolithic or Late Stone Age (5000 B.C.), found mainly in northern areas of the globe. The Keeshond is classed as a Spitz breed, along with the Samoyed, Siberian Husky, Alaskan Malamute, Chow Chow, Norwegian Elkhound, Pomeranian, German Wolfsspitz, etc. The Samoyed is widely credited on canine genealogical charts as being the first known progenitor of Spitz dogs and thus the direct ancestor of the Keeshond.

Based upon legends and lore, it is theorized that the Dutch Keeshond and his German counterpart originally came from the north on ancient water craft. Art objects found in these areas seem to attest to this fact. According to noted Dutch historian and writer George Masselman, ancestors of the Keeshond played a prominent role in the founding of Amsterdam. Indeed, the Great Seal of Amsterdam shows an ancient vessel with a Spitz-looking dog peering over the gunnels of the ship.

The preponderance of evidence indicates that the Keeshond of Holland and the Wolfsspitz of Germany are the same breed. Over a long period, several varieties of Spitz evolved in Germany, ranging in size and coloration

21

Eng. Ch. Ado von Thierlstein, imported from Germany by Mrs. Alice
Gatacre. *(Photo by Fall)*

Baroness Burton's Ch. Dochfour Hendrik, the
first British champion, 1929. (Hendrik van
Zaandam ex Ch. Gesina van Zaandam). Breeder,
Mrs. Digby.

from the Great White Spitz and Grosse Grau Wolfsspitz (large, gray, wolf-colored) to the smaller Pommer (Pomeranian Dog). In the late seventeenth and early eighteenth centuries, a largish White Spitz was raised in Pomerania and other provinces; black and brown varieties in Wurttemberg and elsewhere were used as sentries at vineyards, farmhouses and boats. In addition, the small Spitz (about 11-12 inches) became a popular housedog.

In 1899 German breeders formed the Verein fur Deutsche Spitz (German Spitz Club), a national organization that issued standards and established a stud book and rules governing registration.

Since early times, most barges, farms and carts have had a canine sentry, usually a Keeshond or whatever name he was given in the various countries. "Kees" ("Keezen") and "Spitz" are defined in very early Dutch and German dictionaries as "rabble," a possible indication of the prevalence of the breed in both countries.

Historical events in the Netherlands in the late 1700s, combined with the breed's popularity in that country, made the Keeshond internationally known in Europe. In about 1781, Holland was divided into two political factions: the Orangists who followed William of Orange, and the Patriots (or Keezen, as the pro-Orange men derisively called them). Cornelius de Gyselaar, who had one of these popular Spitz dogs as his constant companion, was a Patriot leader. Because "Kees" is a nickname in the Netherlands for Cornelius, it is believed to have formed the basis for the breed's name. "Kees" de Gyselaar's "hond" became the emblem of the Dutch Patriot party and the breed name was born.

Although not officially the national dog of Holland, the Keeshond did become the symbol of the rebels. When the rebellion was lost, many Kees were destroyed to disavow any connection with the defeated rebel party. Although some barge captains and farmers retained their dogs, it was more than a century later before the Keeshond again came to public attention.

The resurrection of the Keeshond in Holland is generally credited to Miss J. G. Van der Blom, who was actively connected with the breed in Holland, Germany and England and — much later — to Baroness van Hardenbroek van de Kleine Lindt, who showed her first Keeshond in 1891 in Amsterdam.

Breeding stock was imported from England and, in 1907, Keeshonds were divided into English and German-Dutch types in Dutch shows. The next year a standard of points was derived. In 1924 the Nederlandse Keeshond Club was established.

Baroness van Hardenbroek was also an early leader of the Dutch opposition to the persistent German efforts to have the Keeshond in Holland officially named German Spitz. Over the years, many other Dutch breeders contributed much to the breed's progress. Notable among them was Mrs. Alice Gatacre. After her marriage, Mrs. Gatacre became a resident of England — and Holland's loss became Britain's gain.

Ch. Vanderveer of Vorden, her daughter, Tassle of Ven, and her granddaughter, Ch. Vivandiere of Ven—three typical Ven bitches. Owned by Mrs. J. R. Collins.

Commandant of Duroya (Ch. Kester of Wendees ex Duroya Beatrix, whelped 1960, died 1974) holds the record as the sire of 18 U.K. champions. He was bred and owned by Mrs. A. E. Woodiwiss. *(C. M. Cooke)*

3

The Keeshond in England

THE KEESHOND WAS FIRST RECOGNIZED in England as an "Overweight Pomeranian." Three white Overweight specimens appeared in the ring in 1870. The average weight at that time was 21 to 20 pounds. The relationship of the Pomerian to the Keeshond is illustrated in C. M. Hicks' book, *The Pomeranian* (England, 1906), which states that the first "shaded sable Pomeranian" was shown in London in 1899. The dog had been sent as a Keeshond to a Miss Beverly in Britain by friends in Holland, but "Kees," as she called him, caused much discussion in British dog publications as to the correct breed name for him. The general consensus was that he should be classified as a "Pomeranian Dog, Keeshond, Wolfsspitz or Spitz." Although "Kees" was never bred, there is evidence that a number of sable-shaded Overweight Poms were bred in England around the turn of the twentieth century.

The British Kennel Club withdrew Challenge Certificates for Overweight Pomeranians in 1916 and the variety was not officially heard from again until it was accepted for registration in 1925 under the name of Dutch Barge Dogs.

EARLY BREEDERS AND KENNELS

Van Zaandam

A tour of Holland by a young English girl led to the establishment of the Keeshond breed in England. The founder of the breed in England was Mrs. Wingfield Digby, owner of the famous Van Zaandam Kennel. She can well be named the "British First Lady of Keesdom." While yachting in Holland with her parents in 1905, Mrs. Digby (then Miss Hamilton-Fletcher) fell in love with the beautiful watchdogs she saw on the Dutch barges and brought home with her two wolf-gray puppies. Those original Van Zaandams were christened Barkles and Zaandam. Mrs. Digby added others from Holland and a number from Germany for her kennel at Sherborne Castle in Dorset.

The first Dutch Barge Dogs were shown in 1923. They were Mrs. Digby's Breda and Saanie and drew much favorable comment in the British press. The breed was officially renamed Keeshond in 1926 with a Standard much the same as it is today in England and North America. In 1928, the Kennel Club allotted Challenge Certificates for Keeshonds (England's method of acquiring championship titles). To earn a British championship requires receiving three Challenge Certificates under different judges. Current champions are entered in shows in an effort to add more of the coveted CCs to their records and since there is no separate class for champions, a nonchampion dog must triumph over current champions to receive the Bitch or Dog CC. This system is much more difficult than that in the United States and helps maintain a high level of quality in new champions.

When the Dutch Barge Dog Club was founded in 1925 with Mrs. Digby as president, 25 of the breed were registered in England. The next year the club's name was changed to the Keeshond Club and its first specialty show was held in 1933. A second club, the North of England Keeshond Club, was formed in 1936. Both clubs have remained active ever since.

In 1929 Baroness Burton's Dochfour Hendrik, bred by Mrs. Digby and sired by her German import, Bartel Van Zaandam, became the first Keeshond to complete a championship. Mrs. Digby's homebred Gesina Van Zaandam (also by Bartel) became the first bitch to finish.

In 1969, Mrs. Digby published her memoirs in England. This charmingly written book gives an interesting picture of country life in England, starting shortly after the turn of the twentieth century. It is appropriately entitled *My Life with Keeshonden* and has become a collector's item.

Guelder

Mrs. Alice Gatacre came from the province of Guelderland in Holland to reside in England around 1928 and began a breeding program at her Guelder Kennel in Devonshire. From her kennel came foundation stock for early British, American and Canadian breeders. A zealous breeder, fancier and writer, Mrs. Gatacre's pamphlets and magazine articles were outstanding in providing the public with knowledge of the Keeshond. She also authored *The Keeshond*, which was published in London in 1938.

Evenlode

Other Keeshond breeders established kennels that continued to influence the breed through its early days in England and into present times.

Ch. Waakzaam Waalre (Ch. Waakzaam Wotan ex Waakzaam Welriekend), owned by Mrs. Smyth, still holds the record in the breed in England with six champion children.

Ch. Raedels Bernice (Raedels Arminel ex Kwintex Kirsche) was the Top Keeshond Bitch in the U.K. for 1984. Bred by Mr. and Mrs. Riddle, she is owned by Mr. and Mrs. Crawford of Venway Kennels.

Noteworthy of these is Miss Osmunda Hastings, whose Evenlode Kennel is famous for consistently contributing top-quality Kees to the breed's development and history in England and America.

When World War II broke out, Miss Hastings joined the Women's Army and began to disperse her kennel. Miss Barbara Glover, who lived in the country, took the nucleus to keep the strain going until the war ended. The famous Dorcas of Evenlode was among these. Breeding was restricted by the Kennel Club throughout the war and breeders were hampered by a lack of food. However, Miss Glover was able to breed three litters during the war.

Vorden

Mrs. Irene Tucker is known for her illustrious Vorden Kees. Her dogs also served as the foundation stock for many kennels in the United States, included Mr. and Mrs. John A. Lafore's Chantwood Kennel in Pennsylvania and that of Mr. and Mrs. Carl Gettig, also of Pennsylvania. Mrs. Tucker was the breeder of Eng. Ch. Volkrijk of Vorden, winner of Best in Show at Crufts in 1957. In all, Volkrijk took 24 CCs at a time when there were only 14 sets available to the breed annually.

Wistonia

A visit by Mr. and Mrs. Fred Greenwood to see Mrs. Tucker's Keeshonds in 1943 led to the founding of the celebrated Wistonia Kennel in the north of England. The foundation stock behind Wistonia's record-making Kees in England, and the kennel's many exports with spectacular winning records in America, came from various British breeders but the real start of the Wistonia line was Worthy of Wistonia (Zandi Van Zaandam ex Aalik of Wistonia). A total of 38 Keeshonds with English titles were bred or owned by the Greenwoods; of these, 19 gained American titles and four gained Canadian titles. Allendale of Wistonia was the first Wistonia dog exported to America; he became an American champion. The first Wistonia English champion to go to America was Whimsy of Wistonia (Worthy ex Eng. Ch. Mistybank Madonna of Wistonia). She was the first Keeshond bitch to win Best in Show (BIS), all breeds, in America. She became an American champion and top Keeshond in the United States in 1949. She was unbeaten in the breed in the United States.

Many of the Wistonia dogs were exported to the Flakkee Kennels of Mr. and Mrs. Porter Washington in California. Eng., Am. and Can. Ch. Wrocky of Wistonia became internationally famous under the Washingtons' ownership. He was considered to be the best Keeshond ever bred. He had 5 CCs in England, 33 groups and 18 BIS, all breeds, in America and Canada — all in 11 months of showing. He is accepted as the model for depicting the Keeshond Standard and fittingly graces the cover of this book.

28

Ch. Ledwell Dutchman (whelped 1970) was the first Keeshond to win 25 Challenge Certificates. He was bred by Sylvia Scroggs and owned by Mrs. Purdon.

Ch. Gelderland Clipper of Swashway (Swashway No Rush ex Ch. Gelderland Aurelia) is the sire of 11 English champions and five champions abroad. He was bred by Mrs. C. Moore and is owned by Mrs. E. Wilding and Mrs. R. Francis.

In 1964, the Greenwoods and their Keeshonds left England to live in the United States. Not long after taking up residence in Pennsylvania, Mr. Greenwood passed away, but his equally distinguished partner, Nan, carried on the renowned Wistonia tradition in California until her death in 1986 (see Chapter 4).

van Sandar/Ven

When Mrs. Richard Fort moved to the United States from England she set up her van Sandar Kennels in Pleasantville, New York, where her British-bred Keeshonds and their American-born progeny played vital roles in the breed's development. After her marriage to Jere Collins, they returned to England and reestablished their kennel in conjunction with Miss Glover as Ven. In 1963 they imported the first American-bred Keeshond, Am. Ch. Ruttkay Moerdaag. The Collins continued as respected breeders and judges until their deaths, Jere in 1981 and Molly in 1985.

Rhinevale

Through conscientious care and a selective breeding program, Denis and Margo Emerson and their Rhinevale Keeshonden have contributed much to the development of the breed both in England and abroad. Their first Keeshond was a bitch from Miss Hasting's first postwar litter. Tabitha of Evenlode ("Kandy") became the start of the Rhinevale Kennel; all of the Rhinevale dogs are descended from her. Margo never purchased another dog.

The first Rhinevale litter of seven was whelped on August 18, 1947. A second litter produced six dogs, not the bitch that Margo was looking for. However, she fell in love with a beautiful young dog named Eng. Ch. Colin of Ossen and asked to lease his dam to breed to one of Kandy's sons. On November 18, 1950, this breeding resulted in Eng. Ch. Rhinevale Rapunzel. According to Margo, from Rapunzel came the quality and charm of the Rhinevale line. Rapunzel gave Margo 17 years of delightful companionship and produced Ch. Randi, Ch. Rondina and Rhythm, who, in turn, produced Robertina, the dam of Ch. Robinella and Rumbelinda. These two bitches went to Mrs. Scroggs, who founded the Ledwell Kennel.

From their first litter in 1947, Rhinevale produced one or two litters a year. Due to failing health, there have been few Rhinevale litters since 1975. According to Margo, some 30 litters have been bred by Rhinevale, the biggest of which was the "Heavenly Eleven" born in 1977 to Rhinevale Romarina. No bitch has had more than four litters and only then if one had been a very small litter. From these there have been 15 English champions, some international champions, and still others in South Africa, France, Sweden, Finland, Norway, America and Canada.

Ch. Ledwell Lysander (Ch. Ledwell Dutchman ex Ch. Ledwell Heidi, whelped 1974) was bred by Mrs. Scroggs and owned by Mrs. Sharp. In 1981 he won his 25th CC, thus equalling the record held by his sire.

Ch. Gavimir Nighthawk (Kwintex Katterwaad ex Gavimir Verbena, whelped 1980) has accumulated 30 CCs, many show awards and has sired 11 litters. His breeder/owner is Mrs. Pam Luckhurst.

Duroya

In 1955 the first Keeshond joined the Duroya Kennel of Mrs. A. E. Woodiwiss. Two bitches were purchased from Wistonia and from them came Beatrix of Duroya and Eng. Ch. Bekoorester of Duroya. Beatrix was mated with Eng. Ch. Kester of Wendees, a son of Eng. and Am. Ch. Wrocky of Wistonia, and produced Commandant of Duroya. Commandant was the youngest dog to win Best of Breed (BOB) at a championship show and, according, to his owner, with more expert handling would no doubt have won his title. He was born on September 25, 1960 and died on December 11, 1974. His first litter was born in February 1962 and his last in June 1973; during this time he sired 18 English champions — more than any other male to date. There are few pedigrees today in England that do not include his name.

To date, the Duroya Kennel has owned or bred 25 champions. They never keep more than seven Kees at a time; all live with the family and are always owner-handled. Line breeding is practiced with the occasional use of an outside stud. The dogs are named alphabetically in generations so it is easier to trace pedigrees. Mrs. Woodiwiss does not campaign champions after achieving their titles because she feels it is more interesting to exhibit youngsters to test the breeding of the next generation.

Waakzaam

The Waakzaam prefix of Mrs. E. M. Smyth was registered in 1957. This kennel was based on two bitches bought from Mrs. Tucker of Vorden; both carried some Evenlode blood. From these two excellent foundation bitches have descended more than 40 Waakzaam champions, with exports helping to found or strengthen kennels in many countries. In Great Britain many successful breeders have started with Waakzaam stock, and Waakzaam has been named the top kennel in the breed eight times.

Waakzaam has always had more bitches than dogs, but a few males have made their mark. Eng. Ch. Waakzaam Wotan produced some superb bitches, who in turn produced many champions. One of Wotan's daughters, Eng. Ch. Waakzaam Waalre, still holds the record in the breed in England with six champion get. A grandson of Wotan, Eng. Ch. Waakzaam Waag produced 14 champion get.

Sinterklaas

The long-established prefix of Sinterklaas was used by Margaret Collier, who produced Can. and Am. Ch. Sinterklaas Brave Nimrod. He was whelped in 1962, sired by a top stud of that time, Eng. Ch. Big Bang of Evenlode (ex Sinterklaas Lass of Van Keena). "Roddy," as he was known, left his mark on the breed in the United States by producing many champions.

Sinterklaas' last champion was a striking looking male, Eng. Ch. Sinterklaas Kipling, who was whelped in 1975 (Eng. Riesling of Rhinevale ex Sinterklaas Train Beaver). Miss Collier served as a judge at the Keeshond Club of America National Specialty in Dallas, Texas, in 1983 and had the honor of judging Crufts in 1984.

Vaderson

In 1984 Pat and Ron Parkes celebrated the twenty-fifth anniversary of Vaderson Keeshonds. They began their kennel with Gaiety Girl of Evenlode (bred by Miss Hastings), and continued with Eng. Ch. Sinterklaas Test Pilot. Included in Test Pilot's dscendants is Sinterklaas Stirring News (CC and Reserve CC winner, seven BIS, six Reserve BIS).

Ledwell

Mrs. Sylvia Scroggs of Ledwell fame has always been more of a breeder than an exhibitor. Her most successful dogs went to others. The two most famous are the Purdons' Eng. Ch. Ledwell Dutchman and Mrs. Sharp's Eng. Ch. Ledwell Lysander. Dutchman was born on July 24, 1970 and was the first Keeshond to win 25 CCs. He retired after winning the Utility Group at Crufts and passed away on November 20, 1982. The Ledwell strain was founded on Rhinevale originally as was another successful kennel of recent years, Mrs. Luckhurst's Gavimirs.

SUCCESSFUL NEWCOMERS

Gavimir

The foundation for Gavimir Keeshonds, owned by Mrs. Pam Luckhurst, was Rhinevale Roitelet of Gavimir, sired by Eng. Ch. Ledwell Dutchman out of Eng. Ch. Raffetta of Rhinevale and bred by Margo Emerson. Roitelet was bred to Eng. Ch. Surprise of Ven and the first Gavimir litter of nine was born in 1975. In 1979 Roitelet was mated to Eng. Ch. Gelderland of Swashway, top stud for five years running and sire of 11 English champions and five champions abroad. This mating produced seven puppies, one of which was Eng. Ch. Gavimir Reseda of Swashway.

The breed record-holder, Eng. Ch. Gavimir Nighthawk, was born on July 28, 1980, sired by Kwintex Katterwaad out of Gavimir Verbena. As an adult, he continued his winning and accumulated 30 CCs; six Utility Groups, including Crufts in 1983; three Reserve BIS and a BIS at Blackpool in 1985. He has sired 11 litters comprising 47 pups. With his help, Gavimir was the top-winning kennel in 1983 and 1984.

Keesland

In 1972 Bob and Gina Weedon purchased their first Keeshond from the

Ch. Ledwell Lustre of Keesland (Ch. Ledwell Dutchman ex Ch. Ledwell Heidi, whelped 1974) was the foundation of the Keesland Kennel. She was top brood bitch in the U.K. from 1980 to 1982.

Ch. Keesland Highlight (Sam the Candyman ex Ch. Keesland Gypsy) was the top-winning bitch in the U.K. in 1983. She was bred and is owned by Bob and Gina Weedon.

34

Ven Kennels as a family pet. Eng. Ch. Encore of Ven finished her title and Gina's passion for animals was fulfilled by her first litter of Keesland puppies in 1974.

Their admiration for Eng. Ch. Ledwell Charlotte led them to purchase a pick of litter bitch from Charlotte's daughter, Eng. Ch. Ledwell Heidi, who had been mated to Eng. Ch. Ledwell Dutchman. At eight weeks of age, Eng. Ch. Ledwell Lustre of Keesland came to the Weedon household and has been in charge ever since. A delightful, small puppy, she took time to develop and the Weedons decided to breed her to her half-brother, Eng. Ch. Rhinevale Rachmaninov. Bred to Eng. Ch. Gelderland Clipper of Swashway, Lustre's second litter of five males and two females was to break all existing records in England by containing four English champions. Lustre won the Brood Bitch Trophy — the Dorcas of Evenlode Cup — three years running. Lustre was five when she won her second CC; she was brought out of retirement at the age of seven to finish her championship.

Meanwhile, Eng. Ch. Keesland Ember had also been mated to Eng. Ch. Gelderland Clipper of Swashway; this mating produced Eng. Ch. Keesland Gypsy. The Weedons then decided the line needed some "fresh blood" and so mated Gypsy to Sam the Candy Man, a dog of Wistonia and Ven breeding. From this interesting mating came, the big-winning Eng. Ch. Keesland Highlight and her litter brother, Keesland HiJacker. HiJacker was exported to Brenda Brooks of Canada, where he went on to complete both his American and Canadian championshps. Making her debut at 7½ months, Highlight won her first CC in 1983; she was unbeaten in the breed from August 1983 to March 1984, winning ten CCs in total, including the Bitch CC at Crufts in 1984. Her tenth CC was won under the much respected Mrs. Jere Collins.

Neradmik

Another up-and-coming kennel is Jean Sharp's Neradmik Kennel. Her foundation bitch, Davean Cover Girl, was of northern bloodines; her sire was Eng. Ch. Heinz Sparkler and her dam was Eng. Ch. Beatrix of Davean. She was mated to Eng. Ch. Riesling of Rhinevale and thus produced the first Neradmik litter.

Then Eng. Ch. Ledwell Lysander came into her life and, as Jean says, completely reorganized things. Lysander was born on October 14, 1974 by Eng. Ch. Ledwell Dutchman ex Eng. Ch. Ledwell Heidi and bred by Sylvia Scroggs. In 1981 he won his twenty-fifth CC, equalling the record of his sire. On that day he also became the fourth Keeshond to win Best in Show at a championship show. He was then retired from general competition but did in fact win another CC from the Veterans class in 1985.

Ch. Neradmik Didikie (Ch. Keesland Flipper of Lekkerbeck ex Neradmik Christabelle) is the winner of six CCs and seven RCCs. She was bred and is owned by Mrs. Jean Sharp.

Ch. Valsgate Squires Boy (Ch. Ledwell Soloman ex Ch. Valsgate Bonne Chance) was one of the top-winning males during 1983 and 1984. Breeder/owner is Mr. Michael Stockman.

OTHER BREEDERS OF NOTE

Mike Stockman bought his first Keeshond, a grandson of Vandyke of Vorden, in 1946 from Rene Tucker and began the Valsgate Kennel. His second also came from Mrs. Tucker in 1960. Valmijk of Vorden was mated to Waakzaam Wrona (Eng. Ch. Sinterklaas Brushname ex Waakzaam Werewelwind) and produced Eng. Ch. Valsgate Briony; Briony was BIS at the Keeshond Club Open Show in 1972. Briony was then mated to Eng. Ch. Ledwell Dutchman and produced Swed. Ch. Valsgate Oyster Catcher and Valsgate Curlew.

The Kinkeesha Kennel of Mrs. J. Tierney traces back to the Evenlode lines via its two foundation bitches, Eng. Ch. Carlzdryk Carmoni and Waakzaam Waagskuis. Waakzaam Waagskuis' second litter produced Am. Ch. Kinkeesha Kracker and Int. Ch. Kinkeesha Karisma; Karisma is a champion in seven European countries.

The Venway Kennel of Mrs. and Mrs. F. Crawford was started after they had seen a photo of a Keeshond. Already rough Collie breeders, they purchased their first Keeshond in 1976. Goody Snow Shoes became the foundation of Venway. In 1978 she was bred to Kwintex Katterwaad, also owned by trhe Crawfords, and produced their first champion, Eng. Ch. Venway Delph Viking. Mr. and Mrs. Crawford also own Eng. Ch. Raedels Bernice, who was top bitch in the United Kingdom for 1984.

The Vandaban Kennel of Mrs. D. Banfield was founded with the purchase of Gelderland Arabella (by Eng. Ch. Surprise of Ven) in 1973. Arabella was mated to Ch. Ledwell Lysander and in 1977 produced Vandaban Amorella and Eng. Ch. Vandaban 'Allowe'en of Neradmik.

Mrs. Jean Hardcastle bought her first Keeshond in 1954 while working as a kennel maid for Nan Greenwood. She never lost her love for the breed, and in 1969 she acquired Margo of Meadowrock. In 1970 Margo was mated to Eng. Ch. Duroya Guardsman of Ven; this mating produced the first Boreasvale litter. Of this litter, Boreasvale Baarda sired a litter in 1976 with Joan Shaw's Eng. Ch. Vanglede Laughing Jenny. Mrs. Hardcastle purchased a dog from this litter called Sam the Candy Man. Sam was mated to Boreasvale Bellavista, a bitch Mrs. Hardcastle bred by Eng. Ch. Final Edition of Duroya ex Duroya Greta. This mating produced Eng. Ch. Boreasvale Bojangles in 1978; he gained his title at Crufts in 1981, where he was BOB.

John and Sue Arran, owners of the Silberne Kennel, fell in love with Keeshonds when visiting the Waakzaam Kennel and meeeting Mrs. Smyth's two foundation bitches. Waakzaam Were (Eng. Ch. Waakzaam Voljasmijn of Vorden ex Eng. Ch. Waakzaam Waltraute) became one of the Arrans' own foundation bitches. To complement Were, Mr. and Mrs. Alex Shaw allowed the Arrans to have Dalbaro Quest (Dalbaro Burgomaster ex Waakzaam Wolvega) from their Dalbaro Kennel. Quest was mated to Miss

Glover's Welford Nollekyns of Ven (Am. Ch. Ruttkay Moerdaag of Ven ex Welford Ina) and produced in her first litter Ch. Silberne Cavalcade.

The Old English bloodlines gave America its start in the breed. The blend of old and new continues to contribute to the development of the breed worldwide.

Mrs. Wingfield Digby in 1962, with gifts and honors received from admirers around the world in tribute to her 60 years of devotion to Keeshonden.

4

The Keeshond in the United States

THE KEESHOND was first introduced in the United States on the East Coast and in the Midwest. It made its appearance on the West Coast about six years later. Since then the popularity of the Keeshond has increased dramatically and there are now kennels in most of the 50 states. In order to best identify some of the major contributing kennels and bloodlines, we have divided this chapter geographically. The majority of the kennels and dogs identified in this chapter have or will contribute prominently to the breed today and in the future.

Because the kennels, exhibitors and dogs have changed dramatically since the writing of *The Complete Keeshond* by Mrs. Clementine Peterson, space does not permit us to reiterate the information she provided. If your library does not contain this original history of the breed, we cannot urge you strongly enough to acquire it. We will begin our story of the Keeshond in America where Mrs. Peterson left off.

In geographically relating this chapter, we will begin on the East Coast, travel both north and south and then make our way across the country, ending up in California and the Northwest.

EAST COAST

Ruttkay

You cannot think of Keeshonds on the East Coast without immediately thinking of Ruttkay. With the purchase of Brielle of Remlewood in 1946 from Jean Yock of Ohio, Virginia Ruttkay founded the Ruttkay Keeshond Kennel. Already an experienced breeder, Viriginia recognized that the Keeshond answered the dog lover's needs and so began a breeding program that spanned more than 30 years.

Ch. Maverick Son of Ilka (Prince Nichola ex Ch. Ruttkay Ilka Van Roem) was the winner of the KCA Natinal Specialty in 1975. He is owned by Eleanor Lewis.

Ch. Ruttkay Clyde's Cubby, HOF (Ch. Maverick Son of Ilka ex Ch. Ruttkay Misty Morning).

Ruttkay's initial foundation stock and later genetic additions were based on English stock of German and early Dutch origin, as well as early American lines with developments paralleling Ruttkay. Some of the Kees figuring prominently in these key exchange positions have been Am. and Can. Ch. Conwood Kloos; Ch. Ruttkay Roem, ROMX (Register of Merit Excellent); Am. and Can. Ch. Sinterklaas Brave Nimrod, ROMX; Irish and Am. Ch. Karel of Altnavanog, ROM (Register of Merit); Ch. Maverick Son of Ilka and Ch. Ruttkay Moerdaag of Ven.

Later Dutch and German imports were made by Ruttkay but, failing to contribute to the desired type, were discontinued. Most of the above named Keeshonds have actively produced nine to 14 (as of 1982) succeeding generations of progeny. These linebreedings and partial outcrosses, plus inhouse linebreedings, have resulted in a remarkable list of accomplishments for the Ruttkay Keeshonds.

As of November 1984, 202 dogs with Ruttkay sire and dam have finished their championships; another 109 with Ruttkay sire or dam have finished. There have been 28 foreign titles (Eng., Mex., Can., Irish, Dom. Rep., Equador and the only Cuban of the breed). Ruttkay dogs have earned seven Bests in Show, with Ch. DeVignon's Ducomo, HOF (Hall of Fame), accounting for three. Eight Ruttkay dogs have been inducted into the Hall of Fame. There have been nine ROM and four ROMX dogs, and 26 Ruttkay dogs account for 41 specialty winners. On the obedience side, there have been 90 CD dogs, 22 of which were also champions; 29 CDX, ten of which were Champions; seven UD, four of which were Champions, and one Tracking Dog (TD).

In the 1950s and 1960s, part of the breed's gain in public recognition was due to widespread Ruttkay publicity for Keeshonds on TV and radio, in newspaper promotions, as well as in *Popular Dogs* and *Dog World* magazine articles. A major portion of today's Keeshond kennels have Ruttkay stock in their ancestries, resulting from direct acquisitions or from co-owned and co-bred dogs.

Following the death of Virginia Ruttkay in August 1982, a group of fanciers and breeders pooled their talents, consolidated their lessons learned from a talented career breeder, and are carrying on the Ruttkay name.

Sahnsirai

One of the top-winning Ruttkay dogs lent his name to the Sahnsirai Kennel of Betty and Bill Ginsberg of Philadephia. Ch. Ruttkay Sirius, HOF, finished his championship at 18 months of age with four 4-point majors. Siri is the top-winning son of one of the great Keeshond producers, Can.and Am. Ch. Sinterklaas Brave Nimrod (ex Ruttkay Smoky's Heidi Ho). He won 158 BOB, 15 Non-Sporting Group 1s, 75 Non-Sporting Group placements, two all-breed BIS and two BOB at specialty shows. Siri was

Ch. Ruttkay Zabetta (Ch. Ruttkay Johnbear ex Ch. Ruttkay Lady Merry Katherine) was a top-winning show bitch in 1983 and 1985.

Ch. Ruttkay Sirius, HOF (Can. and Am. Ch. Sinterklaas Brave Nimrod ex Ruttkay Smoky's Heidi Ho) was bred by Virginia Ruttkay and owned by Betty Ginsberg of Pennsylvania.

finished to his championship by Dolores Scharff and Betty, but he was shown through his glory years by D. Roy Holloway.

Betty says Siri's temperament could not be faulted; he never made an aggressive move toward another dog. "He was a very all-together guy who ruled the household and who never had to assert himself. He accepted all newcomers, be they pups or mature visitors." Siri passed away in 1983 at the age of 14.

Fairville

In 1959 Marcie Goebel met Virginia Ruttkay at a local dog show and fell in love with the Keeshond. The next day Ch. Ruttkay Nigrescence and Queen Fredrikka van Ruttkay joined what would become Fairville Keeshonds. Marcie soon acquired Ch. Rhapsody of Westcrest, ROM (Eng. and Am. Ch. Wylco of Wistonia ex Ch. Ruttkay Winsome) from Jane West. Rhapsody was BOS at the Capital Keeshond Club Specialty in 1969 from the Veterans Class, a fitting climax for a most illustrious career, which started with the same win in 1962 from the Puppy Class and continued with a Group win from the classes making her the top-winning Keeshond show bitch of 1962.

Marcie was active in all phases of the sport of dogs, as treasurer of the Keeshond Club of America and a charter member of the Keeshond Club of Delaware Valley (KCDV). Marcie will always be remembered for establishing the tradition of KCDV's fabulous trophy table.

Fairville was one of the first kennels in the East to have its dogs certified free of hip dysplasia at the University of Pennsylvania. Each Fairville litter was carefully planned and and as carefully tended. Fantasy of Fairville was Best in Futurity (BIF) in 1966. Fantom of Fairville was BOSIF at the 1966 Keeshond Club of America (KCA) Specialty; Intermezzo of Fairville BOSIF in 1967; and Lucky Leo of Fairville BOSIF in 1969. Marcie's last litter produced Am. and Can. Ch. Pied Piper of Fairville who finished his American championship with three majors and a BOB over specials, and his Canadian championship with four out of five BOBs and a Group 2. Piper is owned by Jean and Tom Toombs.

Sherwood

In 1962 Phyllis Noonan purchased her first Keeshond, Westcott's Crista of Charlinn; her second, Coventry's Robin of Sherwood, followed the next year. This dog became the foundation stud of Sherwood Kennels. Tragically, he was crippled by a tranquilizing shot given him when he was OFA x-rayed. Bred to Crista in 1965, they produced Ch. Rob's MacDuff of Sherwood, a two-time specialty winner; Ch. Just So of Sherwood and Ch. Stauch's Trinka of Sherwood. In 1969 Ch. Sherwood's Cochise of DelVal was Best in Futurity (BIF) and BOW at the KCA National Specialty.

After dropping out of the breed for quite a few years, Phyllis returned and began again. She acquired Ch. Candray Co-Commander, who is a Capital Keeshond Club (CKC) specialty and Group winner, and is once again breeding winning Sherwood dogs.

Larah

Sarah Louie acquired her first Keeshond, Little Lady Rebecca Ann (Ch. Van Fitz the Strutter Modesto ex KC's Princess Mag) from California; she was bred to Ch. Van Storm's Happy Hooligan. Together they produced Ch. Aeneas of Larah, the first real show dog of Larah Kennels. According to Sarah, Aeneas was strong boned and solid and had that special eagerness and presence that pays off in the show ring. He also passed these traits on to his offspring. For his first try as a stud dog, Aeneas was bred to Zonka Dolce of Dorvans, owned by Hugh and Dot Evans; this produced some unforgettable pups: Ch. Ace Larah of Dorvans, Ch. Angie Deb of Dorvans and Ch. Amie Dol of Dorvans. As a result of his few times at stud, Aeneas earned an Award of Canine Distinction from *Dog World* magazine and is in its Album of Great Dogs of the Past and Present.

For the second show dog, Sarah brought home Aeneas' son, Ch. Ace Larah of Dorvans. An impressive young dog, Ace took BOW at the Capital Keeshond Club show in 1973 and again in 1974. He was first Veteran Dog and 1st Stud Dog at the 1980 CKC specialty. Although not specialed until he was six, and under limited specialing with D. Roy Holloway, Ace had an impressive "times shown versus BOB/Group placement ratio." He excelled as a stud and passed on his good movement, bone, dark eyes, beautiful color, contrast and coat texture. He also passed on his love for "hamming it up" in the ring. He was bred to Rockhold Bright Fancy, CD, and produced Ch. Larah's Greta G of Rockhold, CD. Greta, owned by Sarah and husband, Paul Heintel, was shown in both conformation and obedience and earned both titles handily.

Aeneas was later bred to his granddaughter, Calista Larah of Dorvans. This produced Bilbo T Baggins, CD, and Ch. Belva T. Bolka.

Vandy

At Vandy Keeshonden in New York, Carole Henry bases her breeding program on a good dog first — one that is not just finishable but one that also possesses a sharp mind and the ability to produce.

Carole's first Keeshonds were from a pet shop. She showed her second one in obedience and he went on to become Vandy's Thane, CDX. When Thane was unable to finish his UD due to his inability to jump, Carole began her search for a show quality Keeshond. Her search led her to Lynda Doughty of Dow Tees Kees and the dog that would become Am. and Can. Ch. Dow Tees Easy Rider, CDX, Can. CD. Beginning in 1975, Carole

Ch. Dow-Tees Easy Rider, CDX, owned by Carole Henry, was a success in both the conformation and obedience rings.

Carrying on the tradition at Vandy Kees, Ch. Vandy's Breagan, CD, excelled in conformation, obedience and the whelping box.

45

showed him in both breed and obedience. He finished in ten shows, including BOW at the CKC specialty. That same year he won the award for KCA Top Obedience Dog. In 1977 Carole began specialing him and he won the KCA Top Show Dog Award and a BIS that same year. He also finished his Canadian championship in five shows with a Group 1 and Group 3; he finished his Canadian CD in three shows including a High in Trial (HIT) with a score of 199½.

Although only bred a few times, Easy Rider was consistent in producing soundness, good fronts and rears plus super bodies on his bitches. He has sired champions and obedience titlists, including Group placers and HIT dogs. Most of all, his daughters reproduced. His first daughter, Ch. Vandys Argo, CD (ex Dow Tees Little Darling), finished from the Bred by Exhibitor (BBE) Class in only eight shows. In obedience, she followed her sire's success, having the highest national average of Kees in 1979. Her average score was 197½ and she was awarded the Dog World Award for obedience work.

Argo was equally skilled in the whelping box. Bred to Ch. Candray Ghost of Wintergreen she produced Ch. Vandy's Breagan, CD (BOB winner, HIT Specialty winner and Dog World Award Winner); Ch. Vandy's Bayonne, CDX; Vandy's Bayou, CDX; and Vandy's Beta, CD. Her second litter by Ch. Candray the Nobleman produced Ch. Vandy's Deja. Her third and last litter by Ch. Fearless Firstclass produced Can. Ch. Maplekees Harmonie V. Vandy and Ch. Vandy's Havoc.

Breagan's sassy personality, toughness and working ability have made her Carole's constant companion and favorite dog. She was shown to her championship from Bred by Exhibitor and took four BOB and four BOS along the way. She was specialed only eight times, winning four BOB and 2 BOS. In obedience, all her scores were over 195, with a HIT of 198½. She, too, met the Vandy criteria and excelled in the whelping box. Bred to Easy Rider, she produced Ch. Vandys Chanti. Bred to Ch. Tanglewood Mark Frost, she produced Ch. Vandys Elani, a specialty WB winner; Ch. Tanglewood Vandy Jack Frost; and Carrie, CD. There have been only eight litters at Vandy, but they have been eight litters of winners.

Bearpaws

Speaking of winners, Ch. Marcy's Teddy Bear, CDX, HOF, surely qualifies. Owned by Marcy Zingler, Teddy was one of only nine multiple group winning bitches in the last 34 years. She placed in groups in six different years, receiving her last Group 1, owner-handled at the age of 9½ years. During the 1970s she was the No. 1 bitch in the East and was always among the top bitches in the country. To date, according to Marcy, she is the only bitch Group winner with an obedience degree and the only Keeshond admitted to the conformation Hall of Fame with an advanced obedience degree. She earned her CD at 12 months, her championship at 19

46

Ch. Rhadpsody of Westcrest, ROM (Eng. and Am. Ch. Wylco of Wistonia ex Ch. Ruttkay Winsome) was bred by Jane West and owned by Marguerite Goebel. She was the foundation of Fairville Keeshonds and was Top Show Bitch in 1962.

Ch. Marcy's Teddy Bear, CDX, HOF, owned by Marcy Zingler, was a Group-winning bitch even at 9½ years of age.

months and her CDX at three years while being campaigned as a special.

Teddy passed away in 1984 at 13½ years of age. In 1985 Marcy established a memorial trophy for the top-winning Keeshond show bitch in honor of her beloved friend and companion.

KeesLund

Tony and Judy Pomato's KeesLund Keeshonden got its start in 1969 when they purchased their first Keeshond, who was to become Ch. Eastover Wandao Damon (Ch. DoleShar Big Blast ex Ch. DoleShar Wanda the Witch) from Kenneth Van Campen. A few years later they reserved pick bitch from another Van Campen litter by Ch. Dole Shar Lief Erickson and Dole Shar Miss Van Can Do. This litter produced 13 puppies, only two of which were bitches. But Tony and Judy came home with their first bitch, who was to become Ch. Eastover Frosty Dawn. After only three weeks, they were so fond of their new puppy that they returned and bought one of her male littermates; this puppy was to become Ch. Eastover Jason Van Dole Shar.

During the next few years, Tony and Judy raised two litters but devoted most of their time to raising their two sons. When they returned to dog breeding they turned to California-bred stock. These puppies became Ch. Charmacs Fortunate-Lee, Ch. Star-Kees Ironclad, Ch. Klassics Eve of the Storm, Ch. Candray Maxi of KeesLund, Ch. Fearless Flavor For KeesLund, and Ch. A Sure Bet for KeesLund.

Of these, Ch. Fearless Flavor For KeesLund is best known for she excels both in the show ring and in the whelping box. She finished her championship easily and went on to win BOB at the Nor-Cal Keeshond Club Specialty, several BOS specialty wins and group placements. Her Group 1 win at the Palisades Kennel Club show earned her a Hall of Fame designation. "Yummy" has been bred only once to Coventry's Finale for Harry and produced seven pups, five of which finished their championships.

Ch. Klassics Eve of the Storm was bred to Tanglewood Vandy Jack Frost and produced Ch. KeesLunds Kameo Caper, a Group winner from the Puppy Class and BOS at the 1986 KCA National Specialty. Also in this litter is the lovely Ch. KeesLunds Puttin on the Ritz.

The breeding program at KeesLund combines predominantly Fearless, Star-Kees, and Coventry bloodlines.

NEW ENGLAND

Holland Hond

The pedigrees of Holland Hond Keeshonden can all be traced to Ch. Nether-Lair's Damon de Gyselaer, CD, the first Kees that Harriet Cinkosky obtained in 1949 from Nether-Lair Kennels. In 1954, Harriet had a Best in

Ch. Fearless Flavor for KeesLund, HOF, excels in the show ring and in the whelping box. She is co-owned by Tony and Judy Pomato and Helen Cuneo.

Ch. Holland Hond's Merri-K Monarch, owned by Harriet Cinkosky, was Best in Sweeps and BOW at the KCDV Specialty in 1977 and BOB at the HTKC Specialty in 1981.

49

Show Brace with Ch. Nether-Lair's Damon De Gyselaer, CD, and his son, Ch. Har-Curt's Hansel.

Over the years, Harriet produced a number of champions. Having been impressed with Ch. Vereeren of Vorden, Harriet bred her bitch, Ch. Holland Hond Tulip, to Ch. Saremeya Landfall, a son of Vereeren of Vorden. Included in this litter were Ch. Holland Hond Landsman and Ch. Holland Hond Lilac. This breeding was instrumental in developing the Holland Hond type of Keeshond — a dog characterized by a compact, cobby body with good movement, a well-shaped head, dark eyes and a lovely, animated, sunny disposition.

Using the offspring of this leitter as the basic breeding stock, with some outcrosses and line breeding of later generations, Harriet and those associated with her dogs firmly estabished the consistent Holland Hond type that remains today.

Harriet placed Ch. Holland Hond Jonquil, CD, with Frances Boyle, who had obtained another Keeshond from Harriet in 1972 and became involved in the breeding, showing and co-owning of Holland Hond Keeshonden. At the present time, the young bitches suitable for breeding and the Holland Hond Kees active in the show ring live with Frances.

In 1974 Holland Hond Jonquil, CD, was bred to Ch. Holland Hond Landsman, producing Ch. Holland Hond Land Ho, purchased by Jane West; and Holland Hond Bountiful, the dam of Ch. Alecia Kees Whirlwind, CD. A Dutch bitch, Rosebud, was bred to Landsman. Harriet obtained an outstanding puppy from this litter and he became Ch. Holland Hond Landmark, HOF, ROM.

In 1975 Jonquil was bred to Ch. Holland Hond Rolf v. Windfall and produced Holland Hond Ruffian, CD. In 1978 Ruffian was bred to Landmark and produced Ch. Holland Hond Moonflower who was BOSIF at the large 1979 KCA National Specialty.

Although Harriet herself is no longer active in showing and breeding, others are carrying on breeding the Holland Hond type.

Tanglewood

Another Massachusetts kennel got its start from Nether-Lair. Tanglewood Keeshonden were established by Carol J. Aubut in 1960. Her first Keeshond was Nether-Lairs Jon V. Tanglewood, who was a birthday present from the Cowleys, owners of Nether-Lair. After having this dog for only a short time, Carol knew this was the breed for her and so it has been for more than 25 years.

Carol later bought a bitch from Keeshof Kennels in Connecticut. This dog was to become Ch. Bright Promise of Keeshof. From the same kennel, Carol's next two acquisitions were selected. Ch. Herzog V. Herman of Keeshof and Ch. Bingo van Kogi of Keeshof were excellent studs and were multiple BOB and Group winners. Ch. Herzog became the foundation stud

Ch. Holland Hond's Landmark, HOF, ROM is the sire of 22 champions. He was bred by Harriet Cinkosky and is owned by Carol Aubut of Massachusetts.

Ch. Tanglewood Tycoon, owned by Carol Aubut, has 61 BOBs, 27 Group placements and six Group 1s.

dog of the Tanglewood Kennels. His sire was the famous BIS winner, Ch. Nederlan Herman V. Mack, and his dam a litter sister to Ch. Bingo. These dogs were the combination of Vorden and leading American bloodlines.

Although Ch. Herzog had his fair share of champion offspring, Carol found his grandchildren were better than his children. He excelled in the show ring as well and was No. 5 Keeshond for 1969.

In 1975 Carol bred a granddaughter of Ch. Herzog, Ch. Tanglewood Too Much. This was to have been the foundation bitch at Tanglewood but fire ravaged the kennel and she perished. In 1976 Tanglewood acquired and co-owned the outstanding Ch. Holland Hond's Landmark. He is the combination of Vorden, Dutch and American bloodlines. Mark is the sire of 22 champions, has earned his ROM designation and has been inducted into the Hall of Fame. His show record speaks for itself with 75 BOBs, 35 Group placements and 6 Group 1s. As of this writing, Mark is 12 and is still going strong.

Carol later acquired Ch. Jo-Lyn's Brazenly Bold, who goes back to Ch. Nederlan Herman V. Mack. Crossing the Mark daughters to this dog produced some outstanding Keeshonden for Tanglewood. The latest star at the Tanglewood Kennel is Ch. Tanglewood Tycoon, who has so far accumulated 61 BOBs, 27 Group placings and 6 Group 1s.

In the past 26 years Tanglewood has finished 50 champions. Carol takes particular pride in the fact that with a few variations, the kennel has used and worked with the same bloodlines as those on which it was founded more than 25 years before.

Kalmia

Kalmia Kennels, located in southeastern Massachusetts, is the home of Irene Fonseca and Maryellen Grace. Irene and Maryellen acquired their first Keeshond by accident. A naval commander brought his dog from Alaska but, unable to take her with him to Hawaii, left her with an animal shelter. She was seen there by Maryellen's brother and she had a home. At the tender age of 12 "Chicksie" came to live with Maryellen and Irene. Unfortunately, she wandered off and was lost for 12 days during a bitter New England winter. Delighted at her return but still suffering from the shock of even temporarily losing their dog, Maryellen and Irene decided they should get a Keeshond puppy to keep Chicksie company. Kalmia's Auntie Mame of Reeart joined the Kalmia family. Chicksie continued on as head of the household until her death in 1981 at the astounding age of nearly 19 years.

As color was important to Maryellen and Irene, they chose Ch. Reearts Nicholas of Keedox as the sire for Mame's first litter. From this mating came Ch. Kalmia's Holly of Reeart and Kalmia's Lover Boy, CD, both of whom still reside at Kalmia. Holly delights in being a show girl; she was No. 6 Keeshond bitch in 1979 (Keezette) and still does well for herself in the

Ch. Candray Ghost of Wintergreen, ROM, was the foundation stud at the Wanamaker's Candray Kennels in New Hampshire.

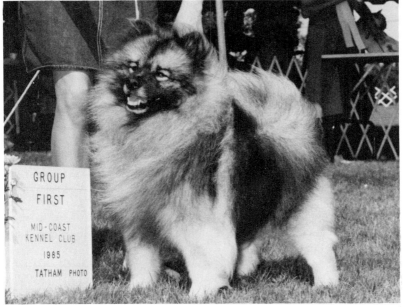

Ch. Dal-Kees Mighty Samson, winner of the 1984 and 1985 KCA National Specialties. Samson was bred by Anne Lowell and Carol Aubut and is owned by Jan Wanamaker.

53

specialties at age 11. Her brother, Love, found an obedience career at the age of eight by earning his three legs in three consecutive shows.

Holly was bred twice to Ch. Thunderoc's Intrepid. From these matings, Maryellen and Irene kept two males who would become Am. and Can. Ch. Kalmia's Yankee Doodle and Am. and Can. Kalmia's The Vagabond King.

Candray

Candray Kennels came into existence in late 1974 when George and Jan Wanamaker, their six children, four Collies and one Keeshond moved to Candia, New Hampshire. They were already active with Collies but their introduction to Carol Aubut of Tanglewood and Linda Cail of Cai-Lin provided the cornerstone from which the Candray line would develop. Candray ideals are to consistently produce attractive, stylish dogs with emphasis on a teddy bear face, sound movement, proud cobby silhouette, both stationary and in motion. They prefer heavier appearing bone and a sweet, attentive expression, select shorter heavier muzzles and prefer lighter shadings for the coat color.

Their goal is a breeding program that will, generation after generation, create recognizable Candray Keeshonds able to compete successfully in the show ring and reproduce their own distinct qualities. They feel strongly that only select dogs represent the Candray name in the ring; very rarely has there been a litter with all or most pups being truly show/breeding quality.

Jan and George find it satisfying that many of the dogs winning so consistently in the ring today for other well known kennels are descendents of Candray. At the KCA National Specialties in 1983, 1984 and 1985, many of the top winners in Futurity, classes and specials were grandchildren of Candray dogs. They feel that specialties are the place to test a breeding program and thus do very little specialing of their champions.

To understand the success of Candray, we will regress to 1973 when Linda Cail took George and Jan to meet Lou and Jean Miller of Wintergreen Kennels. They fell in love with a perky little puppy by Charpats Kristopher ex Ch. Sherwoods Saucy Swinger. He had an expressive face and little ears that just never came off the top of his head. Because of his light color he was called "Casper" and registered as Candray Ghost of Wintergreen, the foundation stud at Candray Kennels. Casper finished his championship and was not specialed more than a few times primarily, according to Jan, because "we were too inexperienced (stupid) to recognize the qualities of this exceptional dog." Fortunately, he was used at stud frequently and sired many multiple champion litters.

Through Carol Aubut the first Candray show litter was whelped. Ch. Pepere's Katrinka of Cai-Lin came to Candray and was bred to Carol's Ch. Tanglewood Rob Roy of Maywood in 1972. From this came Ch. Tanglewood Tiara of Candray and Tanglewood Van Leer. All but three Candray Keeshonds trace directly to these two dogs.

Ch. Tanglewood Tiara of Candray began her show career at nine months of age handled, as Jan says, by her "life-long idol, George,." She finished before her second birthday and was top-winning bitch in New England in 1974 and 1975. "Gretl," as she is called, goes everywhere with George. They keep dog cookies at the bank for her and she insists on going with George every day to make sure she gets one. If he doesn't go to the bank, he has to give her one at the post office to keep her happy.

Jan and George then acquired two granddaughters of Ch. Knova's Moby Avonk — Maywood Tuptims Debutante and Cai-Lin Royal Imp V. Candray. Although Debutante never saw a show ring, she played an important role in the future of Candray and several other kennels. She was a small, beautifully colored silver bitch with a luxurious long coat, small ears, sound movement and elegant neck. In her litter of three by Tanglewood Van Leer was a bitch who would make history for her day. Jan tells us that Candray Cotillion was not a beautiful puppy but from the first time she entered the show ring at nine weeks of age, she was rarely defeated. She completed her championship with four majors at just one year of age. Her first time as a special she was BOB over top-winning male champions. During her show career she had many Group placements and was top-winning bitch in New England and in the top ten nationally for several years. Her grandest moment was winning BOB at the HTKC Specialty in 1979. She produced three champion sons who have also been specialty winners and/or champion producers. She is now retired and is Jan's constant companion. In 1985, however, Jan brought her out for one more spin around the ring at the KCA National Specialty; she waltzed away with BOS in the Veteran Sweepstakes at the age of 12.

The latest star at Candray is Ch. Dalkees Mighty Samson, bred by Ann Lowell and Carol Aubut by Ch. Jo-Lyn's Brazenly Bold ex Ch. Lady Hilliary of Holiday Pt. Sam finished in 1983 and began an historic specials career. That same year he was BOB at HTKC; in 1984 he was BOB again at HTKC, the KCA National Specialty and the American Kennel Club Centennial Show. In 1985 he was BOB at the KCA Golden Anniversary specialty where he triumphed over an entry of 644 Keeshonds. Sam's abilities as a stud dog are also exceptional and blend well with the Candray bloodline. He will be remembered for many generations.

The list of Candray champions and their accomplishments reads like "Who's Who in Keeshonden." In 1977 Jan and George were honored as KCA co-breeders of the year.

Yan-Kee

Peter and Holly Colcord became interested in Keeshonds in 1973 when Peter bought Holly a puppy as a Christmas gift. For fun they took their new puppy to a match; they were hooked. But they found out their puppy wasn't the best Keeshond in the world and so they began a search for a show dog.

Ch. Yan-Kee Starkist, HOF, owned by Peter and Holly Colcord, qualified for her Hall of Fame designation three times over.

Am. and Can. Ch. GreenKees Beowulf V. Ledwell was the No. 1 Show Dog in the Heritage Trail Keeshond Club in 1982. He is owned by Tess and Bill Eckhart.

They bought one of their foundation bitches, Cai-Lin Regal Radiance, from Linda and Bruce Cail. The first Yan-Kee litter was produced in 1976 and from it came the first home-bred champion, Ch. Yan-Kee Inspiration. "Stacey" was BOS at the HTKC Specialty in 1982 and still reigns as kennel boss and chief inspector of litters at Yan-Kee.

Inspiration's sire was Ch. Ghost of Wintergreen and it was through this association that Peter and Holly met Jan and George Wanamaker. They learned a great deal from the Wanamakers, especially the importance of correct structure and sound movement, first and foremost in choosing dogs for breeding and showing. Peter and Holly began to formulate a clear picture of their ideal Keeshond. Casper was the inspiration for the style of Keeshonds at Yan-Kee and his influence is seen in almost all their pedigrees. The goals at Yan-Kee are proper balance and structure, sound movement, good health, happy attitude and their own particular style.

At this point Peter and Holly felt a need for some outside blood and acquired Ch. Woffee Bandit Distraction from Pat Doescher of Woffee Kees in 1981. Although Bandit's grandsire was Casper, his dam's side of the pedigree was a new bloodline for Yan-Kee. He sired three litters including the most successful out of Ch., Yan-Kee Starlet, a favorite of the Colcords.

Starlet, with four champions to her credit, has been one of Yan-Kee's best producers. She is the dam (by Bandit) of Ch. Yan-Kee Starkist and Ch. Yan-Kee Superstar, littermates whelped in 1982, each of which have had exciting show careers. Superstar was BOS in Sweepstakes at HTKC and Capital Keeshond Club Specialties and BOW at HTKC. He finished his championship by taking BOW at the KCA National that same year. Tragically, he was killed before he could realize his full potential.

But Ch. Yan-Kee Starkist is the real "star" — at least in the eyes of Peter! "Chrissy" was Best in Sweepstakes at HTKC and Capital Specialties in 1983; she was also BOS at HTKC the same year. In 1984 she took her first specialty BOB at the Heart of America Specialty; "papa" Ch. Woffee Bandit Distraction was BOS and Chrissy's half sister was BOW, making it quite a day. Later that year Chrissy was BOS at the KCA Specialty. She finished the year as the top Keeshond Bitch (all systems) and earned her KCA Hall of Fame points twice over by the time she was two years old. According to Peter, she has recently qualified for the third time! In 1985 she outdid herself by taking another specialty BOB at HTKC and she was BOS at the KCA Golden Anniversary Specialty. By the end of 1985 she had accumulated 16 Group placements, including four Group 1s, six Group 2s, three Group 3s and three Group 4s. In May 1986 she was BOS at the Nor-Cal Specialty held the day before the KCA National.

The Golden Anniversary KCA Specialty was especially memorable for Peter and Holly for another reason: Yan-Kee Fantasia won the Futurity Stakes in a record entry of 96 puppies. They repeated the win in 1986 with Yan-Kee Neiman Marcus, a Superstar son, taking the Best in Futurity honors.

Since 1977 Peter and Holly have bred and/or owned 17 champions and 11 homebreds have finished since their first in 1980. All homebreds except Starlet (who was finished by Pat Doescher) were finished owner-handled. They are beginning to produce the style of Kees that they envisioned when they began their breeding program. Their goal is an identifiable, high-quality line, consistently producing through the generations the traits they value most.

GreenKees

The breeding program at GreenKees Keeshonden has been solidly English. Tess and Bill Eckhart imported Ch. Ledwell Hyperion (Eng. Ch. Surprise of Ven x Eng. Ch. Ledwell Charlotte) from Mrs. Sylvia Scroggs of England. They also imported Ch. Rhinevale Ribstonpippin (Eng. Ch. Ledwell Dutchman x Eng. Ch. Raffetta of Rhinevale) from Margo Emerson of England. In 1975 Pippin was the Top HTKC member-owned show dog.

The first GreenKees litter produced Ch. GreenKees Pipson Caesar (Ch. Rhinevale Ribstonpippin ex Ch. GreenKees Andrasta V. Ledwell). He was BOW at the National Capital Keeshond Club Specialty. A mating between Eng. Ch. Ledwell Kardos and Pure Honey of Ledwell produced Am. and Can. Ch. GreenKees Beowulf V Ledwell and Ch. GreenKees Kismet V Ledwell.

Tess and Bill then acquired Ch. Ledwell Brittania (Eng. and Am. Ch. Keesland Fisherman, ex Ledwell Quetta). Britt finished in just eight weeks. In 1984 she was bred to Can. Ch. Kendol's Chinook of Gates, Can. CD and this litter produced, among others, Am. and Can. Ch. GreenKees Destiny, who was Best in Match at the Buckeye Keeshond Club A Match held in conjunction with the KCA Golden Anniversary Specialty in 1985. The entry was 171 and was judged by English breeder-judge Gina Weedon. A littermate is Am. and Can. Ch. GreenKees Damien V. Eden, who was BOS in Sweepstakes at the HTKC Specialty in 1985.

South

Dorvans

Dorothy and Hugh Evans of Dorvans Keeshonden acquired their first Keeshonds from Jane West of Westcrest in 1960. They purchased Ch. Keenic's Miss Michelle in 1967 from Rodney Nickerson; she became the foundation of Dorvans. Her first litter, when bred to Ch. Sinterklaas Brave Nimrod, produced seven puppies of their "Z" litter. Dorothy says it was called the Z litter because she put in so much care, worry, concern about their placement, etc. that this was going to be their *last* litter. But thankfully it wasn't and their Zonda Dolce of Dorvans was bred to Ch. Aeneas of Larah. This mating produced four puppies, three of which were Ch. Ace

Ch. Ashbrook's Seawitch, ROM (Ch. Damarkee The Party Crasher, ROM ex Ch. Bonnyvale Afternoon Delight) was BOS in Futurity at the National Specialty in 1980. In her litter by Jo-Lyn's British Sterling, all five of her puppies finished their championshps.

Ch. Ashbrook's Sea Nymph, HOF (Jo-Lyn's British Sterling ex Ch. Ashbrook's Seawitch, ROM) was the first bitch to take BOB at the KCA National Specialty. She is bred and owned by Linda Moss.

Larah of Dorvans, Ch. Angie Deb of Dorvans and Ch. Amie Dol of Dorvans.

In Dorvans "B" litter (Waakzaam Waagskind ex Ch. Amie Dol of Dorvans), all four puppies became champions. Their "C" litter — the last bred at Dorvans — was by Ch. Banacek of Dorvans out of Ch. Angie Deb of Dorvans. This mating produced Ch. Aljun's Chicapee of Dorvans, who was BOB at the CKC Specialty and Group 1 at the accompanying all-breed show.

Following Hugh's death, Dorothy retired from breeding but still enjoys the companionship of her four Keeshonds.

Cai-Lin

Bruce and Linda Cail acquired their first Keeshond in May 1966 when they were living in the northeast. They have since moved to Florida. Over the years, their breeding program has combined Coventry and Rhinevale lines. They keep primarily bitches and their dogs are all housedogs.

They are the breeders/co-owners of BIS winner Am. and Can. Ch. Cai-Lin Regal Rogue and breeders of Ch. Cai Lin Royal Imp V Candray, who was BOSIF in 1975. They are active breeders and exhibitors in both conformation and obedience and Linda has judged several sweepstakes.

Ashbrook

Linda Moss of Ashbrook Kennels has been involved with animals all her life. In 1964 she became interested in showing dogs and began with German Shepherds. When she and her husband Si moved into town, she changed her loyalties to cats but still kept active in dog-related activities. Ashbrook is still registered with the Cat Fanciers of America. When she and Si moved back to the countryside, Linda revived her love of horses and dogs. She soon had accumulated seven dogs and seven horses. In 1978 the family moved to North Carolina and Linda acquired her first Keeshond, Ch. Bonnyvale Afternoon Delight from Darlene Bosch. In the 14 years prior to her introduction to Keeshonds, Linda had never been able to put a point on a dog. She knew she had found the right breed when she walked in the ring with Amy and immediately won a 5-point major. Amy finished in five shows.

Linda bred Amy to Ch. Damarkee the Party Crasher, ROM. This litter produced Ch. Ashbrook's Kenarae Seawitch, ROM, who finished her championship at the Capital Keeshond Club Show. She was BOS in Futurity at the National Specialty in 1980. Linda then bred Seawitch to Jo-Lyn's British Sterling. Five puppies were born and Linda could find no show homes for them so, she kept them all herself! All five finished. Three later went to other kennels but one young bitch stayed at Ashbrook and went on to fame.

Ch. Ashbrook's Sea Nymph, HOF, finished her championship at the CKC Specialty in 1982 by going WB, BOW and BOS in Sweeps. "Bubbles" was No. 6 Show bitch in 1982; in 1983, she was No. 1. In 1983 she became the first bitch in history to win BOB at the KCA National Specialty. This, coupled with her other major wins, earned her the Hall of Fame. She was bred to Ch. Keeslund's Ashbrook Voyager (Coventry's Finale for Harry ex Ch. Fearless Flavor for Keeslund, HOF). From this litter of seven puppies, five have completed their championships; two have received their Canadian championships and one, Am. and Can. Ch. Ashbrook's Hurricane has also completed a coveted tracking degree. At the 1985 KCA National Specialty, littermates Ashbrook's Johnny Reb was BOSIF and Ch. Ashbrook's Hurricane, TD, was RWD.

In 1982 Linda purchased a co-ownership in another foundation bitch, Breezy's Sage, ROM, from Harold and Patti Brizee. Sage was first bred to Ch. Kenarae Silver Edition and produced Ch. Ashbrook's Buccaneer, who was a Select Dog at the 1984 National Specialty and garnered eight Group placements out of 13 breed wins. Both as a show dog and stud, he is proving a true asset to the Ashbrook Kennel.

In 1985 Linda was the breeder or co-breeder of 12 Keeshond champions, making her KCA Breeder of the Year.

Kenarae

In 1969 Ken and Nancy Springer purchased their first Keeshond, who would later become Ch. Mist of Spring. It wasn't until 1972 that they realized dog shows existed. From that point on, Ken, Nancy and Misty learned together and Kenarae Keeshond Kennels was born. Not overly fond of the show ring, Misty was temporarily retired and Ken and Nancy went on to finish other youngsters.

Then Bogart entered their lives. Ch. Damarkee The Party Crasher, ROM (Ch. Dalbaro Beachcomber ex Damarkee Zilver Bairn, bred by Mary Keith Davis) was four years old when he joined Kenarae. He consistently won BOB, and on the same day he finished his championship, he won his first Group 1 and then Best in Show. In very limited showing, he acquired another BIS, four Group 1s and multiple Group placements. In 1977 he was *Kennel Review's* No. 7 Keeshond and in 1978 he was No. 6. During his show career, Bogart was always handled by Ken.

In July 1978 Nancy's mother was dying with cancer; to please her, they decided to bring out her favorite dog one more time and try to earn his Championship. Misty was now 9½ years old and he needed a major to finish. And finish he did by taking BOW. By the cheers at ringside, you would have thought he had taken a BIS! Her dream fulfilled, Nancy's mother died two months later.

In 1976 Ken and Nancy acquired Ch. Keeszar Mint Julep V. Kenarae, ROM (Ch. Rokerig Rebelrouser V. Keeszar ex Ch. Cai-Lin Rebecca V.

Ch. Damarkee The Party Crasher, ROM (Ch. Dalbaro Beachcomber ex Damarkee Zilver Bairn) was a two-time BIS winner. He finished his championship by taking his first BIS. He was owned by Ken and Nancy Springer.

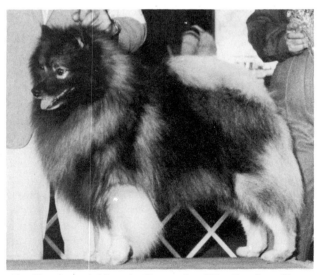

Ch. Karolina Ashbrook Contender (Ch. Ruttkay Commander, HOF ex Ch. Keenote's Jezabell) was the top show dog in 1985. He is owned by Bill and Pat Stroud.

Keeszar). Julie and Bogart were to become the foundation for Kenarae Kennels. Bred together in 1978, they produced a litter of seven males and one bitch; six of this litter finished their championships. The only girl, Ch. Kenarae Pat 'N Pending, stayed at Kenarae and went on to become No. 4 Show Bitch in 1979 (Keezette System). The boys — Ch. Kenarae Beauchamp's Six Pak, Ch. Kenarae the Silver Streak, Ch. Nautica's Kenarae Dark Dream and Ch. Kenarae Silver Edition — all made names for themselves in the show ring. The blending of Beachcomber (Bogart) and Rhinevale (Julie) established the Kenarae line.

Bogart has always been the alpha male and struts his stuff in the ring with great arrogance. When Ken and Bogart last entered the show ring in the Veterans Class at one of the specialty shows, Ken looked down at an aging but still proud showman. Nancy says there were tears in his eyes when an unidentified admirer stopped Ken to say Bogart was the most magnificent animal he had ever seen. Bogart's show career ended on that lovely comment.

Bogart died in 1986, but Ken and Nancy carry on the Kenarae line through Bogart's children and grandchildren.

Chatawa

In 1968 Miss Billie Ann Terry of Tennessee purchased her first Keeshond puppy from Virginia Ruttkay. Ann began training Ch. Ruttkay Paragon Beauty in obedience; she received a Dog World Award gaining her CD and then went on to achieve her CDX. Ann acquired another puppy from Virginia Ruttkay. At her request, Ch. Ruttkay Silver Duchess II, CD, was bred to Ch. Ruttkay Vench's Heir. This mating produced Chatawa Kennel's first litter of 11 puppies, six of which stayed at Chatawa and gained their championships and/or obedience degrees.

One of the puppies, Ch. Creekwood's Sugar N' Spice, was chosen to carry on the breeding program at Chatawa. Bred to Ch. Flakkee High Roller she produced three puppies, all three of which would finish. One of them, Ch. Chatawa Peppermint Patty, CDX, was the winner of the Veteran Bitch Class at both the KCA Specialty in 1985 and the subsequent Canadian Specialty.

Patty was bred to Ch. Chatawa Silver Dutchman from Ann's first litter; from this mating came the brood bitch Ann had been searching for. Ch. Chatawa Tekesta Spring Love, CD, ROM won the brood bitch classes at the Keeshond Club of Dallas, 1985 KCA Specialty and the Canadian Specialty the same year. Bred to Ch. Ashbrook's Buccaneer, they produced a litter from which four out of seven puppies have finished. Ch. Chatawa Sabrina Sioux finished in only six shows with three 5-point majors. She was BOS and BOW at the Keeshond Club of Dallas and finished that same weekend. She was also a Select Award winner at 10½ months at the KCA 1985 National Specialty and Best Puppy in Sweepstakes at the Canadian Specialty.

Ch. Markwright's Square Rigger, HOF, bred by Mary Ellen Marx and owned by Ken Hudson, was BOB at the Keeshond Fanciers of Central States Specialty in 1984.

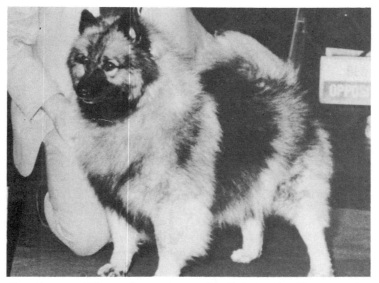

Ch. Chatawa Tekesta Spring Love, CD, ROM (Ch. Chatawa Silver Dutchman, CD ex Ch. Chatawa Peppermint Patty, CDX) is bred, owned and handled by Ann Terry. In her two litters, which produced 14 puppies, six have completed their championships.

At Chatawa, Ann breeds for health, temperament, brains and beauty, in that order.

Karolina

The Karolina Keeshond Kennel is the creation of Dr. Bill and Pat Stroud of North Carolina. In 1977 they acquired Flakkee Double Exposure. Bred to Ch. Fearless Flying Tiger, she produced Karolina's first homebred champions. Then in 1979 they acquired a champion bitch that was to exceed their expectations. Ch. Keenote's Jezabell whelped her first litter in 1982 and, in limited showing that same year, earned the rank of No. 1 KCA Show Bitch. Her litter by Ch. Ruttkay Commander, ROM, HOF, produced Ch. Karolina Ashbrook Kontender, a BIS and multiple Group winner; Ch. Karolina Kommander, BOS in Futurity in 1983; Ch. Karolina Bandit, 1984 BOW winner and 1985 BOB winner at Capital Keeshond Club; and Ch. Karolina Southern Bell, BOS in Sweepstakes at the KCDV Specialty in 1983. Kontender's show record in 1984 and 1985 earned him induction into the Hall of Fame.

Bill and Pat handpick owners of their puppies. Their aims are to produce beautiful puppies of type and soundness with outstanding temperaments as a result of in-home rearing.

Chevron

In Virginia, Katherine Evans of Chevron Kennels has been busy on the international circuit. The titles of two of her four dogs read like a travel atlas: Am., Mex., Bda., Int., Puerto Rican, Can. and Venez. Ch. Chevron's Unsung Hero; and Puerto Rican, Int., S. Am., Venez. Ch. Chevron The Xtabay. These dogs are littermates from Ch. Baronwood's Cloudburst by Ch. Flakkee Taki of Vredendal. Kat hopes to add still more titles to these dogs and her other Keeshonds.

Markwright

Mary Ellen Marx of Markwright Kennels, originally of Wisconsin and now of North Carolina, began showing when she was only 13 years old. She purchased her first Keeshond in 1971. In the next 15 years, Markwright Kennels bred six litters, including nine champions. Of these Am. and Can. Ch. Markwright's Square Rigger, owned by Ken Hudson, is a multiple BOB and Group winner and placer, as is Ch. Markwright's Challenger, CD.

Mary Ellen's two daughters have always been a part of dog showing. In 1984, at the age of ten, Jennifer made her debut as a junior handler. She finished her first year as No. 10 Junior Handler (Keezette). At the 1985 KCA Golden Anniversary Specialty she was in competition with sister Amy, having just turned ten and making *her* show debut in Junior Showmanship. It was Jennifer's day as she took home the award for Best

Junior Handler. Jennifer also had another Best Junior win in 1985, and Amy is working hard to catch up with her sister.

Bischar

Bischar Keeshonden in Virginia was started in 1980 by Shelly Bische Rooks. Her foundation bitch, Yan-Kee Dawn of Bischar (Keeszar Karronade V. Candray ex Yan-Kee Inspiration), was acquired from Peter and Holly Colcord, who have helped and guided her. From Bischar's first litter of Dawn bred to Ch. Brummen of Growling Ridge, Shelly's first Keeshond, came Ch. Bischar's Masked Marvel and Bischars Different Drummer.

In her continuing breeding program Shelly's emphasis is on movement with good fronts, rears and bone.

OHIO

Mar-I-Ben

Marilyn Bender and Eloise Geiger became friends in 1956 when Marilyn was a student and Eloise a teacher at Canton High. One of Marilyn's Keeshond puppies had a "prance on" part in a high school play; this was Eloise's introduction to a breed that would shape her life for the next 30 years. Although only a teenager, Marilyn was already a respected breeder and she placed Ch. Mar-I-Ben Student Prince with Bob and Eloise Geiger. This began a partnership in Mar-I-Ben Keeshonden that continued until Marilyn's death from diabetes in 1974.

Ch. Wil-Los Zoet Zang had two litters — The "Kandy Kids" in 1962, all five of which became champions; and the "Bar Flyers" in 1963, all four of which became champions. In their arrangement, Marilyn would keep the bitches and Eloise the males. So, Ch. Mar-I-Ben Licorice Twist and Ch. Mar-I-Ben Singapore Sling came to live with Eloise; they went on to become a fantastic brace, with six Bests in Show to their credit. Of the two, "Wisty" was the better known and before his retirement garnered 150 BOB, 96 Group placements and two BIS — all owner-handled. When the Hall of Fame was instituted, Wisty qualified easily. Wisty's stud career was also superior and his 11 American champion offspring left him just one short of his ROM designation.

Undaunted by the onset of blindness, Marilyn, with the help of Eloise, continued the Mar-I-Ben breeding program. In 1969 Wisty's daughter, Ch. Midnight Masquerade, was bred to Ch. Dalbaro Beachcomber. All of the four puppies became champions and one, Ch. Mar-I-Ben Feather Duster, was exceptional. She finished her championship at the KCA Specialty in 1970 by going WB, BOW and BOS; she also won the Futurity Stakes the same day. Feather was KCA Show Bitch of the Year in 1970. Another of the

Ch. Mar-I-Ben Singapore Sling and Ch. Mar-I-Ben Licorice Twist exemplify the uniformity of type and quality for which Mar-I-Ben was known. During their brief show career, they won nine Group 1s and four BBIS. They were always owner-handled by Eloise Geiger.

Ch. Keedox's Mischief, ROM, owned by Gerry and Vern Brewer of Bucyrus, Ohio.

"Revolutionary Kids," Ch. Mar-I-Ben Lamp Lighter was bred for his stud potential and a stud he was. His 12 American champion offspring earned him the ROM title that had eluded his grandsire. In 1972 Eloise showed his daughter, Ch. Japar Geraldine, ROM, to Best in Futurity. In 1973 another "Smiley Joe" daughter, Ch. Mar-I-Ben Chatter Box, was BOS in Futurity. There were still more Mar-I-Ben champions and winners along the way. Twenty-eight champions have carried the prefix or been bred by Mar-I-Ben, not including the foundation stock from other kennels finished by Mar-I-Ben.

But Eloise Geiger has contributed much more than quality Keeshonds. She has given abundantly of her time and knowledge, and a great many kennels (including that of these authors) owe a measure of their success to Eloise. She has given of herself unselfishly in her relationships with Marilyn and her own husband, Bob, who was paralyzed by a stroke; she has served many breed and all-breed clubs and was president of the Stark County Humane Society. In 1983 Eloise herself was the victim of a stroke. She passed away in November 1986. It is because of her indomitable spirit, dedication to the breed and love for others that we have dedicated this book to Eloise Geiger.

Keedox

Keedox Kennel, owned by Geraldine and Vernon Brewer, began in 1962 when their first dog earned his championship and CD degree. Raising and showing dogs has always been a family activity at Keedox. Their first lines included Quarter Moon, Ruttkay and Jomito. They added Mar-I-Ben, Wistonia and Rokerig. Ch. Keedox Mischief and her daughter, Ch. Keedox Mischief Bit A Honey received their ROMs. Bred to Ch. Denwood's Gurney Halleck, Honey produced Ch. Keedox Bibbidi Bobbidi Boo, the first American-bred bitch to win a Best in Show.

Denwood

Ch. Keedox's Koka Kola, ROM (Wistonia Winstead, CD ex Ch. Keedox's Mischief, ROM), was the first Keeshond and the foundation bitch of Denwood Keeshonden, owned by Sue Thornton Rucker. Koka produced 13 puppies in three litters, six of which have finished with others pointed. Among her offspring are Group-placing Ch. Denwood's Gurney Halleck, ROM, sire of 12 champions, and Ch. Denwood's Fedaykin and Denwood's Sandtrout, Denwood's multi-BIS-winning brace.

True identical twins, Ch. Denwood's Fedaykin and Denwood's Sandtrout (Ch. Graywyn's Hot Shot ex Ch. Keedox's Koka Kola, ROM) never required much training as they act alike naturally. Sue reports that they always show better together in brace; separately they act as if something is missing. Feda was sold as a young puppy but could never

Ch. Keedox's Mischief's Bit A Honey, ROM, owned by Gerry and Vern Brewer, is the dam of the BIS-winning bitch, Ch. Keedox Bibbidi Bobbidi Boo.

Am. and Can. Ch. DeVignon's Ducomo, HOF (Ch. Ruttkay Bold Venture, ROM ex Ch. Chi-Chi DeVignon). Duci is pictured at 11 years of age taking a Group 1; he retired after ten years in the Top Ten. He was bred and owned by Ann and Frank Vinion of Niles, Ohio.

Ch. Keedox Bibbidi Bobbidi Boo, HOF, bred by Gerry Brewer and owned by Sue Ann Thornton Rucker, was the first American-bred bitch to win an all-breed Best in Show in the United States.

Ch. Denwood's Fedaykin (L) and Denwood's Sandtrout (R) (Ch. Graywyn's Hot Shot ex Ch. Keedox's Koka Kola, ROM) are identical twins. In their brace career, they were awarded many BBIS, including Best Brace at the 1985 KCA National Specialty. They are bred, owned and shown by Sue Ann Thornton Rucker.

adjust to the separation and so was returned to Sue. Entered in their first brace competition, they went all the way to Best Brace in Show (BBIS). They were never defeated in the Breed and only once in the Group. In 1981 they were shown as a brace at six all-breed shows and received six BBIS awards. At the 1985 KCA National Specialty, against heavy competition, they were once again Best Brace. These two dogs truly look and move as one and that is what brace competition is all about.

Sue also owns Ch. Keedox Bibbidi Bobbidi Boo who, at just six months of age, was BOB over six specials. She received another BOB over ten specials her next time in the show ring. She completed her championship at just nine months of age. Her time in the ring as a special ensured her place in history as her owner-handler took her all the way to Best in Show, the first American-bred bitch to take the honor in the United States. She ended the year with one BIS, one Group 1, one Group 2, one Group 3 and two Group 4s, qualifying her for the Hall of Fame its first year in existence.

Klassic

Keedox Kennel also provided the foundation for another kennel when Mary Beeman bought a male puppy for obedience. Little did she know this dog would win WD at the Heart of America Specialty and become Ch. Keedox's Klassy Kid, CD. He finished in six shows and Klassic Keeshonden was born. In limited specialing in 1975, "Smiley" was tied for No. 10 Keeshond. Bred four times, he has sired seven champions.

Mary then began the search for the right bitch; she found her in Ch. Conquest's Contessa, ROM (Ch. Flakkee Gangbusters ex Flakkee Sweet Deal). This sound bitch became the foundation of Klassic Keeshonden and was responsible for several generations of exceptional fronts, good eye shape and very sweet dispositions. Her granddaughter, Ch. Klassic's Dynamic Dame, has five champion offspring.

Mary also purchased Ch. Graywyn's Klassic Kasanova (Ch. Rich-Bob's Stormy Weather, ROMX ex Leespride Charm of Graywyn). He is a Smiley grandson and has sired eight champions. Mary's other young dogs continue to win in the show ring and contribute to the Klassic breeding program.

Paddock Lane

One of the outstanding dogs at the Paddock Lane Farm of Dr. and Mrs. Thomas Hancock was Ch. Ruttkay Ruf-N-Ready V Kathrdon. Born in 1970 by Ch. Ruttkay Thunderation ex Ch. Ruttkay Sugar of Kathrdon, bred by Virginia Ruttkay and Kathryn McNally Bova, he was a multiple Group and specialty winner. Although never actively campaigned, he was No. 10 under *Kennel Review's* system at one time in his career. Always a superb showman, he had a beautiful front, a long elegant neck and a wonderful disposition. Ruffie was owned by Joan B. Hancock and Jeanne Buente-Young.

Ch. Ruttkay Ruf-N-Ready V. Kathrdon (Ch. Ruttkay Thunderation ex Ch. Ruttkay Sugar of Kathrdon) was a multiple Group and Specialty winner.

Ch. Ruttkay Commander, ROM, HOF (Ch. Ruttkay Clyde's Dubby ex Ruttkay Misty Afternoon) is a BIS-winning dog and also producer of 12 champions to date. He is owned by Joan Hancock and shown by Jeanne Buente-Young.

Another outstanding dog is Ch. Ruttkay Commander, ROM, HOF (Ch. Ruttkay Clyde's Cubby ex Ruttkay Misty Afternoon, bred by Virginia Ruttkay. "Manny" joined the Hancock household after his show career had begun. He finished his championship at 14 months in 1979 and was retired from competition in 1983. In 1982 he was KCA Top BOS Keeshond. Handled by Jeanne Buente-Young during his four years in competition, he won one all-breed BIS, three specialty BOB, 82 BOBs, 12 Group 1s, ten Group 2s, seven Group 3s, and 11 Group 4s. Used sparingly as a stud, he has sired 12 Champions to date, including multiple BIS winner, Ch. Karolina Ashbrook Contender, KCA Top Show Dog in 1985.

Mrs. Hancock reports that Manny has great dignity, a mind of his own and holds himself in very high esteem; yet, he is loving and lovable. She says he has very exotic tastes and once won a group baiting on raisins.

Foxfair

If you have limited space for your breeding program but still would like to produce high quality dogs, you might take a look at the Foxfair Kennel. Modeled after the Rhinevale Kennels in England from which their foundation came, Foxfair keeps only four to five adult Kees. Male specials are usually co-owned with the bitches remaining at Foxfair. Debbie Dorony-Lynch and her husband Pat say originally the five dog limit was established due to space constraints; now with several acres, the limit is retained to keep quailty high and to assure time is spent with each dog.

Debbie started showing Keeshonds in 1970 and breeding shortly thereafter, originally with local dogs under the Keemark prefix. "My first Kees was Trinka, Keemark Kandlyt Holi of Wil'O, CD. Since then I've learned a lot about breeding, showing and obviously, *naming* dogs," says Debbie. Trinka and several other bitches that followed were only average producers and so Pat and Debbie began a search for the look they wanted. In 1976 Debbie attended the KCDV Specialty in Pennnsylvania and saw young Am. and Can. Ch. Racassius of Rhinevale, ROMX, who possessed the elegance and substance she was looking for.

Later that year, Debbie and Pat acquired Ch. Vaakers Mary Poppins, ROM, who they then bred to Racassius. This litter produced four champions: Ch. Foxfair Persuasive Friend, ROMX, HOF; Ch. Foxfair Special Sparkle, Ch. Foxfair Popover Peaches (dam of five champions), and Ch. Foxfair Knockout Punch, CD. All the Foxfair dogs are based on this breeding, which established the Foxfair type and temperament; their dominant genetic impact has influenced other lines as well.

The goal at Foxfair is to breed Keeshonds that reflect outstanding type. Of the ten champions bred or co-bred by Debbie and Pat, nine have won BOB, six have Group placements, five have Group 1s, and two have won Best in Specialties. Two Foxfair dogs have won the elusive BIS: Ch. Foxfair Persuasive Friend, HOF, ROMX, owned by Gloria Marcelli; and his son,

Ch. Vaakers Mary Poppins, ROM (Ch. Jomito First Night ex Frosted
Starfire) is shown here on her eleventh birthday. She was bred by Nancy
Edgar and owned by Debbie Dorony-Lynch of Foxfair Kees.

Ch. Jee Jac In Command at Gae-Kee was BOB at the KCD
Specialty in 1983 and 1984. He is owned by Alice Gamache.

Ch. Cedarcrest Quarterback, owned by and co-bred with Carolyn Reinders.

Ch. Foxfair Special Sparkle, littermate of Ch. Foxfair Persuasive Friend, HOF, ROMX, was placed in a junior showmanship home as a puppy; at Debbie's request, he was returned to Ohio to finish his championship. After five long months of care and conditioning, Sparky was ready to enter the show ring. Exclusively handled by Jeanne Buente-Young, he earned his championship in four shows with three majors. Showing Sparky had special significance to Jeanne because ten years earlier, she had shown his dam, Ch. Vaakers Mary Poppins, ROM, to her championship. In limited showing as a special in 1984, Sparky garnered a total of 28 BOBs with 21 Group placements; he was No. 4 Show Dog (KCA) and No. 5 Show Dog (Keezette). He has been shown sparingly since but has added more Group placements and a Specialty BOB win at KCDV in 1985. Sparky is co-owned by Debbie Dorony-Lynch and Jeanne Buente-Young. Since the start of his show career, he has been in residence with Jeanne at Wysperwynd Keeshonden in southern Ohio. When both Jeanne and Debbie are with him, he has a hard time deciding whose lap to jump into or whose face needs to be licked first. As an eight year old, Sparky has the heart, spirit and presence of a youngster.

MICHIGAN

Ronson's

Ronson's Keeshonden are owned by Ron and Judy Fulton of Davison, Michigan. They acquired their first Keeshond in 1968 as a gift from their neighbor for housesitting their dogs. In 1975, they made a family decision to become involved in showing and breeding; since then Ron, Judy and their three sons, Ron, Jr., Todd and Troy, have been active participants.

In their search for a show bitch, they contacted Dave and Barb Connelly and selected Ch. Conquest Penny Pitter Patter. This foundation bitch earned her ROM by producing six American and three Canadian champions. This was the beginning of a very productive breeding program. In the last 11 years, Ronsons's has finished or been involved with finishing 32 American and 20 canadian Champions, five CD, two TD and one TDX. Since 1980 they have consistently placed in the top rankings of Keezette's awards program.

In 1983 Ron and Judy purchased Am. and Can. Ch. Candray's Stormin Normin. Stormy is a BIS winner and a multi-Group placer. Another multi-Group placer at Ronson's is Am. and Can. Ch. Ronson's Benji Boy of Cascadia. Ron tells us that his biggest thrill was at the 1985 KCA Golden Anniversary Specialty when Benji, who hadn't been shown in three years, won Best Veteran in Sweepstakes. Still another winner at Ronson's is Am. and Can. Ch. Ronson's Joshua of Cascadia. He has excelled both as a Group

Ch. Foxfair Special Sparkle began his show career late in life and in limited showing in 1984 won 28 BOBs and 21 Group placements. He is co-owned by his breeder Debbie Dorony-Lynch, and Jeanne Buente-Young.

Ch. Graywyn's Hot Shot, ROM (Ch. Rich-Bob's Stormy Weather, ROMX x Ch. Graywyn's Silver Moonbeam) was bred and is owned by Jo-Ann Gray of Illinois.

placer and as a stud dog, having sired nine American and six Canadian champions.

Geronimo

Geronimo Keeshonden began with the purchase of a Keeshond in 1969 by Bill and Mary Alice Smiley. He was ten months old and his name was Greheim's Geronimo. Gus went on to become a champion both in America and in Canada. He was later bred to a Coventry bitch and Bill and Mary Alice kept the pick female as a pet. According to Mary Alice, "If I could have forseen what would happen to our lives as a result of this puppy, I don't know if we would have continued."

Misty Lady of Kishamo and Mary Alice went to handling school. Misty finished easily, and the Smileys were hooked. Now that they had two champions, they began a search for the perfect stud dog for Misty. They contacted Eloise Geiger and acquired Mar-I-Ben Hobgoblin, who quickly finished his American and Canadian championships.

From the mating of Misty and Hob came three champions: Ch. Geronimo's Hob-Bit, Ch. Geronimo's Shady Lady and Ch. Geronimo's Stormy Weather. Shady Lady went to Bill and Nancy Yant and became the foundation bitch of Keeway Kennels. Misty is now the constant companion of Mary Alice's mother.

The Smiley's purchased several other dogs, including Ch. Magic Myst American Gigolo and Loosenort's Alia of Denwood. The mating of Alia to Ch. Keedox Strawberry Shortcake produced Ch. Geronimo's Maggie O'Keedox, the latest brood bitch at Geronimo. She has produced sound, good-looking champions with excellent temperaments. Through the years, Bill and Mary Alice have tried to breed judiciously with an even, sweet temperament as their highest priority.

An art teacher by profession, Mary Alice's drawings and paintings of Keeshonds clearly illustrate her love and knowledge of the breed. We are delighted that her artistry highlights this book.

Von Rhinegold

The Von Rhinegold Keeshond Kennel of Bill and Lydia Laycook boasts several highly titled Keeshonds and great success both in the conformation and obedience rings. Lydia' was born in Germany and was familiar with Spitz dogs there. So, as an adult in this country, when she decided to acquire a Spitz, she knew exactly what she wanted. In 1973 she contacted Virginia Ruttkay and acquired a three-month-old male. Little did she know what he would become. Echo finished his American championship, and American and Canadian CDs quickly. In 1976 he. completed his Canadian championship and American and Canadian CDX degrees.

Echo hurt his leg jumping and so Lydia decided to discontinue his obedience career. To make up for the disappointment, Bill, Lydia and Echo

Ch. Conquest Penny Pitter Patter, ROM (Ch. Flakkee Gangbusters ex Flakkee Sweet Deal) is the foundation bitch for Ron and Judy Fulton's Ronson's Keeshonden in Michigan.

Ch. Baronwood's Calculated Risk, HOF, owned by Gene and Donna Smith of Missouri, retired with three BIS and 48 Group placements.

decided to take in a show in the Dominican Republic. They came home with a Dominican Republic championship. Naturally, what they started, they had to complete so Echo went on to become the first North, Central and South American champion Keeshond. Next on the list was an International championship. In order to become an International champion, a dog must win four excellent ratings and CACIBs (Certificate of Aptitude, Championship, International Beauty) under FCI (Federation Cynologique Internationale) judges in four countries. On his way to the International title, Echo won eight consecutive times in eight countries.

But that wasn't all that was in store for Echo. Next was the title of World champion. The FCI sponsors a World Show once a year; in order to gain the title of World champion, a dog must win CACIB and BOB all four days of this show. Echo became the first North American-bred Keeshond to do so.

Echo passed away in 1979 but his name and titles live on; he was World, Int. Champion, Dom. Rep., Ecuad., Mex., Can., Am. Ch. Ruttkay Echo von Rhinegold, Am. and Can. C.D.X.

Because they so enjoyed the international shows, Bill and Lydia searched for the perfect bitch to campaign. They found her in Ch. Candray Coronet. Ruffles was to become Int., Am., Can., Puerto Rican, and Venez. Ch. Candray Coronet, Am. and Can. CDX. Bill and Lydia also acquired Am. and Can. Ch. Fearless Flipside.

MIDWEST

Graywyn

Jo-Ann Gray of Illinois received her first Keeshond in 1968 as a birthday present from her husband. "Luckily," Jo-Ann says, "she was purchased from a reliable breeder who had patience and answered a lot of novice questions." Ch. Milmar Nicoleamer, CD, and another bitch, Ch. Milmar's Silver Key of Graywyn, were the foundation for Graywyn Keeshonds. Jo-Ann spent the next several years studying the breed and the sport of dogs and forming her image of the perfect Keeshond. With this image in mind, she began her own breeding program. She bred twice to the great stud dog, Ch. Rich-Bob's Stormy Weather, ROMX. One mating produced Ch. Graywyn's Hot Shot, ROM. "Luke" was special right from the start. He began his show career with a 5-point major at the Heart of America Kees Specialty, where he was also Best in Sweeps. He finished his championship by going BOB over Group-placing specials, all owner-handled. Although not specialed, he has proven himself as a stud, passing on his lovely temperament, intelligence and strong desire to please.

Many Graywyn Keeshonds are serving as foundations and additions to existing kennels. The breeding program at Graywyn strives for Keeshonds with just a little something extra in the show ring and Jo-Ann is proud of her honestly represented, carefully planned puppies that are providing a firm foundation for tomorrow.

Ch. Baronwood's Sling Shot, HOF was specialed 51 times and won 48 BOBs with 27 Group placements and a specialty BOB for his owners, Gene and Donna Smith.

Ch. Woffee Can Can Dancer, ROM (Keli-Kees Woffee Grande ex Misty Silver), owned by Pat Doescher of Wisconsin, has produced seven champions to date; she is the backbone of Woffee Keeshonden.

Baronwood

The Baronwood Kennel of Gene and Donna Smith of Missouri has been more of a show kennel than a breeding kennel. Although they have bred winners, their main interest is in exhibiting, with Donna doing the handling and Gene the grooming.

Their first dog of note was Ch. Baronwood's Flip Wilson, HOF, a multiple Group and specialty winner with 100 BOBs at retirement. He was followed by Peter Witt's Ch. Flakkee Keeboom Diamond Lil, HOF. She remains one of the breed's all-time bitch winners; at retirement she had placed in the Group 14 times and was a multiple Group and specialty BOB winner.

Their next special was Ch. Baronwood's Calculated Risk, HOF, a multiple BIS winner, retiring with a total of 3 BIS and 48 Group placements. He was followed by his son, Ch. Baronwood's Sling Shot, HOF, who was specialed 51 times and won 48 BOBs, with 27 Group placements and a specialty BOB. Concurrently, Sling Shot's dam, Ch. Traveler's Swirling Silver, HOF, who the Smiths co-owned with Sandy Krueger, was finishing her career as a multiple Group winner, plus having been BOS at all the shows on two National Specialty weekends.

Baronwood's primary brood bitch was Ch. Picvale's Miss Vixen of Banks, ROMX. She was the dam of two BIS winners. Gene and Donna had the honor of exhibiting Keeshonds to national top-ten prominence in ten consecutive years, and five of these dogs have been inducted into the KCA Hall of Fame. Since the early 1980s Gene and Donna have curtailed their showing drastically to concentrate on other interests.

Woffee

Woffee Keeshonden in Wisconsin got its start in 1973 when Pat and Roger Doescher purchased a bitch puppy sired by Ch. LaDeJa's Happy Go Lucky ex Car-le-on's Merry Meri of LaDeJa, CDX, bred by Doris and Jim Froman. This puppy grew to be a lovely show bitch and became Ch. LaDeJa's Felicity of Woffee, CD. "Heidi" was bred three times, has four champion get, two sons with CD titles and is behind all but a few of the Woffee Kees.

In 1977 Pat and Roger bought Keli-Kees Woffee Grande (Ch. Star-Kees Batman, ROMX ex Ch. Keli-Kees Erin O'Mist, ROM), bred by Mrs. Sam Kelley. Although not fond of the show ring, his pedigree and soundness contributed to the Woffee breeding program. His daughter, Ch. Woffee Can Can Dancer, ROM, bred by Linda Babcock, produced seven champion get and is most noted for passing on her front, good shoulder placements and proud carriage. Her first litter by Ch. Woffee Silver Reflection, CD (a Dalbaro Beachcomber son), produced Ch. Woffee Sun Dance and Ch. Woffee Native Dancer. This breeding is the backbone of Woffee as it brought together the proud carriage of the dam with the outstanding English type of the sire.

Ch. Woffee Bandit Distraction, ROM (Ch. Candray the Phantom ex Ch. Woffee Native Dancer) at only 5½ years of age, is the sire of 15 champions. He is owned by his breeder, Pat Doescher of Wisconsin.

Ch. Woffee Brazen Detonation, HOF (Am. and Can. Ch. Tryon's Beorn, ROMX, HOF ex Ch. Woffee Native Dancer) excels in the show ring. He is co-owned by Sue O'Connor and Pat Doescher.

Native Dancer was an outstanding bitch and in 1981 was in Keezette's top-ten show bitches in only 12 shows. To continue the Woffee type, Roger and Pat purchased Ch. Candray The Phantom (Ch. Candray Ghost of Wintergreen, ROM ex Wintergreen Candray Katrina) as a potential stud for her. From this litter whelped in 1980 Pat and Roger retained Ch. Woffee Bandit Distraction, ROM. According to Pat, Bandit is "arrogant, bold and showy"; his most outstanding achievements have been as a stud dog. At only 5½ years of age, he has 15 finished champions to his credit, one of which is the lovely Ch. Yan-Kee Starkist, HOF.

To date, Woffee Keeshonden has bred or co-bred 18 champions. All litters are carefully planned, with only the absolute best from each litter destined for the show ring.

Jo-Lyn

Janit Johnson of Oklahoma got off to an exceptional start with the purchase in 1976 of her first Keeshond, Ch. Keli-Kees Kandi, ROMX, the foundation for Jo-Lyn Kennels. She was BOSIF in 1978 and is now the dam of ten champions. Several of Kandi's offspring have been producers themselves. Probably the best known is Ch. Jo-Lyn's Brazenly Bold, owned by Carol Aubut. "Dallas" is the sire of two-time National Specialty winner Ch. Dal-Kees Mighty Samson, as well as Ch. Tanglewood Miles Standish and Ch. Tanglewood Tycoon.

Ch. Ashbrook Sea Nymph, first bitch to win a KCA National Specialty, was sired by Jo-Lyn's British Sterling, littermate to "Dallas." Still another littermate, Ch. Jo-Lyn's Brandy O'Keli-Kees, is showing great promise as the dam of champions.

Over the past decade, Jo-Lyn has produced 20 champions and several obedience titleholders, and has obtained championships on three other Keeshonds. Janit is justly proud of her record as Oklahoma's top-producing, top winning Keeshond kennel.

Bonnyvale

Darlene Bosch began her Bonnyvale Kennels in the midwest and just recently moved to North Carolina. Because she did most of her breeding and winning prior to her move east, we have included her in this section geographically. Darlene began showing Shetland Sheepdogs at the age of 15 and became involved with Keeshonds in 1974. Her first Keeshond was to become Ch. Bonnyvale Glowing Cinder, CD. Bred to Ch. Keenotes Sterling Silver, ROMX, she produced six puppies. Since no one wanted a male, Darlene kept him and two of the bitches. The male went on to become Ch. Bonnyvale Andy, the foundation sire for Bonnyvale Kennels.

Darlene says that Andy was a one-in-a-million companion and, although not raised with children, has a special fondness for them. He is happiest when he can take a child for a walk! Another happy pasttime is

Ch. Bonnyvale Andy (Ch. Keenotes Sterling Silver, ROMX ex Ch. Bonnyvale Glowing Cinder, CD) was the foundation stud for Darlene Bosch's Bonnyvale Keeshonden; he was also her first BIS winner.

Ch. Keli-Kees Kandi, ROMX, was the foundation for Janit Johnson's Jo-Lyn Kennels in Oklahoma. Kandi is the dam of ten champions to date.

destroying Darlene's freshly made bed. She says he "tosses and rolls around, making a mess, and after he has everything in complete disarray, he jumps down and goes to his neat crate to sleep. He is my friend, my clown and my guardian."

Andy is also at home in the show ring and his record includes one BIS, 24 Group placements, four of which were Group 1s, and one Select Award. At 9½ years of age, he lacks only ten points for his HOF, but due to his age and the loss of some teeth, will not be specialed again. With 12 champions to his credit, he has earned his ROM designation

There have been several lovely ladies in Andy's life but two were exceptional. Bred twice to Andy, Ch. Shandell Kiwi of Mistilake, CDX, produced Ch. Shandell Kalvin Klein. Kalvin has 36 BOB with six Group placings in limited showing and is the sire of eight champions. Ch. Jo-Lyn's Ember, bred to Andy, produced six puppies, three of which have already finished and two of which are pointed.

One of Andy's littermates which Darlene kept was also exceptional. Ch. Bonnyvale Afternoon Delight was co-owned with Linda Moss. She had several Group placements and was WB, BOW and BOS at the Capital Keeshond Club Specialty. When she died, she was only four points short of her HOF title.

Darlene has been involved with Keeshonds for more than ten years and owes much of her success to the one she calls the "backbone of the kennel, someone who is always there, the one who never gets the credit for feeding and cleaning up." That person in Darlene's life was her mother. Her mother passed away in 1982 but lived long enough to see their dream come true. Today Bonnyvale has bred 17 champions plus five others Darlene has finished. In her words, "If I never get another Best in Show, at least I did it when it was most important, when Mother was alive to share in the joy."

SOUTHWEST

Magic Myst

While living high in the mountains of Colorado, Jim and Gloria Marcelli acquired their first Keeshond from Debbie Dorony-Lynch of Ohio, and so started Magic Myst Kennels. Although they already had Newfoundlands, the dog that was to become Ch. Foxfair Persuasive Friend, HOF, ROMX, was their first Keeshond and what a Keeshond he was! Friendly has an impressive heritage: his sire was Can. and Am. Ch. Racassius of Rhinevale, ROMX and his dam was Ch. Vaakers Mary Poppins, ROM.

Because the Marcellis had also just acquired a Newfoundland puppy, Friendly and the Newfy bitch grew up together and quite a bit of imprinting crossed over breed lines. According to Gloria, "I now had a Kees pup who

Ch. Foxfairs Persuasive Friend, ROMX, HOF (Am. and Can. Ch. Racassius of Rhinevale, ROMX ex Ch. Vaakers Mary Poppins, ROM) is the sire of 30 American champions, including three BIS dogs. He was bred by Debbie Dorony-Lynch and is owned by Gloria Marcelli.

Ch. Keli-Kees Melody of Kilarney, ROMX (Ch. Waakzaam Winkle, CD ex Ch. Keli-Kees Erin O'Mist, ROM) is the dam of nine champions. She was bred and owned by Sam and Dorothy Kelley.

sat, splashing away, in the middle of the pool I bought for the Newfs. But, I had a Newf that preferred to be on your lap and baited without being stacked." Gloria knew she had to make a decision on one breed or the other and chose the Keeshond. Gloria says Friendly still remembers his youth and goes crazy when he sees a big black dog. This proved to be very embarrassing one day when he won a Group 2 behind a black Standard Poodle. To Gloria's embarrassment, Friendly decided it was true love and attempted to mate the Poodle just as the judge was presenting the ribbons. Friendly is a true stud dog.

In Friendly's short show career, he was a multiple Group placer, won nine Group 1s, an all-breed BIS and, in 1981, a National Specialty BOB. He was inducted into the Hall of Fame and this year will receive his ROMX as the sire of 30 champions. In 1983 he was awarded KCA's Top Stud Dog for siring nine champions during that year. He is the sire of three BIS winners (two in the United States and one in Canada), one National Specialty Winner, two BIF winners, one BOSIF winner, five Grand Sweepstakes winners, and eight Group-placing get that include three bitches. He is also the sire of the KCA 1983 top obedience dog and top obedience/champion dog, and Keezette's No. 1 and No. 2 obedience dogs in Canada for 1985.

After a move to California in 1986, Gloria and Jim carry on their limited breeding program at Magic Myst with Friendly as its foundation.

Keli-Kees

The Keli-Kees Kennel in Texas began when Sam and Dorothy Kelley purchased their first Keeshond, Ruttkay Roeman Princess, from Virginia Ruttkay late in 1966. Princess was bred to Ch. Dole Shar Quarterback and produced the first Keli-Kees litter in December 1967. From this litter came their first champion, Ch. Keli-Kees Gray Mist. Misty, in turn, was bred to Can. and Am. Ch. Sinterklaas Brave Nimrod. From this litter came two champions, Ch. Keli-Kees Erin O'Mist, ROM, who stayed with Sam and Dorothy and Ch. Keli-Kees Kristy of KeeNote, owned by Nancy and Mike Hartegan. She became the first bitch to win BOB at an independent Keeshond Specialty.

Erin was bred to Ch. Waakzaam Winkle, CD, to produce Ch. Keli-Kees Melody of Kilarney, ROMX. She also produced a litter by Can. and Am. Ch. Sinterklaas Brave Nimrod that all finished, all had Group wins or placements and one (Ch. Keli-Kees Replica of Roddy) had two specialty BOBs. Erin, in a later litter by Ch. Star-Kees Batman, ROMX, produced Ch. Keli-Kees Cottontail, ROM. She, in turn, was bred to Ch. Keli-Kees Royal Ra of Roblyn to produce Ch. Keli-Kees Kandi, ROMX, who is owned by Janit Johnson.

Erin's son, Ch. Keli-Kees Royal Ra of Roblyn, is the sire of Ch. Van Mell's Pot of Gold, HOF, owned and bred by Carole Van der Meulen. He is also the sire of Zeta Robeson's Ch. Russ-Mar Fancy Pants, who won two back-to-back 5-point majors at the KCA National and KCD specialties.

Can. and Am. Ch. Sinterklaas Brave Nimrod, ROMX, was the sire of 26 American and seven Canadian champions. He was owned in his later years by Sam and Dorothy Kelley of Texas.

The BIS-winning brace of Ch. Merrikee Wrocky Pooh Bear and Ch. Merrikee Wrocky Tip Topper, owned by Mr. and Mrs. Elmer White of Texas.

Thanks to Virginia Ruttkay, the Kelleys became the owners in 1975 of the great Can. and Am. Ch. Sinterklas Brave Nimrod, ROMX. The sire of 26 American and seven Canadian champions, he was bred by Margaret Collier of England and sired by the great Eng. Ch. Big Bang of Evenlode ex Sinterklaas Lass of Vankeena.

Dog showing and breeding were a family affair at Keli-Kees and, with the help of their daughters Kathy and Cindy and son Don, Sam and Dorothy have bred and raised in their home more than 30 champions.

Merrikee

Merrikee Kennels in Texas had its beginning in 1964 when Orvilline and Elmer White purchased a four-month-old Keeshond appropriately named Von Teufel. A year later Orvilline attended a Keeshond club meeting and was encouraged to show Teufel. According to Orvilline, she "had no idea what to expect but quickly decided all the people were crazy and vowed never again to do anything so stupid." Famous last words for Ch. Von Teufel and Orvilline became familiar figures at the Texas shows. Teufel had many exciting breed and Group wins and Orvilline began to learn the art of showing dogs. With the exception of a few times when her health did not permit, she has handled her own dogs and finished 23 to their championships.

Ch. Flakkee Winsome Miss, CD, ROMX (Ch. Worrall of Wistonia ex Flakkee Starlet), purchased in 1965 from Flakkee Kennels, was the foundation bitch for Merrikee Kennels. A beautiful bitch and a natural showman, she finished her championship and CD the same week, but it is her record as a brood bitch that is outstanding. Bred three times to three different studs, she produced ten puppies, nine of which became champions. The first litter, sired by Ch. Cornelius Wrocky Selznick, ROM, HOF, included Ch. Merrikee Wrocky Pooh Bear, Ch. Merrikee Wrocky Tip Topper and Ch. Merrikee Wrocky Royal Rogue. In addition to their many individual Breed and Group wins, Pooh Bear and Tip Topper won three all-breed BBIS awards and were Best Brace at the KCA National Specialty in 1971 under Judge Clementine Peterson. Royal Rogue, owned by Pete and Inge Davis of Texas, was BOB at the Keeshond Club of Dallas first specialty in 1969. Missy's second litter, sired by Ch. Flakkee Jackpot, ROMX, HOF, included Ch. Merrikee Sunny Debutante, ROM, an outstanding bitch.

The Whites have been actively involved with several Keeshond clubs. They have served as officers of the Keeshond Club of Dallas, the first Keeshond Club to hold an independent specialty. In 1974 Mrs. White was elected to the board of directors of the Keeshond Club of America and served six years, five of them as secretary. Since leaving the board, she has served as the club's education chairman. She judged the Keeshond Club of America Futurity in 1975.

SunniKees

Joan and Skee Czarnyszka of Arizona selected the name SunniKees in 1973, although it did not appear as a prefix until 1975. To date there have been six litters at SunniKees, for a total of 27 puppies; nine of these are finished and others are pointed.

Having been given a Keeshond bitch in 1944 by a Georgia breeder with the Dunwoody prefix, Joan's next Keeshond was purchased, embarrassingly, from the Spiegel catalog. Not surprisingly, he turned out to be less than show quality. Next came a show bitch that was spayed for health reasons just as she was beginning to win in the ring.

Bad luck had to turn into good and so it did when they purchased their first brood bitch, Van Fitz Witch of the West, of English Evenlode and Vorden bloodlines. Bred to Ch. Star-Kees Batman, Witch produced the first SunniKees champion, Ch. SunniKees Winnin' Brew, and their first obedience titlist, SunniKees Witch's Mischief, CD, trained by Skee. Bred to Ch. Rich-Bob's Stormy Weather, she produced Ch. SunniKees Sweet Gypsy Rose, CD, and Ch. SunniKees Stormalong.

SunniKees' second brood bitch, Ch. Rich-Bob's Chrissy V. Modesto, had four litters for a total of 19 puppies. Chrissy's first champion, Ch. SunniKees Chippie, was one of four puppies sired by Ch. Tryon's Beorn. The breeding to Ch. Windrift's Gambler, CD, resulted in eight puppies, five of whom finished. Four other puppies from breedings to Ch. Windrift's Willy Weaver and a repeat to Ch. Windrift's Gambler are now being shown. In 1984 Chrissy was tied for KCA Member-Owned Brood Bitch of the Year.

Charmac

Charmac Kees, also of Arizona, had its beginning in 1973 when Jan and Richard Wilhite purchased "a body by Batman." This young dog went on to become Ch. Star-Kees Ego Trip, CD.

Their next Keeshond became the beautiful Ch. Fearless Fortune Cookie, CD, ROMX. Fortune has fulfilled almost every dream possible in the show ring as well as the producing department. To date, she has 12 Charmac champions. Bred to Ch. Star-Kees Batman, ROMX she produced a litter of seven. One of these is Ch. Charmac's Scatman to Star-Kees, HOF, ROM, a multi-BIS winner. Bred to Wistonia Winter-wind, she produced a litter of six including Ch. Charmac's Fortunate Happening, HOF, and Ch. Charmac's Wheel of Fortune and Ch. Charmac's Kiss of Fortune, both dams of champions. Her breeding to Ch. Kamkees British Sterling produced a litter of two, both of which became champions. Her last litter to Ch. Jee Jac's Academy Award resulted in seven puppies, four of which are champions.

In the show ring, Fortune was the first bitch with a dual title to win a specialty and the second bitch in the history of the breed to win a specialty

Ch. Fearless Fortune Cookie, CD, ROMX (Ch. Painter of Somerville ex Ch. Tryon's Fearless Fruhling, ROMX) was KCA Top Keeshond in 1982. Bred by Helen Cuneo, Fortune is owned by Jan and Richard Wilhite of Charmac Kees in Arizona.

Ch. Charmac Fortunate Happening, HOF (Wistonia Winter-wind ex Ch. Fearless Fortune Cookie, CD, ROMX) was KCA Top Show Bitch and Top Keeshond Best of Opposite Sex in 1985. She is owned by Kathy and Larry Brown.

the day before the National in 1982 at KCSC. She had won the honor of Best in Sweeps at their specialty and came back in 1980 and 1981 to win BOS.

In 1982 Fortune was No. 1 Show Bitch (Keezette) and was awarded the Top Keeshond award by KCA. She and her mother (Ch. Tryon's Fearless Fruhling, ROMX) are to date the only bitches that have received this award. The same year, she shared the spotlight with her son, Ch. Charmac's Scatman to Star-Kees, as he won top Member-Owned Show Dog.

Kalarne

Kalarne Keeshonden was established in 1980 when Kathleen and Larry Brown bought their first Keeshond, Ch. Sobaka Flying Hoofer, from Patricia Katomski-Beck. Hoofer was sired by Ch. Star-Kees Ego Trip, CD. As with other novices in Kees, Hoofer was the love of their lives — the one who took them to their first matches and point show, and the one who accompanied their foster son, Neal Roberts, into his first Junior Showmanship competition and ultimately to his first Best Junior Handler award.

They soon realized that one Keeshond was simply not enough and so Ch. Charmac Fortunate Happening, HOF, came into their lives in 1981. Getting off to a slow start, Happy made up for it in 1982 when she finished her championship by taking WB at the KCA National Specialty. Happy's phenomenal specials career began in 1983 with a Group 1 at the Sahuaro Kennel Club Show in Phoenix.

At 2½ years Happy had developed her own trademark: a cute paw movement that would signal her handler that she wanted bait. In the specials ring she would be known for her flash and showmanship, clear coloration and graceful fleet movement. She finished 1983 as the No. 2 Show Bitch in the country and top show bitch in Arizona's Sahuaro Keeshond Club. In 1984 Happy whelped a litter of five males and two females by BIS winner Ch. Windrifts Producer, HOF. She was first in the Brood Bitch class at the Sahuaro Keeshond Club Specialty the same year. Despite taking six months off for motherhood, she was No. 3 Show Bitch (Keezette) in 1984. In 1985 Happy accumulated two Group 1s, a Group 2 and a Group 4, defeated over 500 Keeshonds and earned over 700 Phillips points. She qualified for her Hall of Fame designation by taking still another Group 1 in November 1985.

At the 1986 KCA National Specialty, Happy was named Top Show Bitch and Top Keeshond Best Opposite for 1985; she also received the Ch. Marcy's Teddy Bear Award for most defeated in Breed and Group. Happy retired from the specials ring in December 1985; she has since whelped a litter of eight by Ch. Timekeeper for Windrift.

PACIFIC NORTHWEST

Royal J

Joe and Cae Sullivan were married in June 1970 and the first thing they did was buy Dexter . . . according to Joe, "a $2.00 blue-merle wire-haired mutt from the City of Seattle Dog Pound." Since work kept them away from Dexter, they began searching for a companion for him. Their research led them to a Keeshond, what appeared to be the perfect family dog and friend for Dexter. They decided to purchase a show-quality dog and so Cha-Mar's Fancii Pantz joined their family. With Fancii, Joe and Cae embarked on what would become an all-encompassing involvement with dog shows, dog clubs, breeding and handling their beloved Keeshonds. Royal J Keeshonden was born.

Fancii's show career was less than impressive and the Sullivan's involvement might have ended there had it not been for the advice and guidance given them by another breeder, Joanne Nixon. They decided the next dog they bought would be an adult whose good and bad points were readily discernible. They finally settled on Am. and Can. Ch. Le Jean's Ramrod. Again they faced frustration as "Yonder" came down with a skin disorder requiring extended care.

Joe and Cae were beginning to wonder if dog showing was really in their future when another dog entered their lives. According to Joe, she was a scrawny little bitch who had been rejected as a pet and had subsequently been returned to her breeder. Cae took pity and purchased her. Little did either of them realize that she would one day become Ch. Boone's Lady Velvet, ROM ("Lil Koko") who would prove to be almost unbeatable on her way to her championship and who would then become the foundation bitch for Royal J Keeshonden, stamping her mark on all Royal J offspring to this day.

The pinnacle of Yonder's show career came in 1979 when Joe and Cae loaded up their dogs for a 2,500 mile trip to the KCA Specialty in Cleveland. The Sullivans thought the trip might be too much for the nine-year-old Yonder but decided to bring him at the last minute. Against incredible competition he placed first in his Veterans class and made the trip worthwhile. Joe was then faced with the decision of handling his young special in the BOB competition or staying with Yonder. Eight years of devotion made the decision easy, and Joe and Yonder re-entered the ring to compete against over 70 top specials. When Dr. Frank Booth chose Yonder as his Best of Breed dog — the only Veteran to ever win a National Specialty — Joe couldn't believe his ears. Joe tells us that "we thank Yonder, not for the glorious and unexpected win, but for the memories. Glorious wins fade with time, but good memories only grow fonder." Yonder passed away in 1982 at the age of 12.

Ch. Boone's Lady Velvet, ROM (Am. and Can. Ch. Kream de Koko ex Party Line's Windream V. Royal) was the dam of seven American and/or Canadian champions. She was bred by Jean and Jack Howard and owned by Joe and Cae Sullivan.

Ch. Royal J's Duke of Crinklewood, HOF (Am. and Can. Ch. Tryon's Beorn, ROMX, HOF ex Ch. Royal J's Gin Fizz Lady, ROM). The latest of the Royal J specials, having won 56 BOB and 30 Group placements. He is bred and owned by Joe and Cae Sullivan.

Lil Koko was bred four times and produced six American and three Canadian champions, thereby earning her ROM. From the breeding of Lil Koko and Yonder has come a kennel producing quality and the distinctive Royal J type.

Royal J's first successful show dog was an offspring of Yonder and Lil Koko. Am. and Can. Ch. Jee Jac's Sir Bors of Royal J finished his show career with 31 BOBs, one Group 1, one Group 2, five Group 3s and four Group 4s. Coupled with his half-brother, Am. and Can. Ch. Royal J's Whiskey Sour, he won eight BBIS awards, including the 1976 and 1977 KCA Specialties.

Lil Koko's second litter, by Ch. Rokerig Rodi V Grayfalls Mews produced another record-setting show dog, Ch. Royal J's Simon Le'Gree V. Abekee. "Chunk's" show career, spanning over nine years, took off when he went to live with Bob and Lois Meszaros in Florida. He retired with 36 BOBs, three Group 1s, three Group 2s, two Group 3s and five Group 4s.

Am. and Can. Ch. Royal J's Whiskey Sour was from Lil Koko's third litter by Am. and Can. Ch. Racassius of Rhinevale, ROMX. His show record stands at 25 BOBs, four Group 2s and three Group 4s. Also from this litter was Ch. Royal J's Gin Fizz Lady, ROM. With a successful show career behind her, Ginny excelled in the whelping box. Bred to Ch. Tryon's Beorn, ROMX, HOF, she produced nine puppies, six of which attained their championships; one of these, Ch. Royal J's Duke of Crinklewood, HOF, has been the most successful show dog in Royal J's history. To date he has accumulated 56 BOBs, six Group 1s, ten Group 2s, eight Group 3s and six Group 4s.

In June 1985 Royal J Keeshonden relocated to Marion, Iowa, where Joe and Cae carry on the breeding and winning tradition associated with their kennel.

Maldolph

Richard and Anna Malet of Washington saw their first Keeshond while on a camping trip to the ocean. Six months later, they acquired a female puppy that was the start of Maldolph Keeshonden. Duchess, a beautiful Ruttkay bitch, was retired after only a few times in the ring to return to what she did best: being a loving family pet. Next Dick and Anna purchased "Beepska" from Jan Ellis. Tryon's Dividend, ROM, possessed the fine qualities of the Tryon line, did respectably in the show ring and passed on her fine qualities to her get. Probably the best known of her get is Am. and Can. Ch. Maldolph's Heidi-Ho of Allan, ROM. Among Heidi's six American and three Canadian champion get is Am. Can. Ch. Maldolph's Calculator, who was No. 1 Keeshond in Canada for 1984 (CKC system).

Jee Jac

Jean and Jack Howard of Washington started Jee Jac in 1962 and the

95

Am. and Can. Ch. Jee Jac's Invader produced many of the champions at the Jee Jac Kennel in Washington.

Can. Ch. Jee Jac's Sparkling Silver, ROM (Am. and Can. Ch. Jee Jac's Invader ex LeJean's Delibal of Jee Jac), bred and owned by Jean Howard.

kennel has been a continuous producer of champions. Jack, always with an eye for a pretty head, liked the Flakkee look and temperament and so Ch. Flakkee Playmate joined the Howards as Jee Jac's foundation bitch.

The foundation stud for Jee Jac was Am. and Can. Ch. Coventry's Diki of Wistonia, an English import bred by Nan Greenwood. Other Coventry and Wistonia dogs were added to form the foundation for the present Jee Jac line. Several other dogs were added that contributed to the Jee Jac breeding program. Am. and Can. Ch. Kreme de Koko had an extremely tight Coventry/Wistonia pedigree and was very dominant for type. When combined with Am. and Can. Ch. Jee Jac's Royal Rogue, they produced Ch. Boone's Lady Velvet, ROM, the cornerstone of the Royal J line and producer of many champion offspring. Another successful blending of Kreme de Koko was with Ch. Childerick Cantada, CD, to produce Childerick Chugalug who, in turn, was bred to Maywood Miss Muffet of Jee Jac. From this exceptional litter came the BIS bitch, Am. and Can. Ch. Childerick's Cherish, Am. and Can. Ch. Jee Jac's Funny Face Childerick and Childerick's Joshua (KCA Stud Dog 1976).

In the meantime, the Howards had acquired another contributor to the Jee Jac type. Ch. Rich-Bob's Stormy Weather, ROMX, was purchased from his breeder, Joanne Nixon. Stormy was bred to Jee Jac's Hello Dolly and produced two notable sons — Ch. Jee Jac's Intruder who went to Alice Gamache of Gae-Kee Kennels, and Am. and Can. Ch. Jee Jac's Invader who remained at Jee Jac to produce many champions for the Howards.

Invader, when bred to Am. and Can. Ch. Jee Jac's Funny Face Childerick produced Can. and Am. Ch. Jee Jac's Orthello v Keeshof, a BIS winner and No. 1 Keeshond in Canada in 1979, and Can. Am. Ch. Jee Jac's Command Performance. Command has produced many champion offspring, most notably Ch. Jee Jac's In Command at Gae Kee ("Man") and Ch. Jee Jac's Academy Award. Can. Ch. Jee Jac's Sparkling Silver, ROM, when bred to Command and his son Man, produced five champion offspring, including the Group-winning Ch. Jee Jac's Platinum Plus.

Jee Jac Kennels has intermittently introduced new bloodlines to augment the type and soundness desired, yet maintaining the Jee Jac line. Jean Howard has twice been awarded Breeder of the Year and the kennel has also won a Top Brood Bitch award. Jee Jac has produced 36 American champions, and dogs from the kennel have become foundation stock for many other breeders throughout the United States and Canada.

Cascadia

Am. Can. Ch. Tryons Beorn, ROMX, HOF, is the focus of the Cascadia Keeshonden breeding program of Judy M. Daugherty and Helen L. Wymore in Oregon. Beorn is the result of a 1975 outcross breeding of Ch. LeJean's Allan A Dale, CD (linebred on Ruttkay) to Ch. Tryon's Pound Sterling, CD, ROM (linebred on Flakkee). A Group winner from the

Am. and Can. Ch. Tryons Beorn, ROMX, HOF (Ch. LeJean's Allan A Dale, CD ex Ch. Tryon's Pound Sterling, CD, ROM) is the focus of the Cascadia breeding program. To date he has sired 43 American champions.

The BIS-winning brace of Ch. Tryons Beorn (L) and Ch. Cascadia Dutch Baron (R), owned and shown by Helen Wymore, are the winners of 12 BBIS and two Best Brace in Specialty awards.

Puppy Class, Beorn completed his championship at 13 months of age. Though never heavily campaigned, this multiple Group and specialty winner was one of the original inductees into the KCA Hall of Fame. In addition, Beorn received the KCA Stud Dog of the Year award in 1981, 1982 and 1984.

A character in the show ring, Beorn took exception to any judge who did not begin with parading the dogs at least once around the ring; he was notorious for creating games to alleviate his boredom and test his handler's abilities. At home, Beorn confines the other Wymore Kees to the yard with the skill and expertise of a herding dog. His favorite pasttime is challenging the Wymore's Arabian gelding to a strutting contest. Down the fenceline one way and then back, necks arched, tails high and with their trotting paces matched, the two animals each defy the other to match his own performance. With a kick of his heels, the Arabian usually concedes the victory to Beorn.

As exciting as Beorn was in the show ring, his performance as a stud dog is even more noteworthy. It is not typical for the product of an outcross breeding to be a prepotent sire, but Beorn breaks all the rules. He is now the sire of 43 American champions, eight of which are Group winners and two of which — Ch. Royal J's Duke of Crinklewood and Ch. Woffee Brazen Detonation — have met the requirements for induction into the Hall of Fame. Line breeding is not essential for Beorn to produce well and several bitches credit their ROM awards to Beorn offspring.

But Beorn is not the total story at Cascadia. The kennel was founded in the mid-1970s when Judy purchased her two foundation bitches, Ch. Tryons Wrock Festival and Tryons Ms Got Wrocks, ROM (Ch. Flakkee Wrockhound ex Ch. Tryon's Pound Sterling, CD, ROM). Cascadia's initial litter of three by Ch. Rich-Bob's Stormy Weather, ROMX, out of Tryons Ms Got Wrocks, ROM, produced Ch. Cascadia Aslan of Narnia (a Group winner) and Ch. Cascadia Dawn Treader, ROM.

At this time, Helen and Harold Wymore and Ch. Tryons Beorn joined forces with Judy to form Cascadia Keeshonden.

The Stormy Weather daughter, Ch. Cascadia Dawn Treader, ROM, plays an important part at Cascadia. She is the dam of five Beorn champions, including multiple Group-winning Ch. Cascadia Dutch Baron. In any other household, Baron would have been the star, but with the Wymores, he has lived under the shadow of his famous sire, Beorn. In addition to his highly successful show career, Baron deserves acclaim as the sire of Ch. Cascadia Double Delicious with whom Melissa Wymore triumphed as top Keeshond Junior Handler in 1984, garnering twice as many points as her nearest competitors.

The 1982 KCA Breeder of the Year Award was won by Judy M. Daugherty when seven Cascadia Kees completed their Championships.

Back in the Wymore household, brace competition was on Helen's

Tryon's Ms. Got Wrocks, ROM, was instrumental in the Cascadia breeding program.

Melissa Wymore has several Best Junior Handler in Show awards. She is shown here with Ch. Cascadia Double Delicious.

mind. Her first brace was comprised of Childerick Silver Wings and Ch. Maywood Hi Fashion of Modesto. This brace received four BBIS awards. Fashion was then paired with Beorn for four more BBIS plus one Best Brace in Specialty. Helen says that Fashion tolerated no slips from her brace partners. Normally sweet-tempered, she was quick to correct lagging or sloppy corners with a nip. Her chameleon-like ability to look like her brace partner was impressive.

After Fashion retired, Helen paired Beorn with his son, Ch. Cascadia Dutch Baron. Together they received 12 BBIS awards plus two Best Brace in Specialty wins.

But Cascadia is also rooted in obedience dogs. The foundation Tryon dogs were all trained in basic obedience and many earned advanced degrees. From Cascadia Stormy Cricket, CD's first litter came Ch. Cascadia Puff O'Smoke, CD, Beorn's first "obedient" son. Smoke quickly and easily earned his first two legs in as many shows and then, according to his owner and handler, Judi James, "became the star attraction at several shows as he invented variations, all hazardous to a qualifying score." Smoke really came into his own while working on his CDX degree. In the open ring he has been known to grandstand the audience and provide a running commentary on the exercises. An excellent (although inventive) performer, he earned both of his degrees with scores exceeding 95 percent of the available points. At age 8, he still agrees to occasional performances and easily clears jumps set for larger dogs.

Smoke's kennel mate, Ch. Cascadia Hawkeye, CD, continues to prove beauty is no stranger to brains. Retired from the conformation ring after a successful career, he teamed up with Judi James and, in five Canadian shows, earned his CD with a HIT. He continued his prowess in the United States by finishing 1984 as KCA's Champion Obedience Dog of the year. Judi has her eye on Hawkeye's becoming Cascadia's first Utility dog.

Cascadia has become synonymous with brains, beauty and the ability to reproduce those qualities.

Tryon

Jean Ellis of Oregon had always been interested in dogs and became acquainted with Keeshonds in the early 1950s. Jean's love for the Keeshond grew but with the arrival of her five children, dog activities had to be put aside.

In 1964 the Ellis family moved to Oregon and decided they needed a family dog; naturally, a Keeshond was the obvious choice. Little Brother Jantje joined the Ellis household and his success in the obedience and conformation rings with Jean's oldest daughter led to the purchase of Lovely Lady of Voornaam, UD, for daughter Carolyn. With both daughters involved in dog showing, Jean yearned for the ring herself. She showed a puppy from their litter of Jantje and Lovely Lady; this puppy became Ch. Tryon's First Try, the first champion for Tryon Kennels.

In 1968 Jean bought a bitch puppy from the Flakkee Kennels. Ch. Flakkee's Choice for Tryon, CDX, set the personality and style that Jean wanted. Gypsy finished both her championship and CD in 1969 and Jean began to search for the right stud dog. She found it in the young Ch. Star-Kees Batman, ROMX. Jean began the custom of naming litters with a theme and so the first of the Tryon dogs were from the "money" litter. Two of these puppies stayed at Tryon — Am. and Can. Ch. Tryon's Coin of the Realm and Ch. Tryon's Pound Sterling, CD ("Sassy").

Andrea Haberman of Gig Harbor, Washington, saw Sassy at a show and bought her on a co-ownership. The relationship was ideal for both Jean and Andrea as it allowed Andrea to raise the litters and Jean to take home the promising puppies to socialize and train.

In 1974, Tryon did its first outcross, choosing Ch. Rich-Bob's Stormy Weather, ROMX. This litter consisted of two puppies — "Toes" and "T'Other." Toes became Ch. Tryon's Tuppence, dam of nine puppies, four of which were champions. "T'Other" was sold to Helen Cuneo and became the famous "Cookie Monster" (Ch. Tryon's Fearless Fruhling, ROMX) — the top-producing Keeshond bitch of all times with 16 champions from 25 puppies in just three litters. A success in the show ring as well, she was the top-winning KCA member-owned show dog in 1976.

For Sassy's last litter, Jean and Andrea did another outcross breeding, chosing this time Ch. LeJean's Allan A Dale, CD. This mating produced Ch. Tryon's Gandalf the Gray and the famous Ch. Tryon's Beorn, ROMX, HOF. Although Pound Sterling was the dam of some of the loveliest of the Tryon Kees, she is no doubt best remembered as Beorn's mother. She was a showy bitch with a beautiful head and expression, correct size, short back and the wonderful Keeshond temperament that kept her Andrea's special companion for her lifetime.

Always interested in obedient Keeshonds, Jean saw to it that each adult dog at Tryon was obedience trained to a novice level and all puppy buyers were encouraged to train their Keeshonds. The real obedience star at Tryon was Ch. Fritz Van Voornaam, UD, HOF. The son of Ch. Flakkee Sweepstakes, ROM, HOF, he joined the Ellis household as an 11 month-old-puppy. He gained his championship easily but the obedience ring was where he shone. His happy attitude, good scores and attractive appearance made him a favorite with show and pet people alike and he became the representative for Tryon Kees.

Jean Ellis has retired from breeding but the Tryon line is being carried on by Andrea Haberman, Judy Daugherty, Helen Wymore and others.

CALIFORNIA

Flakkee

The name Flakkee came into existence in the late 1940's when Mrs. Van Cott Niven decided to start showing a young Keeshond, Patriot van Fitz.

Ch. Maldolph's Heidi-Ho of Allan, ROM, is the dam of six American and three Canadian champions. She is owned by Dick and Anna Malet of Washington.

Ch. Flakkee Jackpot at ten months of age.

Dicky Washington, the first lady at Flakkee, with Eng. and Am. Ch. Worrall of Wistonia.

Ch. Flakkee Sweepstakes, the top-winning BIS Keeshond in history with 46 BIS and 109 Group 1s.

Mrs. Niven contacted Mr. Porter Washington, a prominent handler, to test the dog at the shows. According to Mr. Washington, "Riot was a riot, a natural showman from the word go."

At the first two shows on the Arizona circuit, Riot was BOB; at the third, he took the Non-Sporting Group; and by the time he reached Grand Junction, Colorado, he was a champion. Porter then entered Riot as a special at the coming Los Angeles show and came home with the red, white and blue BIS rosette.

After a short but successful show career, Riot was retired. Mr. Washington and Mrs. Niven came to the conclusion that they needed other dogs to fulfill what they wished to accomplish in the breed. After seeing a photo in an English dog publication, they placed a call to Mr. and Mrs. Fred Greenwood, owners of the famous Wistonia Kennels. After much discussion, Fred and Nan agreed to let Eng. Ch. Whimsey of Wistonia come to America. With Porter on the lead, Whimsey gained her American title in straight shows, going BIS her first time out at San Antonio, Texas. She was shown only 15 times in America and was never beaten in breed competition. She won five Non-Sporting Groups and was twice all-breed BIS. After she retired from the show ring, she was bred to Riot with excellent results.

Shortly, another Wistonia bitch joined Flakkee Kennels. Eng. Ch. Wrona of Wistonia finished rapidly, winning the breed 24 times and garnering 12 Group 1s and two all-breed BIS. As the breed grew in popularity, Flakkee puppies were in demand so it was decided to import a stud dog of similar bloodlines to be used not only with the two Wistonia bitches but with some of the bitches of Flakkee production. Mr. Washington and Mrs. Niven again contacted the Greenwoods, who did not hesitate when asked to send Eng. Ch. Waarborg of Wistonia to America. Waarborg had a very successful show career and was retired with 73 BOBs, 32 Groups and ten BIS awards.

As Waarborg neared retirement, the search began for a young dog to fill the gap at Flakkee. Traveling in Europe with her family, Mrs. Niven flew to England to meet Nan and Fred Greenwood and fell in love with Eng. Ch. Wrocky of Wistonia.

Soon after Wrocky's arrival in America, he blew his coat and it was several months before he could be brought out in California. But word about him spread quickly and the delay in getting him in shape for the show ring created much speculation as to just how good he really was.

His first American show was at the Olympia Kennel Club in Washington. That day he went all the way from the Open Class to Best in Show! He topped the Group at his next three shows and was an American champion in one week.

Mr. Washington says of his first foray into the specials ring

> We kept his success a secret and since I had entered him at the coming Beverly-Riveria K.C. show in Open, we decided to leave him in that class

Ch. Flakkee Snapshot.

Ch. Flakkee Main Event.

106

rather than switch him to a Special. No one knew that he would be coming out at Beverly-Riveria, so when Mr. Bert Heath, owner of *Kennel Review* opened his catalog, he headed for my crates. His first question was, "Do you have him here?" I said, "Yes." He then asked me, "Will he get his ears up?" and I said to him, "Get yourself a good seat at the ring and watch."

When Kees were finally called, I waited until the entire Open Class was in the ring, then I walked Wrocky in on a ten-foot lead. He set himself up in front of the crowd, looked things over as if to say "This will not be too tough," and the show started. He literally walked through that bunch, through the Non-Sporting Group, and we celebrated Best in Show back at the crates.

It was not long after that Mrs. Niven became Mrs. Porter Washington. They celebrated their honeymoon in Canada where Wrocky rounded out his triple championship by adding the Canadian title in straight shows.

This great dog's show career was cut short after only 35 times in the ring in the United States and Canada due to a malignant testicle. Had it been possible to show him further, Mr. Washington believes he would have set a record that could never have been broken. He accounted for 34 BOB, 33 Group 1s and 18 all-breed BIS.

The next dog to arrive from England was Worrall of Wistonia who finished his American championship in short order. Although not campaigned extensively, he did win a few BIS. His main asset was producing and he set the type for Flakkee. Flakkee now had the nucleus to create a breeding program, and they have rigidly stuck to the original bloodlines by line breeding the Wistonia stock with which they began.

Wrocky sired Ch. Cornelius Wrocky Selznick, who, in turn, sired the all-time top BIS winner in breed history. Ch. Flakkee Sweepstakes was campaigned from coast to coast. He was and still is the only Kees ever to win the Non-Sporting Group at Westminster. He was also a Ken-L-Ration award winner and top Keeshond every year shown. His record was 46 all-breed BIS and 109 Non-Sporting Groups.

Worrall was the sire of Ch. Flakkee Jackpot, who appears in the pedigrees of most of the top-winning dogs in America. Other noted Flakkee sires are Ch. Flakkee Instant Replay, winner of 146 Non-Sporting Groups and 45 BIS. He was a Ken-L-Ration award winner and top Kees in America every year he was shown. He undoubtedly could have broken the all-time BIS record held by Sweepstakes, but sentimentally, the Washingtons decided to leave Sweeper as the all-time BIS dog, with Speedy the tops in Group wins.

There have been many other great dogs at Flakkee but space does not permit naming all of them. These great dogs have produced the show record of Flakkee Kennels, a record that will probably never be equalled. To date, Flakkee dogs account for 1,319 BOB, 630 Group 1s, and 188 BIS.

The motto at Flakkee is, "To line breed to the best. Royalty only remains Royal when kept in the Family."

Ch. Flakkee Instant Replay, top Group-winning Keeshond in history with 45 BIS and 146 Group 1s.

Ch. Flakkee Instamatic and Porter Washington of Flakkee Kennels, Reg.

Flakkee's latest star, Ch. Flakkee Hi-Lo Jack.

Eng. Am. and Can. Ch. Whiplash of Wistonia, ROM (Wanjohe of Wistonia ex Winlunde of Wistonia) was the sire of 16 American champions. He was bred and owned by Nan Greenwood of Wistonia Kennels.

Wistonia (in America)

After the death of her husband Fred, Nan Greenwood moved her famous Wistonia Kennels to Lawndale, California, where she continued breeding outstanding linebred Wistonia Keeshonds until her death in 1986. Nan was the winner of the Breeders Trophy in 1974 and 1975 and the Brood Bitch Trophy in 1975. Eng., Am. and Can. Ch. Whiplash of Wistonia, ROM, was the winner of the Stud Dog Trophy for 1966 and tied for third place as top Stud Dog of all Non-Sporting breeds the same year. At that time, he was also one of only two Keeshonds in the history of the breed to hold three champion titles, the other being Eng., Am. and Can. Ch. Wrocky of Wistonia, ROM.

His son, Ch. Wistonia Wylie, ROMX, the sire of 21 champions, was the winner of the Stud Dog Trophy in 1974. Another outstanding producer, Whincindy of Wistonia, ROMX, was the dam of eight champions.

Wistonia dogs have been known for their ability to be shown long after dogs of other bloodlines have been retired from the ring. Proof of this was demonstrated when Eng. and Am. Ch. Winmisty of Wistonia, at 11 years of age, was awarded BOS at the Keeshond Club of So. California Specialty in 1968. She again took BOS at the Beverly Hills Show at over 12 years of age; the judge was Mrs. J. Whitney Peterson.

As a result of her lifelong dedication to the Keeshond, Nan was made an honorary member of the North of England Keeshond Club, the Keeshond Club of America and the Keeshond Club of Southern California. The Greenwood motto of "Win With Wistonia" was most fitting, as well over 100 champions have been bred or sired at Wistonia both in England and the United States.

Star-Kees

Robin Stark of Star-Kees fame became enchanted with Keeshonds at the age of 15 when a customer came into the toy store where she worked toting an eight-week-old Kees pup. It would be four years until Robin would be able to purchase her first Kees. Prince Kodi of Rocky Falls, CDX, never won a point in the conformation ring but he was instrumental in forming the famous Star-Kees Keeshond Kennels. According to Robin, "Kodi's keen intelligence and flawless Keeshond temperament provided me with many hours of enjoyment and love, along with the desire to share such sublime canine companionship with others." This desire eventually led Robin Stark into a breeding program that would produce more than 75 champions as well as many happy, spoiled family companions.

Robin's show career began in 1962 when she acquired a boisterous seven-month-old pup called Otis (Ch. Boko, CD). Since Otis seemed to be having trouble settling down for the obedience ring, Robin decided to give conformation a try. Robin remembers those painful times as a "novice." Nevertheless, Robin's new bulletin board that day sported a blue first place

Ch. Wistonia Wylie, ROMX (Ch. Colonel Cinders of Fairville ex Wincuti of Wistonia) was bred and owned by Nan Greenwood of Wistonia Kennels. Wylie was the sire of 21 American champions.

Eng. and Am. Ch. Winmitzy of Wistonia is shown taking BOS at the Beverly Hills Kennel Club Show under Mrs. Clementine Peterson. At the time of this win, Mitzy was over 12 years of age; she was bred, owned and shown by Nan Greenwood.

ribbon. It was the first of many blue ribbons for Robin and her Star-Kees Keeshonden.

Otis eventually settled down, easily obtained his championship and even became the West Coast's first owner-handled Keeshond to win a Non-sporting Group. He even obtained his CD title! Otis had an outgoing, lovable personality and it was he who was responsible for the long, beautifully arched necks for which Star-Kees' dogs are still famous. He proved to be a successful stud dog by producing four American and two Canadian champions. One of his daughters would become Robin's foundation bitch, Ch. Star-Kees' Forever Amber, CD.

Bred by Phil and Nancy Brakebill, and out of Ch. Dutchess Misty Dawn, Amber was Robin's pick-of-litter stud fee. An outcross, Amber's pedigree had some of the greats from Wistonia and Vorden. She was a beautiful bitch, inheriting her dam's exceptional soundness and her sire's fabulous neck and happy, outgoing temperament.

When Robin first saw the sound and handsome Ch. Flakkee Jackpot, ROMX, HOF, in the flesh, she knew he was the dog she'd been spending years searching for. This was the animal who could solidify and strengthen the soundness she'd already obtained. The mating of Amber and Jackpot was made and on May 2, 1969, Ch. Star-Kees' Batman, ROMX, was whelped.

From 1970 until today, Robin Stark's breeding program has been focused on and centered around her record-breaking, history-making stud dog — Batman. Robin says, "Batman was a gentle dog and didn't have a vain bone in his body. But were those bones ever put together magnificently!" Though he much preferred his chores as a stud dog, he was also a show dog. He was in the top ten of the breed four consecutive years and was a multiple Group winner, multiple specialty winner and consistent Group placer. He won his first BOB at eight months of age at his first show and his last BOB at the age of nine years from the Veterans Class at his last show.

In his stud career, Batman sired 50 American and seven Canadian champions; he was KCA's Top Stud Dog four times, tying once with Ch. Wistonia Wylie, ROMX, and once with his own grandson, Ch. Tryon's Beorn, ROMX, HOF. He won the stud dog class ten times. But these things only tell a part of the story. Because Batman was the product of an outcross bred to an outcross, his producing record was nothing short of a phenomenon. Whether linebred on either side or outcrossed, he produced quality, sound, typey, winning and producing Keeshonds.

In 1980 Jimmy Kranz became a partner in Star-Kees' Keeshonden. The team of Robin as handler and Jimmy as conditioner brought one of Batman's last sons to the fore of the breed. Ch. Charmac Scatman to Star-Kees, ROM, HOF, was bred by Jan and Richard Wilhite out of their lovely Ch. Fearless Fortune Cookie, CD, ROMX. "Skeeter" was Best in Futurity as well as WD/BOW at the 1980 KCA National Specialty. He has won two BIS, three specialties, Select Awards, 18 Group 1s and literally dozens of

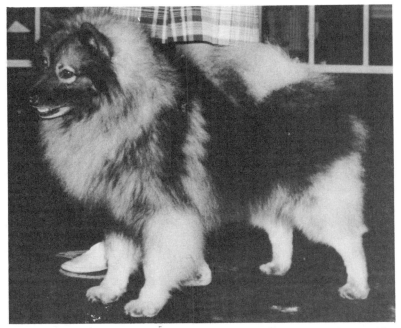

Ch. Star-Kees Batman, ROMX (Ch. Flakkee Jackpot, ROMX, HOF ex Ch. Star-Kees Forever Amber, CD) is shown at four years of age. He was bred and owned by Robin Stark and is the breed's top-producing stud dog.

Ch. Charmac Scatman to Star-Kees, ROM, HOF, owned by Robin Stark, is a Specialty and BIS winner.

Group placements. Skeeter also excels as a stud dog and currently is the sire of 19 American and nine Canadian champions.

In the spring of 1985, Jimmy Kranz, in co-ownership with Alan Leff and John Van Kleeck, purchased a young dog from his breeders, Donna Gierach and Rita Babich. With Robin handling and Jimmy conditioning, Ch. Curacao Chimichanga won a tremendous amount in 1985 and 1986. Nearing his HOF, Chonga is Star-Kees' second BIS-winning Keeshond. Although rarely used at stud, he is currently the sire of four champions.

Shamrock

Shamrock Keeshonds began in 1973 when Shannon Kelly was searching for a foundation bitch in the Wistonia line. Shannon combined the pretty soft expressions, lovely heads and elegance of this line with the solid body and movement of Ch. Star-Kees' Batman, ROMX. From this combination came Shamrock Keeshonds.

Shamrock's foundation bitch was Ch. Somerville Chelsea Morning, ROM (Ch. Painter of Somerville ex Ch. Wistonia Whipadonna, bred by Bonnie Simrell). Chelsea proved herself both in the conformation ring and the whelping box. Out of 14 puppies in three litters, six are American champions, three more are pointed and one has a CD.

From her first litter, sired by Ch. Star-Kees' Batman, ROMX, there were four champions. One of these was Ch. Shamrock Peg O'My Heart who was 1978 KCA Top Keeshond Show Bitch and 1978 Top Keeshond Opposite Sex. Peggy was BOB at the Keeshond Club of Dallas Specialty that same year, plus BOS at Nor-Cal, Sahuaro and the KCA National. Her delightful showy attitude, combining soundness and extremely feminine Keeshond type, made her a favorite of judges, breeders and spectators. Ably handled to most of her wins by Robin Stark, they were a dynamite team.

Using her background and education in genetics, Shannon has built Shamrock around the importance of the pedigree behind one's breeding stock and on the knowledge of not only the dogs used but also their littermates. From this has emerged the Shamrock type. She is a firm believer in the increasing importance of the brood bitch for she not only provides half the genes, but also contributes to the temperament by the manner in which she raises her pups. Shamrock is built as much on line breeding on excellent dams as it is on excellent sires.

An example of the Shamrock head is exemplified in Can. Ch. Shamrock's Finnian (Ch. Charmac Scatman to Star-Kees ex Shamrock Erin Go Braugh), whose photo appears as the frontpiece of this book. He has the elegance, carriage and style that Shannon first admired in the Wistonia line. Specialty winners themselves, each one of Shamrock's producers has produced specialty winners. Consistency in type and correct temperament are of paramount importance. Each litter at Shamrock is carefully researched and planned with a five-to-ten-year projected program in mind,

Ch. Shamrock Peg O'My Heart (Ch. Star-Kees Batman, ROMX ex Ch. Somerville Chelsea Morning, ROM) was KCA Top Keeshond Show Bitch and Top Keeshond Opposite Sex in 1978.

The BIS-winning brace of Ch. Ruttkay Go Man Go, CD, sire of 14 champions; and his son, Ch. Mr Van Sander of Modesto, was owned by Blanche and Floyd Matthews.

with constant surveillance of all puppies in each litter and constant reevaluation of the breeding program.

Modesto

In the late 1930s and early 1940s Blanche and Floyd Matthews were Chow Chow breeders. With the onset of World War II, the Matthews went into defense work and sold their Chows. As a result of a heart ailment, Mr. Matthews was forced to retire in 1956 and they soon felt the need for a dog. Looking through all the dog magazines, the Keeshond caught their eye. Modesto Keeshond Kennels became a reality when, in the fall of 1957, they acquired Ch. Ruttkay Go Man Go, CD, from Virginia Ruttkay. In 1958 from the Dirdon Kennels of Marge and Ed Cummings came a bitch, later to be known as Ch. Dirdon's Leise Van Hanzel, CD. In 1959 from Dicky Washington's kennels came Ch. Flakkee Contessa. A mating of Go Man Go and Contessa produced Ch. Mr. Van Sander of Modesto, one of 14 champions for Go Man Go.

In 1963 Blanche began showing Go Man Go and his son, Mr. Van Sander, as a brace and they won several BBIS awards.

Another of the Go Man Go and Contessa litter was Ch. Junior Miss of Modesto, who achieved her championship in three 5-point shows in 1964. Bred to Ch. Vuurtoren of Vorden, she produced Ch. Van Fitz "The Strutter" Modesto, who was co-owned by Floyd Matthews and Dr. Louis Buente of Ohio. Strutter finished his title in less than one month with five majors in strong east coast competition. According to Blanche, one of her biggest thrills came when Strutter was chosen BOB from the Open Class by English Judge Jere Collins (Ven Keeshonden) and then on to a Group 2. Strutter was handled exclusively by Dolores Scharff.

Other top-winning and producing Modesto dogs have been Ch. Maywood Hi Fashion of Modesto , owned by Helen Wymore; Ch. Rich-Bob's Adorable of Modesto (Ch. LeJean's Allan A Dale, CD ex Ch. Rich-Bob's Dustmop); Ch. The Senator of Modesto; and Ch. Star-Kees Ten-Four V.Modesto (Ch. Star-Kees Aristobat ex Ecru's A Promise Come True), who was WB and BOW at the 1978 Nor-Cal Specialty and BOS at Westminster in 1980.

Blanche and Floyd were both professional musicians. Blanche served the local musician's association as its secretary for many years,so it was fitting that she was also elected secretary of the Nor-Cal Keeshond Club when it was formed; she would serve in this position for ten years. As a result of her dedication to the breed, the Nor-Cal Keeshond Club dedicated its 12th Annual Specialty in 1980 to their first lady of Keeshonden, Blanche Matthews. Blanche passed away in 1986.

Fearless

Helen and Joe Cuneo acquired their first Keeshond in 1964. By the time he reached nine months of age, Helen decided he needed some training and

116

Ch. Rich-Bob's Stormy Weather, ROMX, at eight years of age. A Specialty winner and outstanding producer, he was owned by Helen Cuneo, Fearless Keeshonden.

Ch. Fearless Flintstone, ROM. "Bam Bam" is owned by Helen Cuneo and is the sire of 13 American champions to date.

off to obedience classes they went. That first puppy went on to become Hercules The Big Boy, CDX.

While Helen was showing in obedience, she was watching the conformation ring and befriended Ralph and Sharleen Sims of Zeedrift Kees and Robin Stark of Star-Kees. This led to Herkey's entrance into the breed ring and the addition of a Champion title to his name. In the meantime, Helen had fallen in love with Robin's Ch. Boko, CD and inquired about a puppy. Robin informed her that there was a litter by Otis. Looking for just the right bitch for her new champion, Helen paid the breeders a visit. She came home with her next Keeshond, but it wasn't a bitch! It seems one of the males picked up Herkey's leash and headed for the car; Helen couldn't resist him. That puppy went on to become Ch. Star-Kees Gunther Von Helga.

In 1966 Helen went to a wedding, and came home with Anne's Wispering Lady. In October 1972, Heidi produced the first litter for the fledgling Fearless Keeshonden; the two puppies were aptly named Fearless Fredrick and Fearless Fledermausmann.

Helen was still in search of a brood bitch and so Star-Kees Fearless Fly Helga joined the Cuneo household. Jodi was bred back to her grandsire, Ch. Flakkee Jackpot, and produced Helen's first homebred champion, Ch. Fearless Flashback.

In November 1974, at almost four years of age, Stormy came into Helen's life. He had four points and three champion progeny to his credit. Although he went on to become Ch. Rich-Bob's Stormy Weather, ROMX, and was BOB at the KCA National Specialty in 1978, Stormy hated the show ring. He loved to be groomed, loved to go in the car, loved the show but despised the ring. His real prowess was as a stud and he was KCA's Top Stud Dog in 1978 and 1979. His progeny include many Specialty BOB and BOS winners, and he is the sire of Ch. Tryon's Fearless Fruhling, ROMX, top-producing bitch of all time.

In all, Stormy produced a total of 84 puppies — 46 males and 38 bitches — out of 17 different dams. He was at limited stud with only four breedings per year; Helen now wishes that she had allowed him to be used more for he imprinted his type on many of the dogs that produced the winning foundation for Fearless and countless other kennels. Stormy was a very special dog. His bloodlines were the start of our kennel and we feel privileged to have known him.

Stormy's daughter, Ch. Tryon's Fearless Fruhling, ROMX, was a breeder's dream come true. Whelped November 29, 1974, she soon joined Helen and Joe Cuneo at Fearless. At three months of age, she consumed three pounds of cookies and was immediately nicknamed "The Cookie Monster." Cookie finished her championship at 10½ months of age. In 1976, at less than two years of age, she was awarded Top Keeshond by KCA. This award had never been won by a bitch before; it was won a second time several years later by Cookie's daughter, Ch. Fearless Fortune Cookie.

118

Ch. Tryon's Fearless Fruhling, ROMX. The "Cookie Monster" is the top-producing Keeshond bitch of all time. She is owned by Helen Cuneo.

Ch. Traveler's Zeedrift Carioca was the foundation bitch for two kennels: Joanne Reed's Windrift Keeshonden and Sandy Krueger's Traveler's Keeshonden.

The Cookie Monster was also the first Keeshond to hold Irene K. Schlintz's Gold Certificate of Distinction for Top Producer. Cookie was Top Brood Bitch in 1981 and 1982, top Non-Sporting Producing Bitch in 1981 and tied for Top in 1982.

Bred only three times, she produced 25 puppies, 16 of which are American champions. In her first litter by Ch. Painter of Somerville, she produced eight puppies, four of which finished. These were Ch. Fearless FanciFree of Car-Ron, No. 2 Show Bitch in 1978; Am. and Can. Ch. Fearless Focalpoint, sire of four American and four Canadian champions; Ch. Fearless Flowerchild, producer of Champions; and Ch. Fearless Fortune Cookie, CD, ROM, dam of nine champions including multi-BIS winner, Ch. Charmac Scatman to Star-Kees, HOF. A fifth puppy, Fearless Filibuster, was BIF in 1978, pointed and a BOB winner. Tragically, he died from an overdose of anesthetic at only 18 months of age.

Bred to Ch. Keenote's Sterling Silver, ROMX, Cookie produced eight puppies, six of which became champions. These were Ch. Fearless Flying Tiger, Ch. Fearless Freewheeler and Ch. Fearless Framework — all sires of Champions; and Ch. Fearless Fannyfox O'Bonnyvale and Ch. Fearless Floorshow — dams of champions. This litter also produced Ch. Fearless Flavor for KeesLund, HOF. "Yummy" is a BOB and BOS Specialty winner, Group winner and the dam of five champions.

Cookie's litter by Ch. Fearless Flintstone, ROM, produced nine puppies, seven of which are: Ch. Fearless Floorshow, Specialty WB and dam of one champion to date; Ch. Fearless Firstclass, Specialty BOB, Group 1 winner, Group placer and sire of champions; Ch. Fearless Fox, Select Award winner; Ch. Fearless Fruitcake, dam of three champions; Ch. Fearless Karolina First Lady, Ch. Fearless Felicity and Ch. Fearless Firststorm.

With this record, Cookie enabled Helen to win the Top Breeder award for 1980, 1981 and 1983, and to retire the Kultz Breeders Challenge Trophy after 20 years.

As of November 1985, Fearless had bred or co-bred a total of 17 litters, comprising 63 puppies, of which 32 have gained their championships. Helen and Joe now continue their Fearless breeding program in eastern New York.

Windrift

Joanne Reed has had dogs all her life. While showing her German Shepherd in obedience, she saw a Keeshond happily working in another ring. The search for her own Keeshond ended when she and her friend, Sandy Krueger, acquired Traveler's Zeedrift Carioca. Carioca was the foundation of both Windrift and Travelers Keeshonden. Carioca's show career was interrupted when she was bred to Ch. Flakkee Jackpot, HOF, ROMX. This litter produced four puppies, two of which were the famous

Ch. Star-Kees Dingbat, CD, HOF, ROMX, owned by Joanne Sanford Reed.

Ch. Windrift's Gambler, CD, HOF, ROMX, is owned by Tawn and John Sinclair and was bred by Joanne Reed.

Ch. Flakkee Instant Replay, HOF, and Ch. Windrift's Midnite Masquerade.

Carioca returned to the show ring, finished her championship and garnered several BOBs; she was also BOS at the Keeshond Club of So. California Specialty in 1972 and 1975. Carioca acquired her ROM in style by producing the exceptional winner, Ch. Flakkee Instant Replay.

Joanne's first top-winning dog was Ch. Star-Kees' Dingbat, CD, HOF, ROMX. Dingbat ws the No. 2 Keeshond and No. 10 Non-Sporting Dog in 1974. He has six Specialty BOBs to his credit, including the KCA National in 1974 and again in 1977. Dingbat has also garnered three all-breed BIS, 12 Group 1s, 7 Group 2s, 12 Group 3s, and 5 Group 4s. But Dingbat was equally successful as a stud dog. As of 1985, he has produced 24 champions, one of which (Ch. Windrift's Producer, HOF) is also a BIS winner. Dingbat's stud career was cut short due to a bout with cancer.

The next dog that came along was Ch. Windrift Midnite Special. "Tigger" completed his championship in 14 shows and probably could have been a BIS dog; however, he never really liked to show. He, too, excelled as a stud dog and was the sire of another top-winning Keeshond, Ch. Windrift's Midnite Love, HOF. Midnite was the No. 1 Keeshond in 1976. He won four specialties in 1976, including the KCA National; two in 1977 and another in 1978. Midnite's total record was ten Group 1s, nine Group 2s, eight Group 3s and six Group 4s. As a stud dog, he has sired nine American champions. He was co-owned by Joanne's parents, George and Dorothy Jacobsen.

It is extremely rare that a dam will produce only champions but Windrift's Lovelace, ROM (Ch. Star-Kees' Dingbat, CD, HOF, ROMX ex Windrift's Love of Cari) was such a bitch. Although she had all the qualities to become a champion, she had been maimed at birth when her dam chewed off her rear toes on one foot. She was bred twice to Ch. Rich-Bob's Stormy Weather, ROMX, and produced seven puppies and seven champions.

Ch. Windrift's Love Unlimited, HOF ("Maggie") is owned by Kris Arnds of Winsome Keeshonden. Ch. Windrift's Lover Boy, another of this litter, also did well as a show dog. Campaigned by Joanne, he won three Group 1s and two specialties. Sold to Les Baker of New York, he continued winning and has garnered four Group 1s, one Group 2, four Group 3s, and four Group 4s. To add to his accomplishments, he was BOB from the Veterans Class at the Keeshond Club of Delaware Valley under renowned English breeder/judge Sylvia Scroggs (Ledwell). As of December 1984, "Romeo" has also sired 11 American champions.

Joanne was also blessed with another great bitch. Windrift's Wonder Woman, ROM, was bred to Ch. Star-Kees' Dingbat, CD, HOF, ROMX. This litter produced three very special Keeshonds: Ch. Windrift's Willy Weaver, Ch. Windrift's Honey Bear and Ch. Windrift's Circuit Breaker. Wonder Woman was then bred to Ch. Windrift's Midnite Love and produced two more champions (Ch. Windrift's Annie Oakley and Ch. Windrift's Academy Award), thus completing her requirements for her ROM.

Ch. Windrift's Willy Weaver was bred to Ch. Windrift's Hollywood Squares and produced another record-breaking Keeshond, Am. and Can. Ch. Windrift's Gambler, CD, HOF, ROMX. Gambler is owned by Tawn and John Sinclair of Shoreline Keeshonds. Tawn and John certainly hit the jackpot with their first Keeshond. They had been looking primarily for an obedience dog that could also compete in the conformation ring; they got more than they bargained for. "Kodi" began his show career by going Best in Sweeps at the 1980 Sahuaro Keeshond Club Specialty. He finished his Championship in quick order and then completed his CD in three straight shows. He began his specials career with his breeder handling. In 1982, he won two all-breed BISs, and the KCA and Nor-Cal Specialties. He completed the requirements for his HOF that same year and finished out 1982 as *Kennel Review's* No. 1 Keeshond and No. 10 Non-Sporting dog. Kodi was temporarily retired from active campaigning in 1984; during his two-year specials career, he garnered two all-breed BIS, four Keeshond specialties, 12 Group 1s, ten Group 2s, 16 Group 3s, ten Group 4s, 82 BOBs and defeated 1,879 Keeshonds.

In the fall of 1984, Kodi paid a visit to Sue Gray of Keelane Kennels and finished his Canadian championship in just three shows. In November of the same year, he finished the requirements for his ROM as his twelfth champion offspring obtained her title. As of March 1985 Kodi is the sire of 17 American champions, including several BOB winners and Group placers.

In 1985, bored with retirement, Kodi traveled to Ohio for the KCA Specialty where he was chosen as a Select Dog. He stayed on in Ohio with his new friend and handler, Kathy Hritzo Heimann, and in three months of showing won 24 BOBs with 16 Group placements. His record has of May 30, 1986 stands at: three BIS, four Specialty BOB, 20 Group 1s, 24 Group 2s, 28 Group 3s, 16 Group 4s, and 140 BOBs. He also has sired 26 champion offspring, qualifying him to receive his ROMX.

Adding to the BIS-winning history of Windrift Keeshonds is Ch. Windrift's Producer, HOF. Pro was Dingbat's last son, the dog to carry on in his father's footsteps. And that he did by finishing his championship in 11 shows, being defeated in the classes only once. Pro began his specials career in 1984 and ended the year with an astonishing five all-breed BIS, 12 Group 1s, four Group 2s, seven Group 3s, seven Group 4s, and two specialty wins. According to the 1984 *Kennel Review* statistics, this elevated him to No. 1 Keeshond, No. 9 Non-Sporting Dog and No. 4 BIS Non-Sporting Dog. That same year KCA awarded him Top Keeshond of the Year and Top Show Dog. As a result of his winning record, he completed the requirements for his Hall of Fame in only eight months. Pro was co-bred by Joanne Reed and Jack and Arlene Grimes.

Ch. Windrift's Producer, HOF, is a multiple BIS winner. He is owned by Joanne Reed.

Ch. Windrift's Love Unlimited, HOF (Ch. Rich-Bob's Stormy Weather, ROMX ex Windrift's Lovelace, ROM), was bred by Joanne Reed and is owned by Kris Arnds.

124

Joanne's latest star is Ch. Timekeeper for Windrift (Am. and Can. Ch. Ledwell Alexander x Can. Ch. Windrift's Mercy Sakes, bred by Louise Bakke and Joanne Reed). Timmie completed his championship from the BBE Class in only 11 shows and topped it off by going BOB at the 1985 Kees Club of So. California Specialty from the BBE Class over an entry of 110 other Keeshonds. The next weekend he took BOB and Group 2. He has an exciting career ahead both as a show dog and stud.

As of the beginning of 1985, Windrift Keeshonds has bred more than 60 American champions. There have been 26 BOB Specialty or National Specialty winners and seven inductees into the Hall of Fame bred or owned by Windrift. Joanne and her Windrift breeding program are dedicated to the improvement of the Keeshond breed.

Designer

Rita and John Jacobs of Designer Keeshonds were familiar with Windrift Kennels as they co-owned and co-bred several litters with Joanne Reed. Rita's foundation bitch was Ch. Windrift's Honey Bear (Ch Star-Kees Dingbat, CD, HOF, ROMX ex Windrift's Wonder Woman, ROM). In 1982 she was bred to Ch. Foxfairs Persuasive Friend, HOF, ROMX. From this litter came Ch. Windrift's High Society, HOF, who was BIF at 7½ months. "Snootie" finished at 14 months with three majors.

The following year Windrift's Honeysuckle (Ch. Windrift's Honey Bear ex Ch. Windif's Midnite Love, HOF) was also bred to Friendly and produced the 1983 BIF winner, Ch. Windrift's Spark of Wyldfyr. This bitch finished before she was a year old. In between raising puppies, Honey managed to stay in the top ten show bitches (Keezette). Her show career included BOS Sweeps at the Sahuaro Specialty, BOS at Dallas and Nor-Cal Specialties, and BOS at the 1981 KCA National.

In May 1986 Ch. Windrift's High Society became the second bitch in history to win BOB at the Keeshond Club of America Specialty. In November of the same year, she also became the second American-bred bitch to win a Best in Show. Snootie was bred to Can. Am. Ch. Windrift's Gambler, CD, HOF, ROMX.

Showing at Designer is a family affair and daughter Jamie has finished several dogs to their championships and is an active and winning participant in Junior Showmanship.

Travelers

In 1968 Sandy Krueger, together with Joanne Reed, purchased Ch. Traveler's Zeedrift Carioca, ROM. She provided the foundation for both the Windrift Kennel and Sandy's Travelers Keeshonds. Sandy's interest in Keeshonds came after many years of showing German Shepherds and handling/training other breeds. Sandy and Joanne met when they took their Shepherds to a training class, a class that also included a delightfully elegant, intelligent Keeshond. They decided they would look for a bitch puppy to co-own, show and eventually breed. They found what they were looking for in Cari (Ch. Zeedrift's Kwikzilver, HOF ex Zeedrift Booty). Cari was a born showgirl and, according to Sandy, "could have shown herself without help from any human."

Using the tried and true combination of line breeding on the best ancestor, the most likely candidate for the sire of Cari's first litter was Ch. Flakkee Jackpot, ROMX, HOF. One of their sons, Ch. Flakkee Instant Replay, HOF, inherited much of Cari's style and showmanship. This litter also produced Ch. Windrift Midnite Masquerade and Traveler's Independent Air. Wendy had lovely producing qualities but hated the show ring. She was an ideal house dog, but, always the perfect lady, she felt it beneath her dignity to endure a leash. Sandy decided that Wendy would have to leave her mark in history in the whelping box instead of the show ring.

While many kennels have risen to prominence through an outstanding show dog or top-producing stud dog, the focus at Travelers was on establishing a solid, dominant bitch line by consistently combining close and distant line breeding, predominantly with Wistonia background, to produce color and type, along with overall structural soundness and true Keeshond personality.

Ch. Star-Kees' Batman, ROMX (a Jackpot son) was chosen to breed to Independent Air as Batman exhibited the structural soundness that Sandy found lacking in the breed at that time. This litter produced Ch. Windrift's Dynamic Duo, who went on to sire several good producing bitches, and Ch. Traveler's Fly-By-Nite, ROM. "Bunnie," in turn, was bred to the Batman son, Ch. Star-Kees' Dingbat, CD, ROMX, HOF and produced: Ch. Baronwood's Travlin' Man, the sire of eight champions; Ch. Windrift's Instigator, also the sire of champions; and Ch. Traveler's Ding 'A' Ling, who is nearing her ROM. In an effort to bring in more profuse coat, Bunnie was bred to Ch. Rich-Bob's Stormy Weather, ROMX. This breeding produced Ch. Traveler's Inherit the Wind, Ch. Traveler's Fearless Forecast and Traveler's Flutter-By — themselves all producers of Champions. Ding-A-Ling carried on the Travelers tradition of being an easy-to-live-with fun housedog, a natural showgirl, and an easy breeder and whelper. She is the foundation bitch for Lucy Ober Silvey's Rebo-Kees.

The HOF bitch Ch. Traveler's Swirling Silver (Ch. Star-Kees' Dust Devil x Traveler's Song in the Nite) is once again a product of line breeding on Ch. Flakkee Jackpot on the mother's side, bred to a Ch. Wistonia Wylie son. "Shara" was co-owned with Gene and Donna Smith of Baronwood Kennels and was another born showgirl. Popular with the ringside, Shara went on to win BOS at several specialties, including two Nationals, and was a consistent Group winner. When bred to the Jackpot son, Ch. Baronwood's Calculated Risk, HOF, they produced another HOF titlist in Ch. Baronwood's Sling Shot, HOF, plus Am. and Can. Ch. Baronwood's

Ch. Traveler's Ding-A-Ling was bred and owned by Sandy Krueger of Travelers Kees.

Ch. Traveler's Swirling Silver, co-owned by Sandy Krueger and Gene and Donna Smith, is a multiple Group-winning bitch.

Blackjack and Ch. Traveler's Style Show, the latter a producer of champions.

Am. and Can. Ch. Wistonia Wynscott (Ch. Windrift's Willy Weaver, ROM ex Ch. Wistonia Wyndixie) was purchased as a three-month-old puppy from Nan Greenwood's Wistonia Kennels. At this point, after producing bitches that were closely linebred on known quantities, Sandy felt it was time to find the right male to combine and produce the Traveler qualities of good health and overall structural soundness, coupled with beautiful head type, coat and markings. Already the sire of several champions, Scottie is fulfilling his heritage as a producer.

Although only breeding the occasional litter, Travelers Kees have fulfilled the hope of their breeder — to consistently produce happy, healthy Kees who not only make their pet owners and breeders proud, but go on to produce these qualities.

Sandy passed away in December 1986 after a heroic battle with cancer. Throughout her ordeal, her indomitable courage and enthusiasm rarely diminished; she was a very special lady.

Winsome

In October 1971 Kris Arnds bought her first Keeshond. Dutch Treat IV came from a pet shop and just days afterward began a long battle with distemper. Overcoming this and being convinced by an outsider that Brandy was definitely good quality, Kris decided to breed her. Tragically, when she was x-rayed it was found that Brandy was dysplastic. So, instead of being bred, she was spayed. Not a particularly auspicious start for what would someday become Winsome Keeshonden.

Undaunted, Kris began to look for a friend for Brandy. After contacting the Kees Club of So. California, Kris was directed to Joanne Sanford Reed and acquired Windrift's Midnite Miss. Having been burnt once, Kris had intended to spay "Briar" but, at Joanne's urging, bred her to the handsome Ch. Windrift Midnite Special. Briar became the foundation bitch of Winsome Keeshonden and later attained her ROM from three litters consisting of a total of eight puppies. One of these puppies, Ch. Winsome's Tigger Too, was the National Futurity winner in 1977.

Kris kept two bitches from this first litter. When she attended her first dog show in 1974, one of them won BOS in Sweepstakes, and a month later Best in Sweeps at the Nor-Cal Specialtay and a 5-point major the next day at the KCA Specialty. Kris was hooked.

In 1976 she chose "Maggie" from a litter of five bred by Joanne Reed by Ch. Rich-Bob's Stormy Weather, ROMX, out of Windrift's Lovelace, ROM. Still suffering from bad luck and the loss of a number of litters to an unknown bacterial infection, Kris originally chose Maggie for her breeding potential. Little did she know what was in store for her as Maggie went on to become Ch. Windrift's Love Unlimited, HOF. As of this writing Maggie is 8½ years old, still shows, still wins and still runs Winsome. She has

128

produced five champions, has three other pointed puppies and in 1985 had still another litter. She has won two independent specialties, a number of BOS at specialties, including the 1982 KCA National, a Group 1 and other numerous Group placings. She has done most of her winning owner-handled and Kris is justifiably proud of her.

In her successful breeding program Kris has stayed basically with her original Windrift stock. Recently she has combined it with Rhinevale (Friendly) and Ledwell (Alexander). Winsome's focus is on soundness of body and temperament. As of January 1985 Winsome has bred 13 champions and has owned and finished an additional three. As with many top kennels, Winsome Kees is a kennel in name only; all of Kris' dogs are primarily pets and are raised in a home environment. We totally agree with Kris when she says, "I do not believe our breed does well in real kennel situations, and I hate to think of them in that context. I am sure that the loving, fun temperament that we see is 'true Keeshond character,' and I hate to think of our breed becoming 'institutionalized' and losing that charm."

Kris is active in many dog related activities, in addition to her profession as a high school English teacher. She says, "If I had to attribute my staying active in the breed to any one dog, it would be Maggie. She has been a dream to own, show and breed. I am now trying to find another Maggie, but they haven't perfected cloning!"

Cari-On

The Cari-On Kennel of Dennis and Colleen LeHouillier is responsible for a great many winners and top producers in the breed. One of the most noteworthy is Ch. Coincidence of Cari-On, CD, HOF. "Robyn" won his first points by taking BOW at the 1977 KCA National Specialty; he completed his championship that same year by taking BOW at the Sahuaro Keeshond Club's first independent specialty. He continued with an outstanding specials career and in 1980 was KCA Top Show Dog and KCA Top Keeshond; in 1981 he was again KCA's Top Show Dog. Always owner-handled, his record from April 1977 to September 1981 included two BIS, five Specialty BOB, 14 Group 1s, eight Group 2s, six Group 3s, six Group 4s, 82 BOBs and three BOS for a total of 1,746 dogs defeated.

Ch. Windrift's Willy Weaver, ROM, was WD, BOW and BOS at the 1979 Sahuaro Keeshond Club Specialty, where he was also Best in Sweeps. That same year he was also Best in Sweeps at the KCSC Specialty and BOB at the 1983 Nor-Cal Specialty. As of May 1985, his show record included four Group 1s, two Group 2s, two Group 3s, two Group 4s, 22 BOBs with one specialty win, and five BOS including two specialties, having beaten 1,707 dogs. But his prowess is as a producer of champions. As of the end of 1985, he was the sire of 14 champions, including two offspring BIS winners, Ch. Windrift's Gambler, CD, HOF and Ch. Chalice's Silver Horizon.

Ch. Coincidence of Cari-On, HOF, owned by Dennis LeHouillier.

Ch. Windrift's Willy Weaver, ROM, owned by Dennis and Colleen LeHouillier and bred by P. and R. Hardie and J. Reed.

ABC

Arlene Grimes of ABC Keeshonds began her love affair with dogs as a child in 1955 when she acquired her first purebred dog, a Collie. She entered her in obedience and in 1958 finished her UD with a score of 200+. In 1965 Arlene started the ABC School of Dog Obedience in Davis, California. She acquired her first Keeshond in 1966. The four-year-old Skoci was untrained but that didn't deter Arlene and in 1968 Skoci was Top Obedience Keeshond in the United States.

In 1968 Silver Skoci of Rocky Falls, CDX, Can. CD, was bred to Ch. Wistonia Whiplee. This mating produced the puppy that would become Mex. and & Int. Ch. ABC's Gypsy Silver, CDX, PCE, Can. CD.

In 1969 Arlene and her husband, Jack, moved to San Jose. Gypsy's first obedience trial was the Nor-Cal Specialty in 1970 where she scored a 199+ and was HIT; three weeks later she had a score of 199½ and was again HIT. She finished her third leg the same month with a 197½ and earned a Dog World Award on the way to her CD. The next month they traveled to Canada and Gypsy and Skoci each took a HIT with scores of 198½ and earned their Canadian CD degrees. Gypsy finished her CDX in 1974 with an average score of 198.33.

In September 1974, Jack and Arlene visited Mexico and Gypsy won her first two legs on her PC (Perro Companero) with scores of 198 and 197+. In November they again traveled to Mexico where Gypsy immediately became a celebrity by racking up Novice scores that averaged 199 and Open scores that averaged 198.88; she won 3 HITs and tied for the fourth. She went home with her Perro Companero Excelente (PCE). Her scores and averages set new records for Mexico City's International Shows. While she was in Mexico, proving that she was an all-around winner, Gypsy completed her Mexican and International championship titles as well.

She was the recipient of the William G. Radell Memorial Trophy in 1974 and 1977 for her achievements in the obedience ring. She passed away on September 1, 1977 from a brain tumor.

Not only a top performer but also the producer of outstanding achievers, Gypsy, bred to Ch. Zeedrift Kwikzilver, produced two puppies that stayed with Jack and Arlene and went on to become Can., Mex., Am. and Int. Ch. ABC's Gypsy Zev, CD, and Ch. ABC's Zaffre Gypsy, CD. Zaffre finished his championship in 1975; he earned his CD in 1974 and that same year was KCA's Top Obedience Dog.

Overshadowing Zaffre's Career was that of his brother, Zev. Zev was Arlene and Jack's first BOB dog. He finished his American championship in 1973, his Mexican and International in 1974 and his Canadian in 1975. Finally in 1977, when he was seven years old, Arlene decided it was time to start obedience. He completed his CD in three trials with an average of 194.66, which sure isn't bad for an 8½-year-old Kees. Zev passed away in 1984 just two months short of his thirteenth birthday.

There have been more recent stars in the ABC Kennel. In 1982, they co-owned one of the top Keeshond bitches in the United States, Can. and Am. Ch. Windrift's Academy Award. They were co-breeders of the BIS-winning Ch. Windrift's Producer, HOF, and of Can. Am. Ch. Windrift's Oscar for ABC and Ch. Windrift's Show Stopper. Dog activities are a family function at ABC as well. In 1984 daughter Aimee Marie was No. 2 Junior Keeshond Handler and her sister Janet was No. 3. In 1985 Arlene was granted a license to judge Keeshonds; Jack expects to gain his shortly.

Another international winner also resided in California. Int. Ch. Julday Sara's Schommelaar, CD (Ch. Waakzaam Winkel, CD ex Ch. Julday Treurig Sara, CD) owned by Harry and Vivian Toepfer, began his climb toward the International champion title — a title that no American-bred Keeshond had yet won. In November 1972, he entered his first German show and was awarded an Excellent 1 and his first CACIB. He was also chosen as the West German Champion of the Year, defeating a dog that had won three years consecutively. In June 1973 he was awarded another CACIB in Austria and won their champion title at that show. His third CACIB was awarded in April 1974 in Bern, Switzerland. His fourth and final CACIB was won in Saarbrucken, Germany. He became a German champion on October 29, 1974.

5

The Keeshond
in Canada

ACCORDING TO available information, the first Keeshond in Canada was imported by Miss M. E. Butler of Montreal from Evenlode Kennels in England. Alex of Evenlode was registered in 1929 and ws first shown at the Canine Society of Montreal in June 1930. Another of Miss Butler's dogs, David of Evenlode, became the first Keeshond to win his championship in Canada.

In 1933 Miss Hilda White of Toronto showed seven Keeshonds at a show in Ontario. Mrs. Alice Tool of West Calgary, Alberta, registered six Keeshonds in 1937.

From this early start, a growing interest in the Keeshond flourished in Canada. Today we find many fine kennels in all the provinces and a healthy competitive spirit in the show ring.

WESTERN PROVINCES

Picvale

Following in the footsteps of other pioneers in the breed, Pat and Jean Croken revitalized the breed in Alberta. In 1966 they purchased a young male from Eileen and Howard Currie. Brialin's Nikki of Banks, together with Hanne Lee of Belvern and Belverns Gilded Brandwyn, became the foundation stock for Picvale Kennels.

Of their dogs, several are noteworthy: Can. Ch. Belvern's Gilded Brandwyn, who was the dam of Ch. Picvale's Miss Vixon of Banks; Can. Ch. Picvale's Pepper of Banks, who was 2nd Highest Kees in Canada in

Can. and Am. Ch. Picvales Miss Vixon of Banks, ROM.
Co-owned by Pat and Jean Croken of Canada and Gene
and Donna Smith of Missouri, she became the foundation
bitch of the Baronwood Kennels.

Can. Ch. Keewinds Super Cool (Can. Ch. Keewinds Kountry Studd ex Can.
Ch. Traveler's Keewinds Impulse) was a multiple Best Puppy in Show and
Group winner as a youngster. His breeders/owners/handlers are Ross and
Shirley Henderson.

1970; Can. Ch. Hanne Lee of Belvern, who produced eight champions out of three litters; and Can. Brialin's Nikki of Banks, CD, who received the Keeshond Club of Canada award as outstanding stud dog. Can. and Am Ch. Picvale's Miss Vixon of Banks received the Keeshond Club of Canada award as outstanding brood bitch and ROMX from the Keeshond Club of America. Vixon was jointly owned by Pat and Jean Croken and Gene and Donna Smith of Missouri. Many of Vixon's pups became the foundation stock for other Keeshond kennels in Canada.

In 1971 Pat and Jean, with the help of Rosella and Sam Helwig of Lethbridge, Alberta, and Linda Elliott of Edmonton started the Keeshond Club of Canada (KCC). In 1974 the club applied to the Canadian Kennel Club for recognition as a national club; this was granted in the spring of 1975. The Keeshond Club of Canada held its first specialty at Calgary; 34 dogs were entered. Best of Breed went to De-Jay's Billy Boy of Rich Bob, owned by Joe and Donna Silbernagel.

Jean Croken died in the spring of 1977 and Pat has carried on the breeding at Picvale.

De Jay

De Jay Keeshonden was registered in 1973, the year after Donna and Joe Silbernagel purchased their second Keeshond. "Billy" was purchased from Joanne Nixon of the United States and went on to become Can. Ch. De Jay's Billy Boy of Rich Bob, Can. CD, the first champion in North America for his sire, Am. Ch. Rich Bob's Stormy Weather, ROMX. Although never campaigned, Billy was the BOB winner at the first Keeshond Club of America Specialty and winner of the Veterans Class at two more.

The foundation of De Jay's was Marganna Angie, Can. CD, purchased from Marganna Kennels in 1972. Her lineage went back to Ch. Sinterklaas Brave Nimrod. One of her progeny is Can. Ch. De Jay's Peek A Boo, Can. CDX, Can. ROM, who, along with her sister De Jay's Princess Juliana, Can. CD, took a Best Brace is Show in 1975.

In 1980 De Jay imported a bitch from Darrell and Sharon Buethner of the United States. In limited showing, Can. Ch. Sheminee Gypsy Belle V. De Jay was No. 3 show bitch KCC system and No. 2 Keezette in 1982. Gypsy is now dam to the fifth generation of De Jay puppies.

De Jay also provided the foundation for other kennels in the area. A combination of bloodlines from De Jay and Cascadia provided the start for Gail Holmberg's Shanticlaire Kennel. From Cascadia came Am., Can. and Mex., Ch. Cascadia HR Puff and Stuff, who was no. 2 show male in Canada in 1979.

Komatikee Keeshonden was registered in 1981 by Randy and Patti Pelletier. Their foundation Kees came from De Jay and Maldolph's Kennel in the United States. Their first dog, Can. Ch. Maldolph's Terra of Komatikee, was No. 2 show bitch in Canada (KCC system) in 1982.

Can. Ch. De Jay's Billy Boy of Rich-Bob, CD (Ch. Rich-Bob's Stormy Weather, ROMX ex Salina's Koko of Rich-Bob), owned by Donna Silbernagel of Alberta, was the winner of the first Keeshond Club of Canada Specialty in 1975.

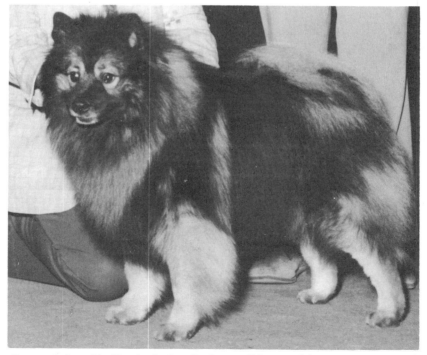

Can. and Am. Ch. Keeshof's Star Performer DJ, owned by Mavis Dunsford of British Columbia, was No. 1 Keeshond in Canada in 1981 and 1982.

136

Keeshof

Mavis Dunsford has owned Keeshonds since 1955. One of her first dogs was Gay-Glades Kornelius, the last of the bloodline of Mrs. Muriel Galicz who brought some of the first Kees into British Columbia.

The most famous of Keeshof's dogs is Can. and Am. Ch. Keeshof's Star Performer DJ. In 1980 he was No. 2 Keeshond in Canada; he ranked No. 1 in both 1981 and 1982. His record included three BIS, 85 Group placings, 12 of which were Group 1s, and 145 BOBs. Another of Mavis' top winners was her import, Can. and Am. Ch. Jee Jac's Orthello, who was also a BIS winner and Top Kees in Canada in 1979.

Keewinds

Ross and Shirley Henderson of Saskatchewan got off to a wonderful start. The cute little puppy they purchased in 1974 became their first champion, Can. Ch. Chan-Star's Midnight Cowboy and Keewinds Keeshonden was born. The purchased their foundation bitch, Can. Ch. Baronwood Sassy Cassy, from Jean and Donna Smith in the United States in 1975. Over the years, Cassy raised four litters that produced nine Canadian champions and two CD winners. Many of her get have been exceptional: Can. Ch. Keewinds Kountry Studd is a multiple Group placer and Keewinds' first Best Puppy in Show (BPIS) winner. Can. Ch. Keewinds Kountry Kowboy was Keewinds' first CD winner; and Can. Ch. Keewinds Super Cool, a multiple Group winner, had three BPIS.

The byword at Keewinds is *quality* instead of *quantity*. Their goal is a sound, healthy dog with a good personality that can become part of family life. A good home for their puppies is their first criteria.

In ten years, the Hendersons have bred nine litters that produced 49 puppies. Out of these, 13 have finished their Canadian championships. They have also championed six other dogs imported into their kennel in the past ten years. Being involved with 19 champion Keeshonds has given them a great deal of satisfaction and pride in what they have accomplished.

Klompen

After an extensive search for the "right" Keeshond, Kathy and Bruce Stewart of Klompen Kennels, began their adventure with the breed in 1978 with the purchase of a puppy bitch who went on to become Can. and Am. Ch. von Ryan's Ragamuffin, Can. CD (Am. Ch. Flakkee Instamatic, HOF ex Can. Ch. Baronwood's Hot Dam). In her first eight shows, Muffin won BIS, three BPIS, two Group 1s and a Group 4 to make her the No. 1 Keeshond Bitch in Canada for 1979.

A success in the whelping box as well, four of her puppies have won BPIS and Group 1 awards; both of her sons are multiple BIS winners.

Two of Muffin's get have done exceptionally well in the Maritime

Can. Ch. Klompen's Tommy Tittlemouse (Can. Ch. Kendol's
Chinook of Gates, CD ex Can. and Am. Ch. von Ryan's Ragamuffin,
CD) was a BIS winner at just 10½ months of age. His breeders/owners
are Kathy and Bruce Stewart of Alberta.

Am. and Can. Ch. Maldolph's Calculator, No. 1 Show Keeshond in
Canada in 1984. He was bred by Anna and Dick Malet and owned by
Dr. Ted Wetzler and Anna Malet of Washington.

Provinces. Can. Ch. Klompen's Limejuice Lill and Can. Ch. Klompen's Sluicebox Sam, CD (Wistonia Winter-Wind ex Muffin) together won a Best Brace in Show. Each was also a Group 1 winner and BPIS winner. Sam was the No. 1 Keeshond in Canada (Keezette system) in 1983 and No. 3 Keeshond for 1984 (KCC and Keezette). Shown sparingly in 1985, he won another BIS.

The current star in the Klompen Kennel is Can. Ch. Klompen's Tommy Tittlemouse (Can. Ch. Kendol's Chinook of Gates, Can. CD ex Muffin). By 10½ months of age, he had accumulated an all-breed BIS, five BPISs and six Group 1 placements. He was No. 5 Keeshond and No. 1 Keeshond Puppy in Canada in 1984. Due to the Stewarts' move from Nova Scotia to Alberta in 1985, Tommy was shown only eight times but it was enough for him to earn the No. 8 spot (both systems). Actively being campaigned in 1986, he is well on his way to becoming one of the top Kees for the year. Another Muffin daughter, Ch. Klompen's Breadline Baby, owned by Irene Ovenden, was the top-winning Keeshond Bitch in 1985.

In the final standings for 1985, five of the top-ten Kees in Canada were bred by the Stewarts.

ONTARIO

Brialin

Brialin Kennels was first registered in 1953 as a Samoyed kennel but in 1965 Eileen Currie became involved with Keeshonds. Her first bitch, Holland Day Hanne de Gyselaer, was mated to Varo V. Myia, a Sinterklaas Brave Nimrod son. From this pair came all but one of the Brialin Kees. A son from this litter was shipped to Pat and Jean Croken and became the first Keeshond champion in Alberta.

In 1975 Mrs. Dolores Hull from Nova Scotia bought Can. Ch. Brialin's Schipper from Eileen. Schipper's progeny led to the formation of other Keeshond kennels in the Maritimes. He is the sire of Can. Ch. Kendol's Chinook of Gates, Can. CD, and grandsire to Can. Ch. Klompen's Tommy Tittlemouse, both BIS winners.

In 1972 Eileen sold Brialin Mieuland Graydawn to Yvette Walton of Newfoundland; she went on to become the first Keeshond champion and CD in that province.

In 1969 Eileen bought Verbar Silver Smoke of Brialin, her first male Keeshond, from Mrs. Verna Stovin of Ontario. Previously Eileen had concentrated on breeding but soon got bitten by the show bug, showing all the Kees that she kept in her kennel to their championships.

In 1981 Thomas and Marion Silverthorne of Brantford, Ontario, whose kennel was founded on Brialin dogs, bred a litter of puppies that included four blacks. Eileen and her husband bought the pick female and, since black is a major fault in North America, began training for the obedience ring.

Can. Ch. Paladin's My-O-My Passionella is shown here at 11 years of age. Still going strong at 17, she is owned by Jack and Madeleine Nugent of Ontario.

Paladin's BIS-winning brace of Can. and Am. Ch. Paladin's Jolly Roger, Can. ROM, and Can. Ch. Paladin's Benji Darnclever, owned by Jack and Madeleine Nugent.

Guymar Velvet Brialin has now finished her CD. Eileen now is dividing her showing between conformation and obedience.

Paladin

The Paladin Kennel of Jack and Madeleine Nugent began in 1968 with the foundation male, Can. Ch. Verbar Maja's Masked Delight, and foundation bitch, Ch. Coventry Maja's Bonny Solo. "Barney" and "Solo" produced a litter of five in 1969, four of which became champions. One of these, Can. Ch. Paladin's My-Oh-My Passionella, Can. ROM is still alive today. While she was actively being shown, Passionella was a multi-BOB winner with Group placings; she was five times best brood bitch in specialty shows. Bred three times, she produced seven champions, including two American champions. Her first litter in 1971 by Rokerig's Rum Punch resulted in BIS Can. and Am. Ch. Paladin's Jolly Roger, Can. ROM. Her third litter in December 1974 by Can. and Am. Ch. Racassius of Rhinevale, ROMX, produced Can. and Am. Ch. Paladin's Deputy Dawg, No. 1 Keeshond in Canada in 1977 who finished at Westminster in 1978; and Can. Ch. Paladin's Dynamic Damsel, Can. ROM, KCC Brood Bitch of 1979 and Best Brood Bitch in Non-Sporting Group in Canada in 1982.

Passionella's daughter Can. Ch. Paladin's Dynamic Damsel, Can. ROM, took over as dam of Paladin's next three litters. In 1978, bred to Am. Ch. Shady Hill's Frederick, she produced Am. Ch. Paladin's Shady Hill Joshua, who finished his American championship undefeated; and Can. Ch. Paladin's Howdy Rowdy, who was No. 3 in Canada in 1983 with only two months of showing.

The Paladin Kees have always been Jack and Madeleine's companions and family pets as well as show dogs. To date they have finished 26 champions, 22 of which have been Paladin-bred. Paladin is also known for its BIS-winning braces and a team of four proven males, the first to be shown in Canada.

Rokerig

Betty Olafson of Rokerig Kennels acquired her first Keeshond from the Van Myia Kennels of Ontario in 1963. Shortly after World War II and during the 1950s and early 1960s, Mary Matchett of Van Myia Kennels had been one of the well-known breeders. In 1963 she imported Sinterklaas Brave Nimrod. He remained with her until her death in 1966, when he joined the Ruttkay Kennels in the United States.

After a trip to England and a visit with Margo Emerson, Betty became seriously interested in breeding and showing. In January 1965 Rugosa of Rhinevale joined the Olafson household. Rugosa acquired her Canadian championship very quickly, despite, Betty says, "her inexperienced handler." She was entered in three KCA shows and took BOS on all three occasions. At the specialty in 1971, she was chosen BOS by judge

Can. and Am. Ch. Paladin's Deputy Dawg was the No. 1 Keeshond in Canada in 1977. "Sprout" is owned by Jack and Madeleine Nugent.

Ch. Brialin's Regal Knight (Ch. Nikita, CD ex Ch. Verbar Hanna) is owned by Eileen Currie of Ontario.

142

Clementine Peterson while Futurity judge Marcy Goebel, chose her son, Rokerig's Rhinn of Kelles, as her BIF dog. Rugosa was KCA's top show bitch in 1969.

Racassius of Rhinevale joined the family in 1968 at the age of ten weeks. "Punch" will be remembered for the many champions he sired both in Canada and the United States, and particularly for the great showman that he was. In 1970 he was the top-winning Keeshond in Canada and he earned his American championship the same year. In 1977 he won the *Kennel Review* award for top producer of the breed in the United States during that year. Am. and Can. Ch. Racassius of Rhinevale, ROMX, made a great contribution to future generations of Keeshonds, including three Canadian all-breed BIS winners. One of his sons, Can. Ch. Reydorp Blast Off, bred by Dr. Peter Woodyer in 1969, was the top-winning Keeshond of all times in Canada. Punch had a long and healthy life and died at the age of 14½ years.

Am. and Can. Ch. Ledwell Alexander is currently the star at Rokerig Keeshonden. Born in June 1981 he came to Canada from England at nine weeks of age. Both Racassius and Alexander were bred by Sylvia Scroggs, of Ledwell Keeshonden, and they stem from the same bloodlines. In his young career, "Toby" has sired several champions both in Canada and the United States. The climax of his achievements came when he took WD at the 1985 KCA Golden Annviersary Specialty Show under Judge Melbourne Downing.

Keesbrook

The Keesbrook Kennels of Brenda Brookes was established in 1972. Brenda's first Keeshond, and the foundation of her kennel, was Can. Ch. Keeboom's Chinook, who emerged a Canadian champion having been undefeated in the classes.

In 1974 Chinook was bred to a young American male, Flakkee's Keeboom Import. This blending of famous bloodlines from both sides of the border produced Can. Ch. Keesbrook's Billigo Bingo. His successful show career included a Group 3 and BPIS his first time out; he remained in the top five for the subsequent four years. At his first American show, the large KCA Specialty in 1979, he was RWD.

Brenda has recently acquired Can. and Am. Ch. Baronwood Black Jack from Gene and Donna Smith in the United States. B.J. was No. 4 Keeshond in Canada in 1981; his son, Can. and Am. Ch. Keesbrooks' Whiskey Jack, owned by Shannon Kelly of California, was WD at the Heart of America Specialty in 1984 and obtained his Canadian championship in one visit to Canada with three consecutive BOBs and two Group placements.

Keesbrook's latest dog is imported from the English kennel of Gina and Bob Weedon. Can. and Am. Ch. Keesland HiJacker made his mark early in his show career by becoming a Canadian and American champion by 13 months of age. He was in the top five Keeshonds in Canada in 1984 and 1985.

Am. and Can. Ch. Rugosa of Rhinevale, owned by Betty Olafson, was BOS at the KCA National Specialty in 1971 under judge Clementine Peterson.

Am. and Can. Ch. Racassius of Rhinevale, ROMX, owned by Betty Olafson of Ontario, is shown here at 10½ months of age.

Keesbrook has bred only four litters for a total of 22 puppies; of these 12 are Canadian champions and two are American champions. Brenda foresees an exciting breeding program emerging from her dogs, each of whom she feels has something to offer the breed.

Maplekees

Maplekees Kennels began in 1980 after Tom and Isabel Ayers saw a photo of a Keeshond in an all-breed magazine. They visited Keesbrook Kennels and were totally captivated by the Keeshond temperament.

Their first Keeshond, Keewinds' Southern Belle (Am. Ch. Baronwoods Sling Shot ex Can. Ch. Baronwood Sassy Cassy) arrived in November 1980. In 1982 she was bred to Can. Ch. Keesbrook's Billigo Bingo and produced two puppies; one of thse puppies was Can. Ch. Maplekees' Melodie, who was No. 5 Keeshond bitch in Canada for 1983.

Tom and Isabel fell in love with Am. Ch. Foxfairs Persuasive Friend and became the owners of his son, Scamp — now Can. and Am. Ch. Jo-Lyn's Excalibur. Scamp was later bred to Keewinds Southern Belle and produced three puppies. Several other Maplekees litters have been bred and are just now making their presence felt in the show rings.

NEWFOUNDLAND

Miss Yvette Walton obtained a female Keeshond from Eileen Currie of Ontario in 1972. Brialin Nieuland Graydawn became the first Keeshond to finish its championship and CD in Newfoundland, according to Mrs. Currie's information. In the spring of 1973 Miss Walton bought Brialin Rocky Shore, who was also shown to her championship and CD. From this pair came other Keeshond kennels in Newfoundland. In 1974 John and Carol Leonard bought Brialin Silver Taffit, who sired the BIS-winning Seabright's Silver Taka.

In 1978 Ron and Dianne Coady bought Can. Ch. Brialin Baron. Baron went on to many Group wins and a BIS. His son, Can. Ch. Diaron's Rook de Bandit, CD, owned by Roland King, won a BIS in 1983. Bandit's dam is Miss Walton's breeding.

NEW BRUNSWICK

Chakka

The Chakka Kennel of Mrs. Flo Beasley was the proud owner of Can. Ch. Reydorp Blast Off, Can. CD. Bred by Dr. Peter Woodyer by Can. and Am. Ch. Racassius of Rhinevale ex Can. Ch. Waakzaam Welsrijp, "Bronco" was first generation "Canadian." Bronco became the top-winning Canadian-bred Keeshond of all time, compiling an amazing record

Am. and Can. Ch. Ledwell Alexander was WD at the 1985 KCA Golden Anniversary Specialty. "Toby" is owned by Betty Olafson of Ontario.

Can. Ch. Keesbrook's Billigo Bingo, owned by Brenda Brookes of Ontario.

146

of 23 BISs, 117 Group 1s, eighth Top Dog in Canada for all-breeds, three times No. 1 Keeshond in Canada and No. 1 Non-Sporting Dog in Canada.

At seven years of age and under the direction of Dr. Maureen Clements, Bronco gained his CD title with high scores in three staight trials. He died in 1980 at the age of ten.

About a year and a half after acquiring Bronco, Flo obtained Bronco's full sister from Dr. Woodyer and bred Can. Ch. Reydorp Better Idea to her. That litter produced eight puppies, six of which gained their Canadian championshps. One of these puppies, Can. Ch. Chakka's Space Cruiser, had three BIS in Canada and one in Bermuda.

Geluk

Dr. Maureen Clements saw a young Can. Ch. Reydorp Blast-Off at a show and decided this was the breed for her. One year later, Can. Ch. and O.T. Ch. Reydorp Carte Blanche arrived to change Maureen's life. Geluk Kennel was born when "Kerry" was bred to Can. Ch. Japar Kommander, owned by Mrs. Beasley. From her two litters to Kommander came Can. and Am. Ch. and Can. O.T. Ch. Geluk is Prince Igor. Igor is a multiple BIS and HIT winner who placed in the top ten dogs in Canada the three years he was shown. He was also top obedience competition Keeshond for two years.

Another of Kerry's get was Can. and Am. Ch. and Can. O.T. Ch. Geluk is Tarantella. Maureen says, "Tara was a super bitch and was good at everything she did." She was a Group winner and was top obedience Keeshond for three years. She also excelled as a brood bitch. Tara produced ten Canadian champions and three American champions; when bred to Blast-Off, she produced BIS winner Can. Ch. Geluk is Kaddaks Big Tough Man, who was top Keeshond in Canada in 1980

Among Tara's other get are: Can. and Am. Ch. and O.T. Ch. Geluk is Allegro, who was top Keeshond bitch in Canada for two years (Keezette system) and under the Canadian system, a multiple HIT and Group winner and now a brood bitch. Can. and Am. Ch. and O.T. Ch. Geluk is King Liam's Fancy is a multiple Group and HIT winner and was top obedience dog in 1984 and third in the Non-Sporting Group in Canada.

Maureen's Geluk Kennel is an unusual one because Maureen's dogs share in all of her activities. They are all house pets, show dogs in both conformation and obedience rings, therapy dogs in her work with nursing home patients and sled team members. Maureen began sledding in 1977 and uses from two to six Keeshonds at a time. She says the dogs love it and crowd around as soon as the sledding harnesses appear. Until her death in 1984, Tara was the lead dog. Subsequently, her son Liam has taken over the duties. Maureen tells about one race where her fellow sledders became concerned at her absence at the finish line. When she finally appeared, she explained, with a red face, that Liam had led the sled to the front steps of a house and into the kitchen where her Kees team had quickly devoured the

Can. Ch. Reydorp Blast-Off, owned by Mrs. Flo Beasley, was the top-winning Canadian-bred Keeshond of all time.

Can. and Am. Ch. & Can. OT Ch. Geluk is King Liam's Fancy, owned by Maureen Clements.

Can. and Am. Ch. & Can. OT Ch. Geluk is Allegro, owned by
Maureen Clements of New Brunswick.

Can. and Am. Ch. & Can. OT Ch. Geluk is Prince Igor, owned by Maureen
Clements of New Brunswick.

local dog's supper! Liam, being the typical social Keeshond, also slowed the team down because everytime the spectators cheered, he would stop to talk!

NOVA SCOTIA

Seawind

Seawind Kennel was born in 1977 when Don Gates presented his wife, Glady, with a Mothers' Day present. Can. Ch. Kendol's Chinook of Gates, Can. CD (Can. Ch. Brialin's Schipper ex Can. Ch. Kristlkees' Karina of Kendol, bred by Dolores Hull) became "Mom's Boy." Chinook is a born showman and won his Canadian championship at the age of 8½ months. In 1981 *his* Mothers' Day gift to Glady was his first BIS at the Dartmouth Kennel Club Show. Before retiring from the ring in 1983 at the age of six years, he had totaled two all-breed BIS, 91 BOBs, 13 Group 1s, 22 Group 2s, 16 Group 3s and 19 Group 4s. He also earned his CD with excellent scores. Chinook was exclusively owner-handled by Glady during his entire conformation and obedience careers.

Chinook also excels as a stud dog and has sired: BIS and HIT winner Can. Ch. Seawind's Lit'l Bit O'Wrock, Can. CD; BIS winner Can. Ch. Klompen's Tommy Tittlemouse; and HIT winners Seawind's First Mate, Can. CDX and Can. O.T. Ch. Seawind's Bold Buccaneer.

In 1980 Can. Ch. Kristlkees' Kelaina of Seawind, Can. CDX, joined the family. Bred by Christine Seidl of Ontario, Kelli is by Am. and Can. Ch. Fearless Focalpint ex Kristlkees' Kute Rags. Kelli became the foundation bitch of Seawind Kennel. She received her Canadian championshp in 1980 at 11 months of age and continued to win as a special, but she was born for the obedience ring and there she excelled. With her owner-trainer-handler, Don, she totaled eight high in class and five HIT while earning her CD and CDX degrees and was No. 2 obedience Keeshond in Canada in 1983.

In 1981 Kelli was bred to Chinook and this mating produced Seawind's September Schatzie, who quickly finished his championship, and a second male who would become Can. Ch. Seawind's Litl Bit O'Wrock, Can. CD. "Ruffin" excelled while still a puppy and finished his championship receiving 15 BPIG and two BPIS awards along the way. In late 1984 Glady brought Ruffin out as a special and in only 19 shows he received five all-breed BIS, 11 Group 1s, two Group 2s, one Group 3 and 16 BOS. Trained and handled by Don, Ruffin also completed his CD degree wih an HIT the same year.

In 1985 Ruffin received four all-breed BIS, 19 Group 1s, 17 Group 2s, five Group 3s, one Group 4 and 44 BOBs which garnered him the No. 1 Keeshond in Canada slot (Keezette system).

In 1983 Car-Ron's Baroness of Seawind (Am. Ch. Foxfairs Persuasive Friend, HOF, ROMX, ex Car-Ron's Constant Comment), joined the Seawind Kennel. "Becki" finished her Canadian championshp handily and

Can. Ch. Kendol's Chinook of Gates, Can. CD, and "Mom," Glady Gates.

Can. Ch. Seawind's Lit'l Bit O'Wrock, Can. CD, owned by Don and Glady Gates of Nova Scotia, was No. 1 Keeshond in Canada in 1985.

Can. Ch. & Can. OT Ch. Car-Ron's Baroness of Seawind is shown here with owner-trainer, Don Gates. "Becki" was the No. 1 Obedience Keeshond in Canada in 1985.

Can. Ch. Car-Ron's Baron De'Markee, Can. CD, owned by Hubert and Julianne Fiander of Nova Scotia, excels in both rings. He was No. 2 Obedience Keeshond in Canada in 1985 and has two BIS to his credit in 1986.

was then bred to Ruffin; both of the puppies from this first litter have now received their championships. Don then began training Becki for obedience and she turned out to be a natural. She completed her CD degree with three HITs and scores of 196, 196 and 198½. In the same year she completed her CDX with scores of 195½, 194½ and an HIT of 196. Her record for 1985 earned her the title of Top Obedience Keeshond in Canada (Keezette system). In 1986, she earned her UD and added the prefix Can. O.T. Ch.

At Seawind, the breeding emphasis is on temperament, type and soundness.

KeeMar

Just down the road is the KeeMar Kennel of Hubert and Julianne Fiander. Getting their start from Seawind, Hubert has focused his attention on the obedience ring (O.T. Ch. Seawind's Bold Buccaneer) while Julianne spends her time on conformation. In 1983 another Car-Ron puppy accompanied "Becki" to Nova Scotia. "Baron" joined the Fiander household and quickly became Can. Ch. Car-Ron's Baron De' Markee, Can. CD. He finished his CD with two HITs in 1985 which earned him the spot as No. 2 Obedience Keeshond in Canada (Keezette). He returned to the conformation ring in 1986 and at this writing has already won two BIS.

Canada has a very active parent breed club and publishes a periodic newsletter to its members on both sides of the border. In 1985, in conjunction with the Keeshond Club of America National Specialty, the Keeshond Club of Canada held its first independent National Specialty, which drew an entry of over 100 Keeshonds. The Keeshond is growing in popularity in Canada, more kennels are springing up and more dogs are excelling in the show ring. The breed has a healthy future among our neighbors to the north.

153

Ch. Katrellie Van Zaandaam and Ch. Rogue of Wildings, two of the first Keeshonds in Sweden.

Swed. and Nor. Ch. Rhinevale Rockefeller is shown here at nine months of age; he is owned by Mai Holmberg of Sweden.

6

The Keeshond in
Other Lands

THE KEESHOND is bred and exhibited in many countries around the world. In Scandinavia, which consists of Norway, Denmark, Sweden and Finland, it continues to be quite popular. Its popularity is growing in South Africa, New Zealand and Australia. Show procedures for gaining championships in these countries are generally similar to the Challenge Certificate system used in England. Dogs can gain their International championships by winning four excellent ratings and Certificates of Aptitude, Championship, International Beauty (CACIB) under Federation Cynologique Internationale (FCI) judges in four countries. For purposes of this chapter, unless other indicated, the champion title refers to the country of residence.

SWEDEN

Early Breeders

The first Keeshonds arrived in Sweden in 1950 when Mrs. Alfrida Lindholm, already well known for her breeding of Finnish Spitz under the kennel name of Reidstahill, desired to add another Spitz breed to her kennel. In discussions with her fellow breeder, Mrs. Carin Slattne of Kennel Slattang, they saw a photo of a Spitz breed called "Keeshonden." Both breeders contacted Mrs. D. Rose of Wildings Kennel in England. Shortly thereafter a male, Rogue of Wildings, bred by Miss Rose, arrived for Kennel Slattang; and a bitch, Voorlicht of Vorden, bred by Mrs. Tucker, arrived for Kennel Freidstahill.

155

In 1951 the first Swedish litter of Keeshonds was bred from these two imports. As Rogue was a beautiful male and the breed went beyond expectations, a wider breeding program was planned. Much to the breeders' delight, they were able to import two adult bitches, both of whom had been bred in England and were in whelp. Katrellie Van Zaandam was bred to Mrs. Wingfield Digby's Eng. Ch. Billo Van Zaandam, and she delivered three pups at Mrs. Slattne's kennel; Yolande of Disenworth, who was bred to Teddy of Wildings, delivered ten pups at Mrs. Lindholm's kennel.

During this time Mr. Lindback imported another bitch from Baroness Van Hardenbroek in Holland. Although bought as a companion dog, she was bred to Freidstahill's Boris from Yolande's first litter. Another male from Yolande's litter was exported to Miss Elsa Nielsen, Kennel Tryggevaelde in Denmark. The breed was advertised as "Dutch Chow-Chows."

Although the breed was unknown in Sweden, the first imported Keeshonds soon received their championships. Breeders encouraged their puppy buyers to show and spread knowledge of the breed in the country.

Despite their attempts, there was little growth in the number of registered dogs until 1965 when new breeders came on the scene. Mrs. Inga Ahlberg moved to southern Sweden and brought her two adult bitches, Peggy and Hokdalen Kickan. Peggy was bred to Bjorkenas Herr Karlsson, and Hokdalen Kickan was bred to Freidstahills Kimme; this was the start of the Torparlickan Kennel. Mrs. Ahlberg decided to expand her kennel and imported a male, Husar of Ven (by Am. Ch. Ruttkay Moerdaag of Ven), from Mrs. Jere Collins in England.

At the same time, Mrs. Lillebil Dahlquist imported two Keeshonds, Van Bergen of Ven and Blazon of Ven, from Mr. and Mrs. Collins. Van Bergen was also a son of Ruttkay Moerdaag but out of a different bitch. The half-brothers were very different in type, with Husar being much darker, like his father, and Van Bergen carrying a huge silver coat. Both passed their types on in subsequent breedings.

Van Bergen, later to become a Swedish and Danish champion, was the first Keeshond to go BIS at a Scandinavian championship show. Several years later his great, great-granddaughter, Int. and Nord. Ch. Noble House Susan, did the same thing. They remain the only two BIS Keeshonds in Sweden.

Stiiberg

In 1965 Van Bergen and Blazon were bred and from this litter Mai Holmberg bought a bitch called Black Girl, who later became an International and Nordic champion and the foundation for Stiiberg Kennel. Mai is one of the few breeders from the 1960s who remains actively breeding and has 40 champions to her credit.

Int. and Nord. Ch., Finnish Winner 1981, Nordic Winner 1984 Duroya Junker, owned by Mrs. Mai Holmberg.

Int. and Nord. Ch. Keestorpets Excellent (whelped 1980) is owned by Mona Karlsson.

157

Mai planned future breedings of Black Girl but could find no suitable studs in Sweden; she turned her attention to England and acquired Rampant of Rhinevale. "Bimbo" became an International and Nordic champion and the only Kees ever to finish in all four countries — Sweden, Norway, Denmark and Finland.

Yet another English import made an important contribution to the breed in Sweden. Rhinevale Rockefeller, bred by Mrs. Margo Emerson, was delivered to Mai and Sten Holmberg. His sire was Eng. Ch. Foxburgh of Rhinevale and his dam was Ronalisa of Rhinevale, daughter of Eng. Ch. Robinella of Rhinevale. Rockefeller became the sire of 20 champions, a record that still stands. He also became a Swedish and Norwegian champion and earned eight CACIBs.

Stiiberg's Kennel was again in search of a new stud dog and so Mrs. Woodiwiss' Duroya Junker (Eng. Ch. Swashway No Rush ex Eng. Ch. Duroya Imogen) arrived in Sweden in 1978 and earned his International and Nordic championships. He is the sire of 15 champions in three countries.

Thaagarden

Ruth Svensson began her Thaagarden Kennel in 1958 with Ingerbo Vivi as her foundation bitch. From Holland she imported a male, Ma-Lings Hans-Arno. In 1969 Int. and Nord. Ch. Stiibergs Kommendant of Baloo joined the kennel as well as two more English imports, Sivad Silver Fox and Vandaban Athelstane (Eng. Ch. Ledwell Lysander ex Gelderland Arabella of Vandaban).

Repeta

Inga-Britt and Bengt Johansson of Kennel Repeta, also imported their breeding stock from England. From Mr. and Mrs. Collins came Repeta of Ven (Eng. Ch. Surprise of Ven ex Wellford Onrinda of Ven), which was the foundation of their kennel. Repeta of Ven was instrumental in the progress of the breed as she produced champions each time she was bred to different types of dogs.

Vaderson Sieglinde was bred in England by Mrs. Pat Parkes to Ch. Rhinevale Robin Hood. The litter was whelped in August 1975 and produced Antouanette, who later became an international and Nordic champion. With 14 BIS and 24 BOBs, he was Keeshond of the Year three times. He also proved to be a good producer with 16 champion offspring to date.

Lohamra

Gerd Bastholm of Kennel Lohamra bought her first bitch, Thaagarden's Ahita Sussie, from Ruth Svensson. She later acquired two more bitches,

Stiiberg's Nanou and Stiiberg's Orchide, a Rockefeller daughter, from Mai Holmberg. Nanou became a Swedish champion and Orchide received a Nordic championship. Nanou was bred to Rockefeller and one of the offspring, Ch. Lohamras Bay City Roller, a strong male with beautiful coloring, is their current stud. The Lohamras Kennel is renowned for their long line of beautiful bitches.

Keestorpets and Wesaborg

Two breeders who began their kennels with bitches from Inga Ahlberg are Mona Karlsson of Keestorpets Kennel and Pia Anrep-Nordin of Wesaborg's Kennel. Keestorpet's first bitch was Torparflickans Zsa-Zsa, who was later bred to Inga Ahlberg's imported Ch. Wrester of Waakzaam. This resulted in two champions — Int. and Nord. Ch. Keestorpet's Colombo and Nord. Ch. Keestorpet's Cherie, who was later sold to Finland. Colombo was bred to Ch. Valsgate Oyster Catcher and produced Int. and Nord. Ch. Keestorpet's Excellent. He in turn was bred to Int. and Nord. Ch. Keestorpet's Brilliant and this resulted in Int. and Nord. Keestorpet's Kavaljer, owned by Eva Isaksson . . . three generations of International champions!

Wesaborg Kennel began its breeding program with Torparflickan's Zingo. She in turn was bred to Torparflickan's Kaupouschi. A male in this litter, Ch. Wesaborg's Semlon, became Wesaborg's stud and has produced many good offspring. Recently Pia Anre-Nordim has imported Gavimir Pecan and Eng. Ch. Traza Teasel from England to add to her breeding program.

In Sweden few Keeshonds are shown in obedience, but those who do have had good success. An obedience trial champion bears the designation LP and there are very few of them in Sweden. The most famous is Repeta Happy, owned by Ann Louise Ahlgren. Happy won her title in 1982 at the age of three. She has qualified to compete in the Swedish championship trial two years in a row and was district champion in 1983 and 1984. A double champion, Swed. and Norw. Ch. LP Ch. Stiiberg's Dear Cousin Jenny, is owned by Lena Hindersson. Another Keeshond, Teddy-Bjornen Fredriksson, was selected as a leader-dog for the blind and fulfilled that assignment for his owner Boris Lamby beautifully.

Keeshondringen, the Keeshond Club of Sweden, was organized in 1965 and recently celebrated their twentieth anniversary. From a small membership of 15, the club has grown to include aproximately 500 Keeshond fanciers. Sten and Mail Holmberg served the club since the beginning as president and secretary respectively until, Mai says, "the club had to be taken over by younger and stronger persons." The club also publishes a quarterly breed magazine, *Keeshond Posten*.

Swed. Obed. Ch. Repetas Romeo and Repetas Ragtime, a
Swedish and Norwegian show champion. Ragtime and
Romeo have competed successfully in obedience trials.
Romeo was the first Keeshond in Sweden to gain a
Swedish champion title in obedience.

Int. and Nord. Ch. Thaagardens Jay Silver and Nord. Ch. Thaagardens Sharriana
were two winning Keeshonds in the 1970s. They were bred by Ruth Svensson of
Kennel Thaagarden, one of the oldest and most active kennels in Sweden.

NORWAY

In Norway, Emma Knardahl purchased a bitch, Thaagarden's Liebestraume, in 1966; she also acquired Torparflickan's Buffalo from Inga Ahlberg and Kennel Knarrebo was born.

Norway's best known early breeder was Jens Semb-Nygaard. He began breeding Keeshonds in 1967 under the kennel name of Bjornheim. His foundation bitch, Kissin Cousin of Ven (Eng. Ch. Sinterklaas Big Noise of Evenlode ex Cousin Kate of Ven), was imported from Mr. and Mrs. Collins. She received her International and Nordic championship in no time, and was later bred to a Norwegian male, Ruggen (sired by Int. and Nord. Ch. Ricko from Sweden whose background went back to the original imports to Sweden). The combination of these two was remarkable and resulted in a long list of International champions. Unfortunately, Kennel Bjornheim is no longer in existence.

Marit Wanggaard, bought a bitch, Knarrebo's Kees, from this kennel. She was later bred to Rhinevale Rockefeller. Three of these offspring, under the kennel name of Wangbo, became champions. Happiness had no end when Ch. Wangbo's Tammy Girl traveled to Sweden to compete at the Keeshondringen Show and went BIS.

Marit, one of the most prominent breeders in Norway at this time, does very selective breeding and raises only one or two litters a year in her home. In 1984 Norw. Ch. Wangbo's Tammy Girl was bred to Norw. Ch. Keestorpet's Galant. This resulted in a litter of seven puppies. Rondi Tyler, who was visiting her homeland of Norway from the United States, saw the puppies and fell in love. Wango's Prince of Norway was handcarried aboard the plane by his new owner and arrived in the United States in April 1984. There he joined the other Keeshonds at the Tyler household and added a U.S. championship when he finished at 18 months of age, in less than six weeks, with four majors to his credit.

Although breeding in Norway is limited, the Keeshond has received some royal attention. In the 1970s King Olaf of Norway was given a Keeshond bitch as a present from his children. The king, as well as the Norwegian people, are very sports minded and it was common to see King Olaf cross-country skiing in the mountains with his beloved Keeshond faithfully trailing him. In the summer, he would go for long outings, always followed by the little Kees bitch. There were constantly pictures of the "King and his dog". In the December 1978 issue of the Norwegian dog magazine *Hundesport*, Norw. Ch. Wangbo's Tammy Girl was pictured on the front cover, with a long article on Keeshonds, as well as an article on the "King and his dog." So today in Norway, the Keeshond is recognized as a Keeshond and not a "long-haired Norwegian Elkhound."

FINLAND

In previous years few Keeshond puppies were born in Finland but when there was a litter, Irene Lilja was usually involved. Both as a breeder and president of the Finnish Keeshond Club, she has taken the lead in Finland for the Keeshond.

In the 1960s two Keeshond bitches, Raoul and Ralana of Rhinevale, were imported from Mrs. Margo Emerson. Both became champions in a short time and, together with a Finnish male, Ch. Marijken Hilarik, became the foundation for Kennel Alkestitan. Later, Irene Lilja received two more bitches from Mrs. Emerson, the highly beloved Ch. Raketta of Rhinevale and Ch. Rhinevale Rosemarie.

Nord. Ch. Stiiberg's Pierina arrived in Finland in 1976 with owner Susanne Heinonen. This bitch was bred to Rhinevale Rockefeller and out of this litter Susanne kept a male, Solbjorn, who became a champion, and also a bitch named Solvarg, who lent her name to the Kennel Solvargens.

The next time Pierina was bred it was to Ch. Stiiberg's Utter. This proved to be a good breeding, producing Ch. Solvargen's Unik. In recent years, Susanne Heinonen has been working in conjunction with Kennel Lohambra in Sweden.

HOLLAND/NETHERLANDS

The Dutch Kennel of Oet et Laand van Aleer was begun by Esther Zuidema in the late 1960s. Esther had extremely good fortune with her first litter. Claus and Cupido became International champions, Christian a Swiss champion and Christel both International champion and champion of Monaco. Although slow to develop, Claus was destined to become the most famous member of his litter and one of the most outstanding representatives of his breed on the continent. He won his championships in Belgium, France, Italy, Monaco and Switzerland, retiring the Swiss Tessin Challenge cup by winning it three years in a row.

At this point Mrs. Zuidema again felt the need to import and so acquired the South African bitch Kavancha Blithe Spirit from Chris and Pam Fedder.

Until her death, Mrs. Zuidema was also the breeder of white Keeshonds, having imported Int. Ch. Kavancha's Now or Never from the Fedders. The white Kees stays white and should have a black nose and dark eyes. In Europe, whites are only bred to whites. The white Keeshond is recognized by the FCI. Mrs. Zuidema's whites have been very successful and have included: Int. Ch. Optima Bianca oet et Laand van Aleer, who was a champion of Luxembourg, Holland, Germany, and World Champon FCI in 1976; Int. Ch. Adonis Bianco oet et Laand van Aleer, who was a champion of France and Luxembourg; Int. Ch. Aurora Bianca oet et Laand van Aleer, champion of Belgium, France, Luxembourg and Germany; and

162

Int. Ch. Aurora Bianca oet et Laand van Aleer, and Int. Ch. Adonis Bianco oet et Laand van Aleer — white Keeshonds bred by Mrs. Esther Zuidema of Holland. Their sire was Int. Ch. Kavancha's Now or Never, imported from Chris and Pam Fedder of South Africa.

Hina of Summerlease and Trusty van Zaandaam, the first two Keeshonds to be shown in South Africa.

Int. Ch. Adonis Bianco oet et Laand van Aleer, French and Luxembourg champion.

SOUTH AFRICA

The first Keeshond registered in South Africa belonged to owners in Cape Town, but it was not established if this dog was ever shown. Trusty van Zaandam and Heena of Summerlease, imported by the late Michael Lupton in 1951, were the first breeding pair. Other people became interested and began to exhibit and in 1959 Casper van Zaandam won the first Keeshond BIS at Bloemfontein. The Luptons later changed their kennel name to Sedbergh and imported many Kees from England and Ireland. One bitch from Ireland, Ch. Geronina of Brytondale, carried the white gene and threw an occasional white pup amongst the grey. One of their more famous dogs was Ch. Tiger of Sedbergh, who won BIS twice and contributed much to the breed as a stud dog.

Later Mrs. Eva Ficker began the van Saaftingen kennel by importing two Keeshonds from Holland, Ch. Sigelinski's Siem and Sigelinski's Marjan. Siem won BIS at Goldfields in 1961 and was one of the top stud dogs in the country. This kennel disappeared with Mrs. Ficker's death.

The Keeshond Club of South Africa was begun in 1962 with Michael Lupton as chairman. The club's first championship show was in 1968. In 1963 Kavancha's Tanja van Wilda became the first Keeshond to join the Kavancha Kennel of Chris and Pam Fedder of Welkom, Orange Free State. Their first litter, out of Kavancha's Cherrie Chika of Zamenhoff, was born in 1964. Soon thereafter another bitch, Kavancha's Mariella of Zamenhof, was bred to English import, Maxwell of Mazelands, a son of Eng., Am. and Can. Ch. Whiplash of Wistonia. Five pups were whelped on October 30, 1966, and two went on to become Kavancha's first home-bred champions.

In 1969 the Fedders purchased a white Keeshond and mated her to Ch. Tiger of Sedbergh. Two white pups and one grey pup were born. One of the whites was exported to the Dutch kennel of Esther Zuidema and later became Int. Ch. Kavancha's Now or Never and the foundation for Oet et Laand van Aleer's white breeding program.

Chris and Pam purchased Rhinevale Rocamodor who became a S.A. Champion and the top-winning Keeshond in South Africa. Sadly, "Dusky" died before he could realize his real show potential. On a visit to the United States in 1979, Chris and Pam searched for a replacement for Dusky. The returned to South Africa with Tanglewood Magic Marker of Kavancha. Markie had a spectacular show career until his untimely death.

In 1985 Chris and Pam made another trip to the United States where Chris judged the Veteran Sweepstakes at the KCA Golden Anniversary Specialty. Shortly thereafter Kavancha imported two more American dogs, Am. Ch. Fearless Fruit of the Loom, who is now a South African champion as well, and KeesLund's Promises to Keep. They continue their very

S.A. Ch. Rhinevale Rocamador of Chattaronga was the top-winning Keeshond in South Africa. He was owned by Chris and Pam Fedder, Kavancha Keeshonden.

S.A. Ch. Kavancha's Gotcha (Ch. Tanglewood Magic Marker of Kavancha ex. Ch. Kavancha's Anneline) was Keeshond of the Year in 1984. He is owned by Pam Fedder.

successful breeding program based on a combination of English, Dutch, South African and American lines.

In 1980, Ian and Elaine Stubbings emigrated from England to South Africa with their two English champions, S.A. and Eng. Ch. Final Edition of Duroya and S.A. and Eng. Ch. Duroya Josephine of Vandersee; these were the two top-winning Keeshonds in England at the time. Their Vandersee line will also leave its mark on the Keeshonds in South Africa.

NEW ZEALAND

The earliest record of the Keeshond in New Zealand was 1939, when five were registered with the New Zealand Kennel Club. However, at a meeting held by the Executive Council on March 6, 1940, they were de-registered because, after inspection, it was said that their breeding was doubtful and their ancestry obscure.

There were no more registrations of Keeshonds with the New Zealand Kennel Club until 1950 when Mrs. O'Rorke imported the dog Arnhem Rascal from Australia. Arnhem Rascal was the first Keeshond to be shown in New Zealand and the first to gain his Championship Certificate.

In 1957 at South Otago Greenslade Dandy Lad became the first Keeshond to take a Best in Show.

Imports during the 1960s, 1970s and early 1980s have all played their part in improving breeding programs. Registrations have steadily grown until 1983-84 when 122 Keeshonds were registered

In January 1983 the New Zealand Keeshond Club was formed and has grown from a membership of 22 to over 150. The officers of the club are situated mainly in the Auckland area and other centers have area representatives to keep Keeshond owners in touch and to organize activities.

Permission was given by the New Zealand Kennel Club to hold an Open Show in 1985. Permission to hold championship shows should be granted in the near future. The club also publishes an informative magazine every two months.

In recent years there have been a number of imports from Australia and a few from the United Kingdom. With these bloodlines to help the breed, the future of Keeshonds in New Zealand looks rosy. One of the reasons for importing mainly from these two countries is that there are no quarantine restrictions; quarantine laws for dogs imported from the United States are very strict and make it prohibitive.

The Keeshond is coming into his own in the show ring now, winning Groups and BIS awards. Much of this credit is due to careful breeding by dedicated breeders, better handling in the show ring (interestingly, owners generally show their own dogs as professional handlers are not permitted in New Zealand) and a greater understanding of the breed as a whole.

Ch. Colijn Van Hals, owned by R. and K. Frew, was Best Dog at the New Zealand National Dog Show in 1983; and Ch. Brown-Derby Maire Joy, owned by Dave Clark, was judged Best Bitch at the same show.

Ch. Sonny Ledwell of Keechow, CD (whelped 1977) is one of the few New Zealand Keeshonds to have gained his championship status and CD. He is owned by Jenny Freemantle.

167

One of the prominent kennels in New Zealand is Gildenwyn. Started in 1979 by Gwen and Dave Clark, it is located in a beautiful rural area north of Wellington. At the present time they have three stud dogs and two brood bitches. Kaiserin Silver Earl is a New Zealand champion. Alshain of Gildenwyn has five CCs and their English import, Malmeck Zhivago, at this writing, is on his way to becoming a New Zealand champion. Both bitches, Brown-Derby Maire Joy and Alchiba of Gildenwyn, are New Zealand champions and have produced some fine litters of puppies. Ch. Brown-Derby Maire Joy has been named Best Open Keeshond Bitch for the past two years with the New Zealand Keeshond Club; to date she has over 30 CCs and is presently retired from the show ring for breeding.

AUSTRALIA

The development of the Keeshond in Australia really began in 1949 when Mrs. Bourne emigrated from England. She brought with her four Kees, three of which were Ch. Airking of Arnhem, Airamber of Arnhem and Babette of Willowden. These dogs became the foundation of the Australian lines throughout the 1950s and into the 1960s.

Keeshonds were first exhibited at the Royal Easter Show in Sydney in 1952 and at the Royal Melbourne Show two years later. Thse exhibits were the progeny of Mrs. Bourne's original imports.

During the 1950s and early 1960s Keeshonds slipped into relative obscurity, until in 1967 two breed clubs were formed. With the founding of the Keeshond Club of Victoria and the Keeshond Cub of New South Wales (NSW), interest in the Keeshond increased again. Mrs. Ruth Taylor, a founding member of the Keeshond Club of Victoria, imported Ch. Ensign of Duroya, who was to leave an indelible impression on future pedigrees.

Mrs. Taylor's Kendari prefix is synonymous with Keeshonds in Australia and many good dogs today trace their roots back to Ensign and his son, Ch. Kendari Cover boy, who was one of the earliest Keeshonds to win a BIS in a show career spanning eight years.

Interest in the Keeshond continued to grow. During the 1970s both the quality and quantity of Keeshonds increased. Current involvement with the Keeshond continues to expand and the few foundation kennels have grown to include many newcomers to the breed.

Colijn

Mrs. B. Douglas of Colijn Kennels admits that the Keeshond has been a big part of her life, helping her make new friends, enabling her to see much of Australia and influencing travel overseas. She did well in the show ring with Ch. Lett Beron, her first show Keeshond; she did ever better with her second, Ch. Kendari Kijdag.

Mrs. Douglas later acquired a bitch, Ch. Karuah Venus. "Sam," as she

Aus. Ch. Bovenste Rashond, pictured at two years of age, was the winner of the Puppy of the Year (Victoria) for 1983. Bred by Mrs. B. Taylor and owned by Mrs. Sue Emary.

Aus. Ch. Vendorfe Prim N Proper was Best of Breed at the Melbourne Royal 1982 Show and bitch CC at the 1983 Keeshond Club of Victoria show. She was bred and is owned by Sue Emary.

was called, was bred to Ch. Kendari Kijdag and produced four Australian champions. Mrs. Douglas purchased another dog, Spaarnehof Adonis, from Mrs. Taylor. After arriving at Colijn, he went on to win three BIS and many other Group and BOB wins.

In an effort to improve her breeding program, Mrs. Douglas acquired Ch. Ledwell Intrepid and Ch. Ledwell Jasper. Jasper was used extensively in Mrs. Douglas' breeding program and greatly improved her line. His get proved to be consistent winners in the show ring earning many Challenge Certificates and BIS awards.

Mrs. Douglas' next import was Ch. Gavimir Ubacaan. In addition to being a superb stud dog, he has done well in the show ring and holds the record for the most Challenge points on the Kendari Encouragement Trophy. Her latest import is Ch. Duroya Janessa of Dargrant, who was mated to Ch. Swashway No Rush before she left England.

Mrs. Douglas says, "After breeding about 70 champions and many noteworthy dogs, it has been very gratifying to win the New South Wales breeders' trophy for ten years in a row."

Deldacmeer

Mrs. Del Walker of Deldacmeer Kennels has been involved with dogs since 1966 when she began breeding Dachshunds. In 1967, inspired by a photo of Ch. Ensign of Duroya, she acquired Ch. Rominea Sharon. In 1970 she acquired Ch. Harzwald Atlas, who went on to win several BIS awards before his death in 1981.

Ch. Waakzaam Weismuller came to Deldacmeer in 1975 from England and won many BIS awards. In 1978 she purchased Ch. Grachthond Azranee from Karen and Bob Findlow; she went on to win many Group and BIS awards, including BIS at the Keeshond Club of NSW championship show in 1981.

Delft/Boventste

In 1967 Barbara Taylor (nee Ingram) acquired Keish Sam from Janice McCurrie. This dog went on to become an Australian champion in just a few months. Barbara married in 1968 and, with Geldrop Marijke as her foundation bitch, formed Delft Kennels. Then Ch. Waakzaam Wolthius (Eng. Ch. Ledwell Dutchman ex Eng. Ch. Waakzaam Wursel) and New Zealand Ch. Waakzaam Walsoken (Eng. Ch. Waakzaam Waag ex Eng. Waakzaam Waalre) became part of the Delft family. Barbara continued breeding and showing some of the top-winning Keeshonds in Australia, until she was forced to give up her kennel in 1980 following a divorce.

In 1981 she began again with a new prefix (Boventste) and a new bitch (Grachthond Marijke). In 1984 Boventste Kennels moved back to Barbara's home state of Victoria, where she now continues 18 years of breeding on sound, typey bloodlines.

Aus. Ch. Colijn Miss Miska was BIS three times at the Keeshond Club of New South Wales Championship Show. She was bred by Mrs. B. Douglas and is owned by Rem. Parker.

Aus. Ch. Delft Blauw Roullette (Ch. Delft Blauw Driftkop ex Alkmaar Circe) is a winner in Group and in Show. She is the dam of six champions from two litters. Bred by L. Ingram, she is now owned by Bob and Karen Findlow.

Grachthond

In 1977 Bob and Karen Findlow acquired Ch. Delft Blauw Driftkop from Barbara Ingram (Taylor). He has been very successful in the show ring and at stud. In his first litter was Ch. Delft Blauw Roullette, the bitch who became the foundation of Grachthond Kennels. Driftkop has sired nine champions, including Ch. Grachthond Azranee, owned by Mrs. Del Walker, the second bitch to win BIS at the Keeshond Club of NSW Specialty.

Ch. Delft Blauw Roullette was bred to Mrs. Douglas' Ch. Gavimir Ubacaan; this litter produced four champions. Ch. Grachthond Volbrengen became the first Keeshond to win BOS Puppy in Show at the 1982 Royal Easter Show in Sydney. His litter sister, Ch. Grachthond Bloemrijk, owned by Mrs. Sandra Creighton, has won Top Keeshond in Victoria for three years.

Just before their transfer to the air force base in Darwin, the Findlows imported two Kees fronm England, Aust. Ch. Vandaban Fanfare, a son of Eng. Ch. Gelderland Chlipper of Swashway, and Aust. Ch. Keesland Hailey, a litter sister to Weedon's Eng. Ch. Keesland Highlight.

Although a small kennel with a limited breeding program, Grachthond has bred 11 champions and looks forward to a bright future by combining the best of the Australian lines with an infusion of English stock.

Alkmaar

The Alkmaar Kennels of Ron and Mabs Cleverly got its start in 1972 with the purchase of Kimberton Ronaldo, a grandson of Eng. Ch. Commandant of Duroya. Their interest in the breed grew and in 1974 they acquired a bitch puppy from Mrs. Gwen McGowan. Taimeyr Tulip Time became one of the most successful bitches to be exhibited within Victoria, obtaining her first CC at six months and her title at 9½ months of age; she was the first bitch to win the Top Keeshond Trophy for two years.

Vendorfe

Mrs. Sue Emary first became involved with Keeshonds in 1974 and acquired a young bitch, Rutherine Kenmia. Soon after she acquired her first male, Snowski Venlo, who finished his championship in 1976. A breeding of these two dogs produced Vendorfe's first litter and first homebred champion, Ch. Vendorfe Ascot Lady. Mated to New Zealand and Aust. Ch. Waakzaam Walsoken, she produced Ch. Vendorfe Van Nessa, who, in turn, produced Ch. Vendorfe Prim N Proper, the pride of the Vendorte Kennel. In 1982, over an entry of 48 Kees and 6,405 dogs at the Melbourne Royal, she went CC, BOB and Best Puppy in Show.

In 1982 Sue acquired Ch. Bovenste Rashond, who was Keeshond Puppy of the Year in 1983. Over the years Sue has bred and owned seven

Aus. Ch. Delft Blauw Driftkop is a BIS winner, has four CCs at Royal shows and is the sire of nine champions. He was bred by L. and B. Ingram and is owned by Bob and Karen Findlow.

Aus. Ch. Grachthond Bloemrijk was winner of the Top Keeshond of Victoria award for three straight years—1982, 1983 and 1984. He was bred by R. and K. Findlow and is owned by G. and S. Creighton.

champions and has had three generations of bitches win at the Keeshond Club of Victoria championship shows. Her breeding is along the Waakzaam lines, blended with the English Hanovarian and Gavimir blood, and Vendorfe Keeshonds are prominent for show and export.

7

Official Breed Standard of the Keeshond

As adopted by the Keeshond Club of America, and
approved by the American Kennel Club, July 12, 1949.

GENERAL APPEARANCE AND CONFORMATION

The Keeshond is a handsome dog, of well-balanced, short coupled body, attracting attention not only by his alert carriage and intelligent expression, but also by his luxurious coat, his richly plumed tail, well curled over his back, and by his foxlike face and head with small pointed ears. His coat is very thick round the neck, fore part of the shoulders and chest, forming a lionlike mane. His rump and hind legs, down to the hocks, are also thickly coated, forming the charcteristic "trousers." His head, ears and lower legs are covered with thick short hair. The ideal height of fully matured dogs (over 2 years old), measured from top of withers to the ground, is: for males, 18 inches; bitches, 17 inches. However, size consideration should not outweigh that of type. When dogs are judged equal in type, the dog nearest the ideal height is to be preferred. Length of back from withers to rump should equal height as measured above.

HEAD

Expression—Expression is largely dependent on the distinctive characteristic called "spectacles" — a delicately penciled line slanting slightly upward from the outer corner of each eye to the lower corner of the ear, coupled with distinct markings and shadings forming short but expressive eyebrows. Markings (or shadings) on face and head must present

175

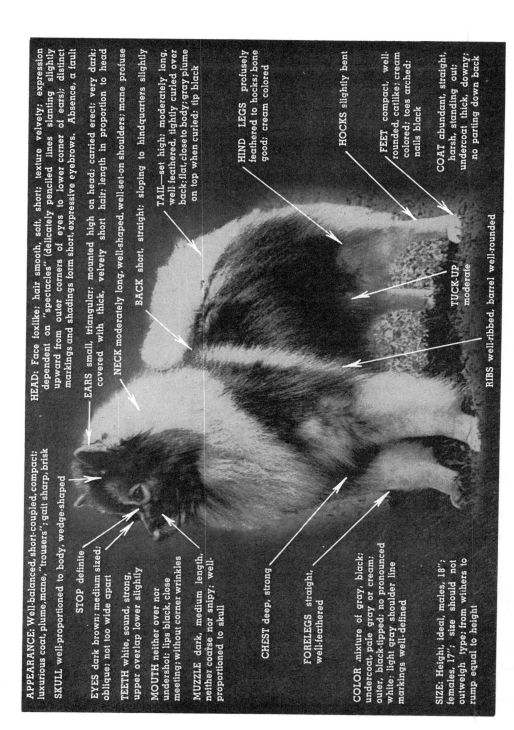

APPEARANCE: Well-balanced, short-coupled, compact; luxurious coat, plume, mane, "trousers"; gait sharp, brisk

HEAD: Face foxlike; hair smooth, soft, short; texture velvety; expression dependent on "spectacles" (delicately penciled lines slanting slightly upward from outer corners of eyes to lower corner of ears); distinct markings and shadings form short, expressive eyebrows. Absence, a fault

SKULL well-proportioned to body; wedge-shaped

STOP definite

EYES dark brown; medium sized; oblique; not too wide apart

TEETH white, sound, strong, upper overlap lower slightly

MOUTH neither over nor undershot; lips black, close meeting; without corner wrinkles

MUZZLE dark, medium length, neither coarse nor snipy; well-proportioned to skull

EARS small, triangular; mounted high on head; carried erect; very dark; covered with thick, velvety short hair; length in proportion to head

NECK moderately long; well-shaped; well-set-on shoulders; mane profuse

BACK short, straight; sloping to hindquarters slightly

TAIL—set high; moderately long; well feathered; tightly curled over back; flat, close to body; gray plume on top when curled; tip black

HIND LEGS profusely feathered to hocks; bone good; cream colored

HOCKS slightly bent

FEET compact, well-rounded, catlike; cream colored; toes arched; nails black

COAT abundant, straight, harsh, standing out; undercoat thick, downy; no parting down back

TUCK-UP moderate

CHEST deep, strong

FORELEGS straight, well-feathered

COLOR mixture of gray, black; undercoat, pale gray or cream; outer, black-tipped; no pronounced white; light gray shoulder line markings well-defined

SIZE: Height; ideal, males, 18"; females, 17"; size should not outweigh type; from withers to rump equal to height

RIBS well-ribbed, barrel well-rounded

a pleasing appearance, imparting to the dog an alert and intelligent expression. *Fault*—Absence of "spectacles."

Skull—The head should be well-proportioned to the body, wedge-shaped when viewed from above. Not only in muzzle, but the whole head should give this impression when the ears are drawn back by covering the nape of the neck and the ears with one hand. Head in profile should exhibit a definite stop. *Fault*—Apple head, or absence of stop.

Muzzle—The muzzle sould be dark in color and of medium length, neither coarse nor snipy, and well-proportioned to the skull.

Mouth—The mouth should be neither overshot nor undershot. Lips should be black and closely meeting, not thick, coarse, or sagging; and with no wrinkle at the corner of the mouth. *Fault*—Overshot or undershot.

Teeth—The teeth should be white, sound and strong (but discoloration from distemper not to penalize severely); upper teeth should just overlap the lower teeth.

Eyes—Eyes should be dark brown in color, of medium size, rather oblique in shape and not set too wide apart. *Fault*—Protruding round eyes or eyes light in color.

Ears—Ears should be small, triangular in shape, mounted high on head and carried erect; dark in color and covered with thick, velvety, short hair. Size should be proportionate to the head — length approximating the distance from outer corner of the eyes to the nearest edge of the ear. *Fault*— Ears not carried erect when at attention.

BODY

Neck and Shoulders—The neck should be moderately long, well-shaped and well-set on shoulders; covered with a profuse mane, sweeping from under the jaw and covering the whole of the front part of the shoulders and chest, as well as the top part of the shoulders.

Chest, Back and Loin—The body should be compact with a short, straight back sloping slightly downward toward the hindquarters; well-ribbed, barrel well rounded, belly moderately tucked up, deep and strong of chest.

Legs—Forelegs should be straight seen from any angle and well feathered. Hindlegs should be profusely feathered down to the hocks — not below, with hocks only sightly bent. Legs must be of good bone and cream in color. *Fault*—Black markings below the knee, penciling excepted.

Feet—The feet should be compact, well-rounded, catlike, and cream in color. Toes are nicely arched, with black nails. *Fault*—White foot or feet.

Tail—The tail should be set on high, moderately long, and well-feathered, tightly curled over back. It should lie flat and close to the body with a very light gray plume on top where curled, but the tip of the tail should be black. The tail should form a part of the "silhouette" of the dog's body, rather than give the appearance of an appendage. *Fault*—Tail not lying close to the back.

Action—Dogs should show boldly and keep tails curled over the back. They should move cleanly and briskly; and the movement should be straight and sharp (not lope like a German Shepherd Dog). *Fault*—Tail not carried over back when moving.

COAT

The body should be abundantly covered with long, straight, harsh hair; standing well out from a thick, downy undercoat. The hair on the legs should be smooth and short, except for a feathering on the front legs and "trousers," as previously described, on the hindlegs. The hair on the tail should be profuse, forming a rich plume. Head, including muzzle, skull and ears, should be covered with smooth, soft, short hair — velvety in texture on the ears. Coat must not part down the back. *Fault*—Silky, wavy, or curly coats. Part in coat down the back.

COLOR AND MARKINGS

A mixture of gray and black. The undercoat should be very pale gray or cream (not tawny). The hair of the outer coat is black tipped, the length of the black tips producing the characteristic shading of color. The color may vary from light to dark, but any pronounced deviation from the gray color is not permissible. The plume of the tail should be very light gray when curled on back, and the tip of the tail should be black. Legs and feet should be cream. Ears should be very dark — almost black. Shoulder line markings (light gray) should be well defined. The color of the ruff and "trousers" is generally lighter than that of the body. "Spectacles" and shadings, as previously described, are characteristic of the breed and must be present to some degree. There should be no pronounced white markings. *Very Serious Faults*—Entirely black or white or any other solid color; any pronounced deviation from the gray color.

SCALE OF POINTS

General Conformation and Appearance 20

Head

Shape	....	6
Eyes	....	5
Ears	....	4

.... 20

Body

Chest, Back and Loin		10
Tail	....	10
Neck and Shoulders	.	8
Legs	....	4
Feet	....	3

.... 35

Coat 15

Color and Markings 10

TOTAL 100

179

8

Blueprint of the Keeshond

THE DESCRIPTION and Standard of Points adopted by the Keeshond Club of America and approved by the American Kennel Club is the official, written "blueprint" of the ideal Keeshond by which the breed is judged in the United States. This same Standard is used in Canada. It is based mainly on the British Standard.

Thorough study of the Standard and pictorial depiction in Chapter 7, together with study of the illustration of "Rights and Wrongs" contained in this chapter is important for everyone who now raises and shows Kees, or who may do so in the future.

Fortunately, the Keeshond Standard is generally clear and complete. Nevertheless, there are important fundamental aspects in judging the overall quality of dogs, whether in the show ring or at home, that must be considered in conjunction with all Standards. Some of these are discussed in greater detail in the paragraphs that follow.

BALANCE

When a dog is well-balanced, each part of the animal is in proportion to all of its other parts and in accordance with the conformation called for in the breed Standard. For example, a Keeshond may have a perfect head, but if the head seems too small or too large in relation to the body, the dog lacks balance.

Another factor in regard to balance or lack of it in a Keeshond is the neck, vaguely described in the Standard as "moderately long, well-shaped and well-set on shoulders." To clarify the description, the authors submit that the neck should be set far enough back on the shoulders and be long enough to form an arch or "crest" as it is called, so that when the dog is at attention, the back of the skull is in line with the backs of the front legs (see illustrated Standard).

A short neck, or one not based well back and thrust forward, is a deterrent to a properly-balanced appearance. This is usually accompanied by a faulty "top-line," i.e. a level back or one which slopes downward toward the withers (top of the shoulders). These structural faults make a dog seem to pitch forward instead of correctly sloping from the withers down toward the hindquarters, and breeders should — through selective breeding — make every effort to breed them out.

Where the Keeshond's tail is based, and how it is carried, are also vital to a balanced picture because the tail must be part of the dog's silhouette. The tail's base should be well forward from the rear protuberance of the pelvic bone (rump), and the whole tail lie curved flat on the back, the tighter the better. It should never seem to be an appendage held either up on a loop above the back (wheel tail) or hanging off the dog's rear.

SOUNDNESS

The question of which is more important, "type" or "soundness" in dogs, seems to be a recurring subject of discussion among both novice and experienced dog fanciers in all breeds. To these authors, if a dog is "typey," he is a correct representative of his particular breed, conforming to all points of the Standard, and displays temperament characteristic of the breed. Judges and knowledgeable exhibitors advisedly put great emphasis on the necessity of a dog being "sound," which refers to its physical structure and the resultant gait and stance. In the authors' opinions, a dog will move and stand correctly if it conforms to the Standard. Therefore, soundness is actually an essential part of type.

In regard to legs and gait, the Keeshond Standard states: "Forelegs should be straight, seen from any angle." On the hindlegs, "hocks should be only slightly bent." Moreover, "Dogs should show boldly and keep tails curled over the back. They should move cleanly and briskly, and the movement should be straight and sharp (not lope like a German Shepherd Dog)." This may be a bit confusing so let's look at what contributes to sound movement and stance.

When moving and standing, front feet and legs should turn neither in nor out. Elbows should be close to the body. The pasterns, or wrists, should not bend backwards, and the legs should be straight and at right angles to the feet.

On the hindlegs, what appears to be the elbows are actually the dog's true heels, and are called the hocks. Viewed from the rear and side when standing, the hindlegs from the hocks down should be straight, parallel to each other and at right angles to the ground. "Spread" hocks turn outward, a defect that contributes to hind feet coming too close together or

181

overlapping when moving. Hocks should *never* point or swing toward each other at any time, i.e. "cow-hocks." Cow-hocked Keeshonden of any age should be definitely avoided as breeding or show prospects. Angulation at the hock joints should be sufficient for a Keeshond to trot freely without stiffness or roll in its gait. Proper action also requires that all four legs move straight forward in line with the direction of travel. When that is not the case, the fault is described as "crabbing" or "side-winding."

TYPE

The true-to-type Keeshond, in accordance with the American Standard, is a sturdily-built, medium-sized dog distinguished by its beauty and elegance. The Standard describes the ideal height at the withers to be 18 inches for a male and 17 inches for a bitch. The official American Standard also says: "Size consideration should not outweight that of type. When dogs are judged equal in type, the dog nearest the ideal height is to be preferred."

We are currently seeing a variety of sizes in Keeshonds, ranging from the small (16 inches for males) to the overly large (20-21 inches). While both extremes can still retain the typiness essential to the breed, one should keep in mind that the Standard clearly defines the preferred height and therefore the correct Keeshond. The future size and consequent type of Keeshond called for in the Standard is the responsibility of everyone who raises a litter.

COLOR

Under *Color and Markings* our Standard states: "A mixture of gray and black. The undercoat should be very pale gray or cream (not tawny). The hair of the outer coat is black-tipped, the length of the black tips producing the characteristic shading of color. The color may vary from light to dark, but any pronounced deviation from the gray color is not permissible."

The Standard's statement is concise and easily understood. We all know the color of fresh cream and that very pale gray and very pale cream are *almost* white. The dictionary defines "tawny" as the color of a lion. Therefore, the only permissible coloring is mixtures of shading from almost white, through gray to black.

HEAD, EXPRESSION AND EYE COLOR

All parts of a Keeshond's head should be in pleasing proportion to its own parts, and to the whole dog. The skull should be wedge-shaped and somewhat flat, never "domey." There should be a definite dent (or "stop" as it is called) between the eyes, just above where the skull seems to meet the muzzle. Inadequate stop is penalized. The muzzle should be of medium length in relation to the depth of the skull, and be neither unattractively coarse nor so narrow as to be "snipey."' (Bitches' muzzles are usually not as wide as males'.) The jaws must meet in front in a "scissors bite" with the upper teeth just overlapping the lower.

Small, triangular-shaped ears, mounted high on the head and carried erect at attention, are essential. When Kees are expressing happiness and affection they usually hold their ears folded back into the ruff. But ears should never droop or fold forward from the tips, and big ears, or those which point away from each other like a bat's, ruin expression and are bad faults.

The Keeshond's expression is exceedingly important. According to the Standard it "is largely dependent on the distinctive charcteristic called 'spectacles'— a delicately penciled line slanting slightly upward from the outer corner of each eye to the lower corner of the ear coupled with distinct markings and shadings forming short but expressive eyebrows. *Fault*— Absence of spectacles."

This description of face markings in the Standard sometimes confuses people. However, to visualize the effect, just imagine a pair of dark-rimmed spectacles (without a nose-piece) on the dog's face. In other words, light gray areas around the eyes are outlined by dark hair to delineate the spectacles' rims, and are joined by dark, penciled lines from the outer corners of the eyes toward the ears that might be considered the side-pieces.

The eyes play a vital part in the breed's typically gentle expression. They should be deep, dark brown, the darker the better, somewhat oval in shape and of medium size. If eyes are light colored or have a light band around a dark center, they produce an ugly, glaring expression which is utterly untypical, and should be penalized accordingly. Also penalized should be round, bulging eyes.

COAT

When in full bloom, at from two to three years old and on, the Keeshond is a strikingly handsome breed, distinguished by the subtle markings in its luxurious, off-standing coat. To achieve the right effect, the whole coat must be dense, consisting in reality of two coats — a thick, downy undercoat and very harsh, straight guard hairs as an outercoat. Silky, drooping, or wavy coats are faults.

TEMPERAMENT

The typical Keeshond has an outgoing personality, a friendly attitude toward people and dogs, and is sensible and affectionate. Although these characteristics are not mentioned in the Standard, they are nonetheless essential in the typical Keeshond. If a Keeshond does not have a good disposition in every way, it is not true to type.

Keeshond Rights and Wrongs

Photographs by Evelyn Shafer

These depictions were first presented in August 1963
issue of Popular Dogs, Philadelphia, Pennsylvania, U.S.A.,
and are included here with special permission.

A well-balanced Keeshond head; note "spectacles," stop, shape of eye, ear placement, muzzle proportion.

Eyes should be oblique — never round and not too wide apart; this round eye should be faulted.

A poor head; note light muzzle marking, light eyes and lack of "spectacles."

Another poor head; note the too-wide-set ears, also the light eyes; both detract from expression. Ears too big; insufficient ruff.

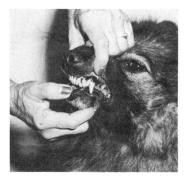

An excellent bite, upper teeth just overlap lower.

An extremely poor head, completely lacking "spectacles." Note insufficient stop; muzzle is too long.

An excellent front.

A "fiddle" front; wrong.

Poor; flat feet, bowed front.

Front too narrow; poor.

185

A good rear; good tail placement and plume; feet good; note short back.

Note straight stifle; poor tail carriage, no plume; lacking "trousers."

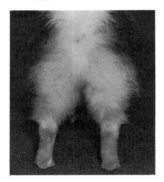

A good, sturdy rear with good bone.

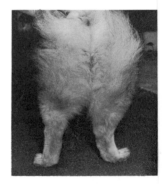

Cowhocked (hocks turning in and feet out); a poor rear.

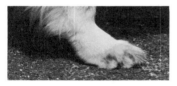

A poor foot, neither compact nor rounded; down on pasterns.

An overlong body with a topline too straight; topline should slope from shoulder to rump; wavy coat on back is wrong, as are the poor pasterns.

186

9

Choosing a Keeshond Puppy

CONGRATULATIONS! After careful research you have decided to acquire a Keeshond puppy. There are now several things that you must take into consideration. First of all, when you acquire a Keeshond you actually are gaining a new member of the family. It is essential that *everyone* in the household be in favor of this, and that responsibilities for the dog's care and training be predetermined. We strongly suggest that an adult be responsible for the initial care and training. The first few weeks are critical to the development of the dog, and training should not be entrusted to a child at this point. To depend on a child's continued care of a new dog is wishful thinking. The initial enthusiasm wears off and the dog can often be neglected. Lack of training and a decrease in attention can result in a puppy seeking other ways of amusing himself — most of which will not be considered acceptable behavior.

Keeshonds of all ages are loving and eager to learn. The amount of their knowledge and training should be limited only by that of their new owner. Before you choose your puppy, study the official Keeshond Standard and the Breeders Code of Ethics. Obtain all possible information about the breed and breeders. Decide what age and sex you want and what your goals are for your new puppy.

MALE OR FEMALE

In Keeshonds, there is little difference in temperament between a male (dog) and female (bitch). Both are loving and loyal. In our own household we seem to have acquired more males (14) than females (5). We find the females a bit more independent but still very loving. The males are not particularly territorial and it is possible to raise several males together with no aggression problems. All our males were raised together and live together with no more than an occasional grumble. The females, on the other hand, tend to be more domineering. If you are considering more than one dog in your househld, working knowledge of pack behavior is essential.

If you decide on a male puppy, don't expect that people who own a female will come knocking on your door in search of a stud dog. There are hundreds of quality show dogs available for stud around the country. The breed is not highly popular and puppies are not in great demand. If you have no intention of showing your male Keeshond, we suggest that you have him neutered.

If your new pet is a female and you have no intention of breeding or showing, it is far better for your bitch, your own lifestyle, and that of your neighbors, to have her spayed. A bitch in season sends out a signal over the entire neighborhood and can cause more problems than you desire. She could also accidentally escape from your yard and present you with a litter of unwanted mongrels. For these reasons, we strongly suggest that you spay a bitch you do not plan to breed or show.

SOURCES OF SUPPLY

The best sources of supply are, of course, Keeshond breeders. Whenever feasible, you should go to the kennel, see the mother (and father, if possible) and the entire litter. The environment in which the puppy is born and spends its first few weeks of life is as important as its pedigree. An unsocialized puppy, with little love or training during the first important eight weeks, is not the best choice.

Fortunately, there are many breeders who are devoted to the breed and its welfare. Above all other considerations, the objective of conscentious breeders is to raise healthy, good-quality dogs with proper temperament, bred selectively to the Standard and the laws of heredity. These breeders give personal care and attention to their dogs; they take pride in them and make every effort to be helpful to novices and puppy buyers.

There are several ways to locate responsible Keeshond breeders. The American Kennel Cub, 51 Madison Avenue, New York, NY 1010, can furnish you with the name of the secretary of the Keeshond Cub of America and other Keeshond clubs in your area. They can also tell you if there is a publication for the breed. The current one is *Keezette International*, published by these authors. In its tenth year of publication, *Keezette* contains articles and information for Keeshond owners, as well as a source of responsible breeders and puppies available.

The Keeshond Club of America can furnish a listing of litters available as well as the name and address of a Keeshond club in your area.

We strongly urge that you *not* buy your puppy from someone who raises litters on a wholesale basis, without regard to their welfare or the acceptability of the puppy buyers. Far too often the dogs have not been properly cared for, have been raised in an unclean and certain uncaring environment and have not been properly socialized. Even if these puppies survive, the unknowing buyer could face growing veterinarian bills as the puppies mature. It costs no more — in fact, usually much less in time and money — to purchase a healthy puppy of good quality from a reliable breeder than it does a mediocre, poorly cared for animal from a questionable source.

MINIMUM AGE FOR SELECTION

The Code of Ethics of the Keeshond Club of America specifies that no puppy may be sold before that puppy reaches the age of eight weeks. Experienced breeders generally agree that from eight to 12 weeks is a good age for appraisal of the potential quality of Keeshond puppies. By that time the bone structure and other characteristics are fairly well discernible. However, many a promising puppy has not matured as its breeder hoped. If someone promises that a particular puppy is "guaranteed" to become a champion, take it with a large grain of salt.

"PET" OR "SHOW"

Most breeders predetermine which of their litter are "pet" quality and which they choose to reserve for buyers intending to show. If you are even the least bit interested in showing, advise the breeder and purchase the "show-quality" dog. If you are buying your puppy strictly as a pet, advise that as well. The only differences between show and pet puppies are faults that would make it difficult for that dog to compete in the dog show ring. Perhaps the bite is off, the ears too big, the tail too low set or the feet black. None of these things detract from the dog's health or general appearance; they simply make him less competitive in a very competitive show ring.

Be prepared when you see the litter or when you inquire about a puppy to be informed that the breeder has only one or perhaps no pet puppies for sale. Don't be discouraged; most breeders want the best for their puppies and will consider selling a show puppy to a pet home if the people and the environment are best for the dog. Some breeders will also sell a show Keeshond with an option to show the puppy themselves. If your breeder suggests this, be sure you understand fully what is expected of all parties before you make such a decision.

HEALTH

The puppy you buy should have had a proper physical start in life. Before it leaves the breeder, it should have been wormed (if necessary), and given the preventive inoculations against distemper, hepatitis, leptospirosis and parvovirus appropriate to its age. It should have been on a diet including meat, vitamins, milk and proper dog food. The breeder should furnish you with the puppy's veterinary record and instructions on proper care and feeding.

A healthy puppy is full of pep. His eyes are bright and have no discharge. The nose is clean, cool and slightly moist. Bowel movements are formed, not runny. The coat stands out from the body and has a fluffy, lively appearance with no flaky skin; it is clean with no black spots of flea dirt. He should be plump with bones well covered. A "pot-bellied" puppy may not be fat; he may be suffering from malnutrition, worms or other troubles. An accepted method of testing for proper plumpness is to feel for the top of the pelvic bone on the back in front of the tail's base. The areas should be well rounded and firm, with bones scarcely perceptible.

If there is any question in your mind about the health of the puppy you have your heart set on, you should ask to have it checked by your own veterinarian. Any responsible breeder should be delighted to have you do so, and some will insist on it.

TEMPERAMENT

At any age, the typical Keeshond is friendly and usually not afraid of anything or anybody. The varying degrees of those characteristics depend on the puppy's genealogical background and its own contact with people. Seeing either or both of a litter's parents can give you helpful clues on the future development of your puppy. One word of warning, however: Don't be shocked by the dam's appearance. By the time you see her (when the puppies are eight to ten weeks of age), she will probably have lost her coat as a result of the pregnancy and nursing and will look absolutely awful. The good disposition and structure will still be readily apparent, but ask the breeder to see a photo of the dam at her best to determine her coloration and extent of coat.

A Keeshond puppy that piddles when you pick it up or pet it is a rarity and indicates unnatural nervousness. If you clap your hands loudly, most little Kees will look up in surprise and curiosity. Look at all the puppies in the litter. They should be alert and full of devilment. They should come quickly and joyously to you when called. Their ears and tail should be up and each should be trying his best to convince you to choose him to be your own.

If you tell the breeder what you are looking for in a puppy, perhaps he or she can help by telling you some of the mannerisms of a particular puppy. But which of the litter will turn out to be the best and most devoted as your dog is anyone's guess. The main thing is to decide which puppy you find most appealing . . . and which one likes you best!

SELECTING BREEDING AND/OR SHOW PROSPECTS

Whenever puppies are to be selected for breeding and/or show, a thorough study of the breed Standard is a must. It is also valuable to have a knowledge of genetics and of the individual Keeshonds in the pedigree. The good points and faults in every dog are inherited from the parents and ancestors, and, in turn, are transmittable to the descendents. Learning about a litter's ancestry takes a bit of doing but is well worth the effort. The Keeshond Club of America publishes a "Breeders Guide" containing photos and pedigrees of hundreds of dogs; it is an excellent reference guide. The breeder can probably also furnish you with photos and show records of some of the dogs.

While it is true that champions may range in quality from excellent to mediocre depending upon the competition they encountered and the number of shows they attended, a championship title does indicate some degree of recognized merit.

Another important aid to prospective breeders and exhibitors is to watch Keeshond judging at shows, with regional or national Keeshond specialty shows being especially helpful. The secretary of the Keeshond Club of America should be able to furnish you with a list of these shows and their dates. This gives you the opportunity to compare a number of Kees together in the ring, and to gain an awareness of the various degrees of quality in the breed. Read books on dog breeding and showing (see Appendix for a listing). Ask breeders and exhibitors for advice, and study pictures of winning Keeshonds published in the dog magazines. Then give yourself a chance to absorb all the information you have acquired. The longer you raise dogs, the more you will find that there is always more to be learned.

STRUCTURE AND GAIT

At eight weeks of age, the structure of the Keeshond is usually a miniature version of an adult. The puppy should have a short back, sloping slightly from the top of the shoulders (at the withers) to the hips. A back that slopes toward the head is a fault and is not likely to improve with age. The rib cage should be well rounded, not "slab-sided," and there should be good depth of chest and width between the front legs. All legs should have plenty of bone without coarseness.

Although some allowance can be made for "puppy looseness," soundness of gait and stance are essential in Kees of all ages. To check a puppy's action and stance, watch how it trots to its breeder and back to you when called, and note how it stands naturally when at attention. Remember, even a poor specimen can be made to look like a world-beater if it is "set up" on the floor or a table by someone who knows how to manually place the dog's legs, tail and head for best effect. Frolicking little

191

puppies are difficult to evaluate, but a well-constructed dog of any age should be able to set itself up properly.

TAIL

To form the correct Keeshond silhouette at eight weeks of age, the base of the tail must be set well forward from the points of the rump and lie close to the back. Puppies' floppy tails can tighten up as they mature, but after eight weeks of age a Keeshond's tail should never curve upwards from its base (wheel tail) or appear to be an appendage. It should always be part of the dog's outline.

FACE, EYES AND EARS

Proper face markings, eye shape and color and the ear size and placement that typify a Keeshond are discernible in eight- to 12-week-old puppies. A potentially good puppy has a black muzzle. If there is an intermixture of gray or, worst of all, tawny hair, with the black, the muzzle will undoubtedly later become incorrectly light colored or "streaky." The light gray areas around the eyes and dark lines forming the required "spectacle" markings should always be present.

Eye color, shape and placement are important. Oval (almond shaped), very dark brown eyes are required; light eyes are a definite fault. Eyes that are round and bulge, or are placed too far apart or too close will not improve with age and are definite faults. But to judge what color a puppy's eyes may be at maturity is something else again. All Kees puppies' eyes seem dark at first glance, but look at them closely with a good light. Their eyes are actually dark blue when very young. The depth of blue throughout the eye is a clue as to what shade of brown the eyes may be in the future. Whenever youngsters' eyes are not deep, dark blue, or when a lighter band of color is perceptible around the perimeter of the eye — beware!

The ears should be small, triangular in shape, mounted high on the head, carried erect and covered with velvety black hair. Very big or wide-set ears in a puppy are faults that should definitely be avoided if looking for a show prospect. If the ears are not all the way up, a helpful way to check ear placement and size in proportion to the head is to lay the puppy on its back so that the ears fall back into somewhat the position they may have later. At 12 to 16 weeks, ears should definitely be up. While Kees puppies are teething, at about five months of age, their ears sometimes droop temporarily. An adult Keeshond's ears should *never* fold forward or point away from each other like those of a bat.

ORCHIDISM

In most eight- to 12-week-old Keeshonds, both testicles can be found in or right near the scrotum. If that is not the case, you would be well advised

192

to inquire about the litter's sire and other male forebears' development in this respect. There occasionally are Kees dogs that mature more slowly than normal, but by six months of age at the latest, a Keeshond should have both testicles descended.

An adult dog of any breed whose testicles are not both in the scrotum is disqualified from the conformation breed ring. A cryptorchid is a dog who has abnormally retained both testicles in the abdominal cavity; a monorchid dog has one descended testicle and one that remains undescended. Authorities point out that when congenital (not from an injury, etc.), these physical defects are considered inheritable.

HEAD

Very young puppy heads are apt to seem too big for their bodies, but the skull should be wedge-shaped and must have a definite indentation (stop) between the eyes. Be sure the jaws meet in front in a scissors bite (upper teeth just overlapping those of the lower jaw). An undershot or overshot mouth is an inheritable fault; while not a disqualification in the show ring, it would be detrimental and should not be considered in a show prospect.

COAT TEXTURE, COLOR AND MARKINGS

Puppies' coats should be dense, with a thick, downy undercoat and coarse guard hairs. When you run your hand toward the head, the fur should show a light gray or pale cream undercoat beneath black-tipped outer hairs, and feel slightly harsh. A young bitch's fur is sometimes softer than a dog's.

Coat development varies from one bloodline to the next. Some puppies will develop their guard coat by growth of all the same length. Others will have a soft lambs-wool undercoat with the guard hair coming in like porcupine quills. Both are correct and the end result should be the same.

In eight- to ten-week-old puppies, the overall coloring and markings called for in the Standard should be well indicated. The relatively minor faults of "smutty" colored, darkish legs, black "thumb marks" below the knees, black toe markings and creaminess around the ears often — but not always — clear up as the puppy matures. It is most important that the coloring of the puppies be from shades of lightest gray or very light cream through medium gray to black. The general effect in the whole dog can legitimately vary from light gray to dark. But at eight to ten weeks of age, tawniness in areas that should be light gray and/or a brown cast in the hair wherever black tipping should be present could develop into serious faults in a mature Kees.

WHAT TO REQUIRE OF THE BREEDER

All breeders should give the buyers of their dogs the following *written* information:

- Details of the dog's diet and feeding schedule. A sudden change in the amount and kind of food can cause diarrhea.

- Data on all wormings; the inoculations given against distemper, hepatitis, leptospirosis, parvovirus, etc. and any medical problems encountered prior to delivery to the purchaser.

- The name, address and phone number of the treating veterinarian.

- The Keeshond's four-generation pedigree.

- With any dog represented as purebred, Chapter 3, Section 5 of the *American Kennel Club Rules and Regulations* requires that the seller must complete and deliver to the buyer the AKC's official forms necessary for registering the dog (generally a blue litter registration form) unless otherwise agreed to by the seller and buyer in written, signed agreements.

- A bill of sale and/or contract of sale.

- A veterinarian's health certificate, if the puppy is being shipped.

- A copy of the veterinarian's statement of his or her findings relative to x-rays of both of the dog's parents indicating the absence of any potentially inheritable bone malformation such as hip dysplasia or slipping stifles (loose kneecaps).

As a practical, routine procedure for the benefit of everyone concerned, all financial and other arrangements between the seller and buyer should always be clearly defined in written agreements signed by both parties. Many contracts of sale are very strict and are designed to protect both the puppy and the breed as a whole. Some breeders will choose to reserve stud services, puppies or breeding rights. Read the contract closely and discuss it in detail with the breeder. This rule also applies for such transactions as stud services or leasing dogs or bitches on breeding or showing terms. No matter how honest and well intentioned the people may be, verbal agreements can lead to unfortunate misunderstandings and subsequent problems.

Another area of potential misunderstanding is the naming of the new puppy. Most breeders request — or perhaps require by contract — that their kennel name be included in the registered name of the puppy. Many have "theme" litters or identify the puppies in each litter by a letter of the alphabet (i.e., the "A" litter, etc.). Clarify this with the breeder in advance so there is no misunderstanding later. Once a name is listed on the AKC registration papers, it cannot be changed. Remember that your dog may someday be in the show ring or appear on another puppy's pedigree. Choose your registered name to reflect the personality of your puppy and your pride in the breed. The call name of your dog can be anything you choose but it is often related to his registered name. Call names of only one or two syllables are best, especially if you are considering training your dog for obedience. By the time you call out, "Abracadabra, come!", the dog will be long gone!

Remember, when you buy your first Keeshond, you may think you will never raise a litter, use your dog at stud or enter dog shows. But as time goes on and your beautiful puppy matures into a handsome dog or lovely bitch, you may change your mind. So, for every reason, buy the best puppy possible!

M. SMILEY

The travel type bowl is most suited for your puppy since Keeshonds love to play in their water. *(Swanson's Photographics)*

You must ensure that your puppy has the proper toys to keep him occupied. If he becomes bored, he may revert to activities that you do not consider acceptable . . . like separating the receiver from the telephone! *(Mary Ellen Marx)*

196

10

Living With Your Keeshond

Y OU HAVE FOUND the right breeder, weighed all the criteria and made your selection of the perfect Keeshond puppy. Now it is time to introduce your newest family member to his new home.

For those of you who think a Keeshond puppy would make a wonderful Christmas gift under the tree, we urge you to consider the puppy instead of your child. Christmas is a very exciting time for a child and perhaps is just *too* exciting a time for a puppy to adjust to his new lifestyle. The right time to bring a puppy home is when you have properly prepared for his arrival and can devote your full attention to this needs and training during the first few critical days.

PREPARING FOR THE PUPPY'S ARRIVAL

Prior to bringing your new puppy home, there are several things you should purchase or prepare. First of all, the puppy should have a place of his own to sleep. We highly recommend the use of a dog crate or sky kennel. While these may seem cruel to the novice dog owner, the dog will regard it as his own little haven. It is a tremendous help in housebreaking since Keeshonds generally do not like to soil their living quarters. For households where both adults work, the crate is essential provided the dog is not required to be in it for extended periods of time. The crate should be large enough for an adult dog to comfortably stand and turn around. Your breeder can help you choose the proper size.

If you choose not to utilize a crate for your puppy's sleeping quarters, then a small area should be identified and blocked off for this purpose. We do not recommend giving a new puppy the run of the house. As the puppy's housetraining progresses, he can be introduced to more and more of your home as you see fit.

The other items you will need for the puppy's arrival include food and water bowls, a collar and leash and a good nutritious dog food, preferably what he has previously been fed. Again, your breeder can give you excellent advice on these things. With regard to food bowls, we recommend the very hard plastic ones (similar to crockery but unbreakable). Keeshond puppies are very fond of water and are notorious for playing in their water bowls. We recommend the travel type of bowl which will make the puppy's water games a bit more difficult (but not impossible!).

BRINGING THE PUPPY HOME

If you have chosen your puppy from a local breeder, transportation should present no problems. If you have a vehicle large enough to accommodate the puppy's crate, we suggest you use that to transport him to his new home. Put in a blanket or towel and position the crate so that you can soothe him during the trip. If your vehicle is small and the trip a short one, you can probably get by with someone holding him in their arms.

If your new puppy will be coming by air, an airline crate is essential. These arrangements should be made well in advance with the breeder. No puppy can be shipped under the age of eight weeks. If at all possible, the flight should be nonstop and scheduled at a time when traffic is light (not holidays or peak travel times) and weather conditions neither too hot nor too cold. We do not suggest that the puppy be tranquilized. You should plan to arrive at the air freight terminal by flight time even though you will undoubtedly have to wait for the crate to be brought from the plane. Don't hesitate to impress the airline with the fact that this is a very young puppy and that you are most anxious for his safe delivery to you.

Have your collar and leash and some water ready as the puppy will definitely need to be exercised and will probably want something to drink after his long trip. Do not be unduly concerned, however, about the rigors of airplane travel on such a young puppy. Several of ours came from the West Coast and bounced from their crates will no ill effects. We find that Keeshonds of any age travel better than their human companions.

THE RIGHT START

The right start for your new puppy is very important. As you introduce him to his new home, gently identify those areas where he is allowed and those where he is not. Show him his sleeping area and where his food and water are. Take him outside and show him where you want him to go to the bathroom. Try not to do too much at a time since he will tire easily and his attention span is very short. Constant gentle reminders of your rules are required. Because the puppy is very small and humans are very large to him, it is important that you play with him on *his* level frequently. This applies to adults as well as to children.

The first night is often difficult. The puppy has had a confusing day. He has been uprooted from his home and mother, has traveled great distances by air or car, is in totally new surroundings and perhaps overwhelmed with attention. Suddenly, everyone abandons him and goes to bed. What does he do? Cry, of course! The natural reaction is to go to him and comfort him, but don't do it. A Keeshond puppy is very smart. He will quickly learn that to get more attention, all he needs to do is cry. In several days he will have *you* very well trained. Unless you want him to sleep in the bedroom with you, we suggest you stay out of his sight but loudly and firmly tell him that this is not proper behavior and that he should be quiet. A radio softly playing is an excellent idea not only for puppies but for adult dogs as well. We leave radios on all over the house during our absence, not only as company for the dogs, but also to cut down on any neighborhood noises (children playing, car doors, etc.) that might encourage unnecessary barking.

HOUSEBREAKING

The secret to housebreaking is supervision and training. From the time you bring him home until he is trained, take him out every hour and especially when he first awakens, after eating and before bedtime. Show him the proper place to exercise and praise him when he does what he is supposed to do. Never leave your puppy outdoors unattended. Small bodies can slip out small openings, and there are people who might steal your puppy should the chance present itself. So, proper caution is definitely the watchword.

If there is no one at home during the day, supplemental newspaper training is the solution. Our dogs are trained to utilize the papers if absolutely necessary during our absence or to wait for our return, if possible. With your new puppy, set up an area slightly away from his crate or bed. Line this area with several layers of newspaper. When the puppy first awakens or after eating, show him the newspapers and encourage him to utilize them. When he does, praise, praise, praise. It will not take long for him to understand what you want.

If the puppy makes a mistake, do *not* rub his nose in it! This serves no purpose other than to destroy his dignity. Immediately correct him with a firm "No" and carry or lead him to the correct spot.

The same techniques apply to other household behavior. If you wish to prohibit the puppy from entering a particular room or jumping on the furniture, now is the time to set the behavior pattern. Remember, though, that if you do not allow your Kees up on the furniture with you, you frequently need to come down to his level to play. As the puppy begins to teethe, furniture, rugs, and somtimes you, become fair game. Make certain that your puppy has safe things of his own with which to play and chew. If

At 2½ weeks of age, the eyes are open and markings are clearly visible. *(Cash)*

By three to four weeks, the fur has fluffed out and they resemble soft seals when asleep. *(Pelletier)*

200

he persists in misbehaving, the firm "No" and a slight shake should reaffirm the correct pattern.

The most important thing in training and housebreaking your new puppy or dog is *consistency*. You cannot allow him to do something once and then scold him for the same thing later. Unacceptable behavior is unacceptable *all* the time. Do not expect him to understand that he can come in the living room when you are there, but not when you have company. Make the rules and stick to them.

STAGES OF DEVELOPMENT

At birth, average Keeshonds weigh about seven to 12 ounces and look like small, very dark rats with heads that are proportionately too large and long, straight tails, but cheer up . . . by the second day, their coats fluff out, shadings begin to appear (including shoulder stripes and perhaps spectacles) and they begin to look like Keeshonds. From then on, the rate of growth is astounding.

In ten to 15 days, their eyes and ears begin to open. They respnd to you more and more. A bit later, teeth poke through the gums, and tails fluff out and begin to turn over their backs.

At six weeks ears begin to come up and from here to 12 weeks is a glamorous age. Kees puppies are absolutely irresistible at this age and resemble black and silver teddy bears.

By about 16 weeks of age, the second teething begins and from that age until six months most Keeshonds go through a gawky, adolescent period. Commonly referred to as the "baboon stage" or the "uglies," they hardly resemble the cute little puppy you chose several weeks before. They seem to be all ears and legs; their stop disappears, the muzzle is very dark, the rest of the dog can take on a strange coloration and the coat is very dense and short (like lamb's wool).

The adult coat will come in quickly. By the time the dog reaches six to eight months, he should have all the required, typical silver-to-gray-to-black shadings and markings. Some puppies (and bloodlines) develop faster than others, and those that mature slowy may turn out to be the best at two to three years of age when the average Keeshond is in full bloom.

Some puppies retain their baby teeth as the adult teeth grow in. By the time they reach six months of age, all baby teeth should have disappeared. If they have not, contact your veterinarian so that the baby teeth can be removed. This can usually be done without anesthetic and is necessary to prevent the bite from being thrown off by the extra teeth.

CRITICAL DEVELOPMENTAL STAGES

The first critical period in a puppy's life is the first 20 days. During this period it needs warmth, food, massage and sleep. The second critical period

At five weeks, some puppies will have their ears up and may resemble tiny bears. *(Kamman)*

At eight weeks, this puppy is full of devilment and ready to go to his new home. *(Harrigan)*

is from 21 to 49 days of age, during which time the puppy learns from its mother, its littermates and from its envrionment. The third critical period, from 49 to 84 days (seven to 12 weeks) is the best time to form the man-dog relationships and to begin training.

From 12 to 16 weeks of age is the fourth critical period in socialization. This is the age of "cutting." The puppy cuts new teeth, both figuratively and literally. This is the time when man and dog decide who is boss, the time when serious training can begin.

The critical developmental stage is so short (from 21 to 112 days, 13 weeks in all) — and once it is gone it can never be retrieved. It is up to the breeder and the new owner to make the best of it.

SOME KEESHOND IDIOSYNCRACIES

Living with more than one Keeshond is like living with a houseful of small children in dog suits since they do not seem to recognize that they are dogs. They are inquisitive, devoted, extremely playful and very loving. You will soon find you have developed a black-and-gray shadow. Once you have gained the trust and love of your dog, he will want to be with you — constantly. Regardless of their size, Keeshonds think they are lap dogs. If you don't want a 45-pound bundle of fur in your lap when you are trying to read the paper, this, too, should be taught early in life. Since we enjoy the affection of our dogs, this is one lesson we never taught; watching television can be quite an experience at our house!

Keeshonds are people-lovers and cannot discern that some might not like their affectionate advances. In general, Kees tend to jump in greeting and if you consider this inappropriate behavior, you should correct it when your Kees is a puppy (see Chapter 12)

Do they shed? They sure do! A puppy will usually go through a major "blow" prior to his first birthday. From then on Keeshonds usually lose their coat in the spring and fall. At these times they lose the fluffy undercoat but generally retain the long guard hairs. Although one dog is less of a problem, you can expect to see some "tumbleweeds" of undercoat in the corners of your house. In between major "blows," there is always a stray hair that somehow finds it way into your butter. Once you decide that finding hair in everything is normal, you will find a nonchalance you never imagined you had.

The Keeshond is known as the "Smiling Dutchman" and he is expert in various displays of the curled lip. Generally, the Dutch "grin" is accompanied by a dropping of the head and much wagging of the tail. Usually, Kees will grin when they have been found out! Sometimes they will grin when they see someone or something they are particularly fond of. The "Kees grin" is a sign of submission. Your dog is acknowledging that you are the leader. Our first Kees, Akela, greets people at the door with his teeth completely bared. It works wonders on salesmen but is a bit disconcerting

From seven to 12 weeks of age is the best time to form the man-dog relationships and to begin his training. This nine-week-old Star-Kees puppy is already working on his CDX dumbbell training.

By about 16 weeks the second teething begins. From this age until about six months, most Keeshonds go through a gawky, adolescent period commonly referred to as the "baboon stage." They hardly resemble the cute little puppy you chose several weeks earlier.

to uninitiated friends. If the baring of the teeth is not accompanied by a deep growl, it is undoubtedly a grin and should not be punished. Some dogs never develop the grin and others begin as very small puppies. It is just another charming characteristic of the breed.

A not-so-charming characteristic is the fact that many Keeshonds "talk." It takes some practice to differentiate between growling — which comes from low in the chest — to talking which is a dog's way of orally communicating. Many of our dogs are talkers (it does seem to be hereditary. Watch the tail and the dog's body English; they are better indicators of behavior than the noises they often make.

The Keeshond was never bred to be anything other than a companion. You may hear that Keeshonds were used as "guard dogs" on Dutch barges. Not true. *Watch* dogs, yes, but never as guard dogs. With their keen eyesight and acute sense of hearing, they are excellent sentries. Our own dogs will bark at strange noises such as a neighbor closing the car door two houses away, hearing the noise through the walls and over the television. When a stranger (or even someone they know) comes to the house, they *will* bark (and that *is* what you want them to do); once the person has been accepted in the house (and has paid the dog an appropriate amount of attention), your Kees will settle down.

Many people will admit to being "owned" by their Keeshond, instead of the other way around. To a certain extent, the Keeshond does own those with whom he lives. Due to the intelligence inherent in the breed, your Keeshond can and will make his wants and desires known and can easily "train" his owner. It is up to you to determine who is the boss.

Owners of Keeshonds (and in general, all dogs) have been known to assign human attributes to them, saying things like, "Oh, she's being vindictive," or "He's feeling guilty." While Keeshonds are admittedly very intelligent, they are not human. All dogs are amoral — without moral principles. They only know right from wrong when reminded of their sins by their owners. Their attention span is very short and must be reinforced by consistent corrections. A well-trained, obedient Keeshond is more preferable to share your home than would be the untrained dog with a mind of its own. Just remember that training should be constructive and not heavy-handed; you do not want to injure the spirit and personality that makes the Keeshond so unique.

Keeshonds in general adapt quite readily to other dogs, cats, birds, etc. Over the years we have added animals to our household with little adjustment. Because Keeshonds are not hunters, they usually have no animosity toward other animals. Our dogs share their yard each spring with a mother rabbit and her babies and easily coexist with our two cats. Just remember, when you do introduce a new pet into your household, take it slow. There will be an adjustment period and you must remember to give the previous pet(s) equal attention to avoid jealousy.

Keeshonds are generally at their peak of maturity around two years of age. At 20 months of age, Ch. Foxfairs Persuasive Friend, HOF, ROMX, exemplifies the beautiful silhouette of the Keeshond.

(Marcelli)

Keeshonds are true people lovers and take every opportunity for a face-licking. This photo of young Troy Fulton and his puppy illustrates the close bond between Keeshond and youngster.

PACK BEHAVIOR

If you have several dogs, it is strongly recommended that you spend some time studying pack behavior. Animal behaviorists make a living solving problems that could have been prevented had the owners done their homework. In our home, the study of pack behavior became a necessity soon after we acquired our third dog. In most homes that have one or two dogs, pack behavior study is not required; but if you are really interested in why dogs do what they do, the study is fascinating. If the proper study of man is ape, then the proper study of dog is wolf.

Groups of wolves and groups of dogs have commonality in that they are both "packs" and have a definite pecking order. Of our 14 males and five females, there is a dominant male and female who would normally be called the "alpha" male and female. The female holds dominance over other females, and the male is the leader. Instead of allowing this to happen, we have become the alpha figures to our dogs and are afforded the respect given to those positions. Our more dominant dogs have dropped to sub-alpha roles. On the other hand, the "omegas," the lowest in the structure, are given little respect by the other animals; these are generally the younger and smaller dogs. One word of caution: The dogs will constantly challenge roles among themselves, and with you. You must *never* relinquish the alpha role as you may find it difficult to regain.

Obviously, dogs are domesticated while wolves are feral (wild), but many of their actions bear remarkable similarity. For instance, when we let our pack out into the exercise yard, they run out en masse. When they hit the back yard, they stretch out single file, much as wolves do when moving cross-country on a trail. Our dogs also initiate the "wolf-kiss," or nuzzling and licking the muzzles of dominant members of the pack. Since we have become the alpha male and alpha female of our pack, our dogs often attempt to give us the wolf kiss in greeting.

We will not attempt to go fully into pack behavior here, as many who are more knowledgeable have already written volumes on the subject. For those who wish to further expand their knowledge, we recommend the following books: *The Wolf: The Ecology and Behavior of an Endangered Species* by L. David Mech (University of Minnesota Press); *The Order of Wolves* by Richard Fiennes (Bobbs-Merrill); *Of Wolves and Men* by Barry Holstan Lopez (Schribners); and *The Soul of the Wolf* by Michael W. Fox (Little, Brown).

If you study pack behavior, and you should if you have more than one or two dogs, you will find that you will better understand canine behavior. You come to an understanding with them that allows for a much more satisfying relationship for both human and dog.

The Keeshond is known as the "Smiling Dutchman" and he is expert in various displays of the curled lip. Often misunderstood, this grin is just another charming characteristic of the breed.

(Buente)

Because of the easy-going Keeshond temperament and the fact that we have become the alpha members of our "pack," the Car-Ron dogs all live together harmoniously. We have always traveled with them and they are true diplomats of dogdom.

208

11

Care and Grooming
of the Keeshond

$\mathbf{K}$EESHONDS ARE inherently healthy and require little grooming. This does not mean, however, that you can neglect your dog's needs. It simply means that you needn't spend hours and hours caring for him.

As you have already read, Keeshonds are people-oriented. For generations they nave been bred as house (or barge) pets and it is extremely important that they be closely associated with their owners. For this reason, we do not recommend that a Keeshond be strictly a kennel or outside dog. Owners who find it necessary to house a number of their Kees in a kennel environment usually bring two or more of their dogs into the house each day to take turns as housepets on a rotating basis. Many breeders, ourselves included, will not sell a puppy into a home where it will be other than a housedog.

OUTSIDE EXERCISE AREAS

One of the questions asked most often of prospective puppy buyers is, "Do you have a fenced-in yard?" For obvious reasons, this is most desirable. Your Keeshond is a family member and for the same reason you would protect a child with a fence, so too should you protect your dog. If you are planning to purchase a fence for your yard, bear in mind that many Keeshonds are jumpers and still more are escape-artists. The fence should be high enough (at least five feet) and secure enough to prevent escape.

If you have no plans to utilize a fence, remember that your Keeshond does need exercise so plan to take him for frequent walks. It is good exercise for both of you and will undoubtedly present the opportunity to make many new friends.

Although the Keeshond's double coat acts as insulation against both heat and cold, care must be taken to prevent the consequences of either extreme. In the heat of summer, shade must always be available; in winter, a warm place should be provided if your dog will be outside for any length of time. Because our house is air conditioned, our dogs spend little time outdoors in the summer. But in the wintertime, they love the cold. With the first snowfall, they gleefully run around, burying their noses in the snow like bulldozers. However, we limit their time outdoors because sub-zero temperatures and wind chill factors are equally dangerous to animals unused to the cold. Prolonged exposure to these conditions can cause frostbitten feet, noses and ears.

One very strong admonition: *Never shave your Keeshond.* The double coat acts as insulation against the sun and heat. If you clip this coat off, you could seriously endanger your dog's life.

Because of the heavy coat, Keeshonds pant more and require large intakes of water. Always make sure that your dog has a full bowl of clean, cool water.

FEEDING

As a rule, Keeshonds are eager, nonpicky eaters. But, like any other dog, they can become spoiled by well-meaning owners. To maintain good, healthy eating habits, puppies and grown dogs should only be given proper sized, balanced meals. If they do not eat their food within a few minutes, pick it up and feed them nothing until the next regularly scheduled meal. This is emotionally hard on owners but should achieve the desired results. When a bitch is in season, the males will barely touch their food. Don't panic; they won't starve. Just feed them less for a few days and when they are interested in food again, increase it to the normal amount. However, if a dog's appetite continues to fall off for no apparent reason, you should consult your veterinarian promptly.

Feeding at regularly scheduled hours is best for both dogs and owners. It allows you to maintain your own personal or work schedule and still be there when your dog requires exercise following his meal.

People will often say that their dog is well fed because it gets leftovers or tablescraps. They may be tasty but they do not provide enough daily, balanced nourishment for dogs. It is wiser to feed a good-quality, commercial dog food or additive based on years of professional research on canine nutrition. Stay away from generic brands of dog food and refrain from buying whatever is on sale; choose a good-quality dog food and stick with it.

One additive that we use is corn oil. In the winter months when your dog is indoors and the furnace dries out the air in the house, your

If you do not want to invest in a fenced-in yard, it is important that you spend time exercising your Keeshond. Mary Alice and Bill Smiley take long walks in the woods with their canine companions.

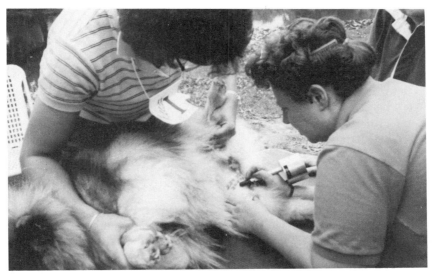

Tattooing the inner thigh of your Keeshond will prove your ownership and facilitate his recovery should he be lost or stolen. The identification numbers can be your social security number or his AKC registration number.

Keeshond's coat and skin can become excessively dry. A tablespoon of corn oil in his food every day or so will alleviate some of the problems.

We would also like to pass on a hint that Nan Greenwood gave to all Wistonia puppy buyers: Elevate your dog's food and water dishes. Now this may sound silly but it accomplishes two things: it keeps your dog up on his toes so that his pasterns (wrists) do not collapse, and it aids in digestion since food doesn't have to go uphill to get to the stomach. Our dogs eat from small step-stools and appear quite indignant when asked to eat from floor level.

The subject of bones for dogs is a controversial one. In general, bones are not good for dogs; but, oh how they love them. Our veterinarian has allowed us a compromise: We purchase the large marrow bones (leg bones) from the butcher shop and then cook them in garlic-salted water for at least an hour. These bones will last for months. One word of caution: Sometimes there will be a small splinter bone on the side of the larger bone; this must be removed before you give the bone to the dog.

Under no circumstances should you give pork, steak or chicken bones to your dog. These splinter and could easily pierce your dog's stomach or intestines. It is safest to use one of the substitutes sold in pet supply stores. Rawhide bones or chews are generally good but we also caution that rawhide is not particularly digestible and too much of a good thing can cause intestinal blockage and other digestive problems. So, with either the marrow bones or substitutes, good common sense is the best practice. Whatever toys or bones you give to your dog should be large enough to avoid lodging in the dog's throat.

HEALTH

The Keeshond suffers from few of the hereditary maladies affecting other breeds. However, there are several problems of which the Keeshond owner should be aware.

Hip Dysplasia

The incidence of this hereditary, disabling malformation of the hip joints has been greatly reduced through the x-raying of all stock by conscientious breeders prior to actual breeding. However, retail outlets and puppy mills may not be as ethical. Hip dysplasia often does not manifest itself until the dog is two years of age; this can be confirmed by x-ray. Sometimes the situation can be remedied by surgery but it is very expensive and not always successful. The safest policy is to buy a puppy only from parents who have been x-rayed clear of H.D. Needless to say, should your dog be afflicted with H.D., it should not be bred.

Subluxation of the Patella

"Slipping stifles" simply means slipping of the kneecap in the rear legs.

212

This condition may be hereditary or it may be caused by trauma. The tightness of the patella can be determined by a veterinarian upon palpation of the knee. Dogs that "hop-scotch" in the rear may be candidates for a slipping stifle problem. Patellar subluxation is correctable by surgery but because of the hereditary aspects, they should not be bred.

Reproductive Problems

While Keeshonds are not known for specific reproductive problems, they do suffer from the same afflictions that beset all dogs. Bitches, especially those which have not been spayed, are prone to vaginal infections. If you notice that your bitch licks her vaginal area, urinates frequently and/or has a discharge, a trip to the veterinarian is in order.

One of the infections that plague bitches is pyometra. This is a life-threatening disease of the uterus which occurs most commonly in bitches over six years of age. A bitch with pyometra refuses to eat, appears depressed and lethargic, drinks a great deal and urinates frequently. Often there is abdominal enlargement and a low grade fever due to the abscessed uterus. If your suspect your bitch might have pyometra, you must contact your veterinarian at once.

Spaying used to be the only remedy for pyometra; however, recently a treatment has been developed that not only permits recovery without spaying but may allow your bitch to conceive. This treatment is controversial and is practiced by veterinarians with expertise in the area of reproduction. Our own veterinarian, Dr. R. V. Hutchison, is one such expert.

The males are not immune from reproductive problems either. Your dog can suffer from prostatitis or an enlarged prostate. Signs of prostatitis are fever, an arched back or tucked-up abdomen and pain on urination. Sometimes blood or other secretions may be emitted from the penis. If you observe any of these symptoms, contact your veterinarian immediately. If caught in time, this condition can usually be treated with antibiotics.

Miscellaneous Problems

There have been other cases of myocardial infarctions (heart problems), von Willebrand's Disease (essentially hemophilia), hypothyroidism, skin disorders, hormonal problems, flea allergies, juvenile cataracts, juvenile diabetes, epilepsy and other maladies plaguing all dogs; but these are not the norm. If you have purchased your Keeshond from a reputable breeder and give it proper care, your veterinarian bills should be low and your canine friend should be with you for many years.

Because your Keeshond is a member of your family, it is important that he be kept in good health. He should have inoculations at least yearly for distemper, hepatitis and leptospirosis (DHL) as well as for Parvovirus.

Keeshonds love the snow and delight in burrowing through it. However, special care must be taken when temperatures are low as your dog's feet and ears can easily become frostbitten.

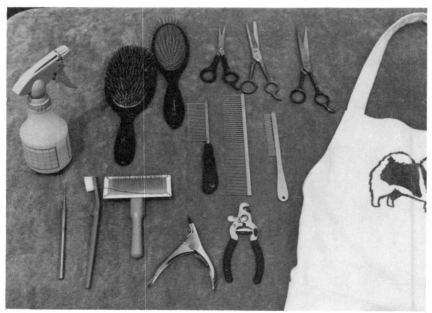

These are the basic tools you will need to keep your Keeshond well-groomed.

Rabies vaccinations are usually good for three years. If you live in an area of the country where heartworm (carried by mosquitos) is a problem, your Keeshond should be on preventive medication and checked at least yearly.

We will not attempt in this book to give veterinary advice about injuries or illnesses that you might encounter during your pet's life. We strongly suggest, however, that you have in your home at least one home veterinary book for easy reference. Suggested reference material is identified in the Appendix of this book.

TATTOOING

We know that you will take care of your new Keeshond and make certain that he is protected at all times, but what if he isn't? The world is full of unscrupulous people who might steal your pet, either for themselves or to sell to an experimental laboratory. Someone could forget to close the gate or door, and your beloved Keeshond disappears. If your dog was ever lost or stolen and then recovered, how could you prove it is really *your* dog? There have been many lawsuits over dogs simply because there was no physical proof of ownership.

Tattooing is the answer. There are several registration agencies with whom you can file your dog's identification number. This identification number can be your social security number, your dog's AKC registration number, etc. It is tattooed on the inner left thigh and, if done properly, will remain readable all your dog's life. Some of the local kennel clubs sponsor tattooing clinics to which you can take your dog, or perhaps your veterinarian can recommend someone, if he does not do it himself. It is painless and will provide extra security for both you and your dog.

GROOMING THE KEESHOND

by Jeanne Buente-Young

The Keeshond is fortunate to be graced with a lovely, easy to care for double coat. People are often first attracted to the breed by the dog's beautiful, profuse silver-to-black shaded hair, but are concerned about the amount of care it will require. If done on a regular basis, you need only spend a moderate amount of time grooming your Keeshond. Grooming not only serves the purpose of coat care and maintenance, but it also is a monitor of your dog's health. The time spent grooming your dog stengthens the bond between you and your pet. Since the Keeshond does shed his coat, grooming helps to minimize the problem of loose dog hair on carpets, furniture, clothing, etc.

The Keeshond does not require professional grooming or trimming. With a minimum amount of instruction and a few quality grooming tools, the new Kees owner should be able to maintain the abundant coat.

215

Your puppy should be taught to sit quietly on the grooming table while you brush him.

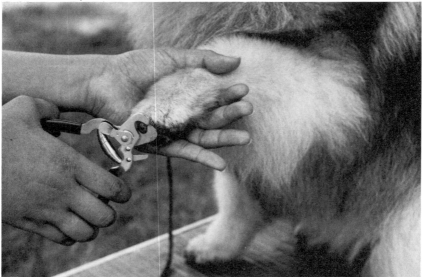

Toenails should be trimmed frequently, possibly as often as once a week. The tip of the toenail can be snipped off with the use of a scissor type (pictured here) or guillotine type nail clipper.

216

Grooming is only one factor contributing to a beautiful, luxurious coat. Heredity plays a major role in determining the length, thickness, texture and color (shading) of the dog's hair. Health, nutrition and exercise are also of vital importance in the fitness of your dog's coat, as is freedom from both internal and external parasites.

As previously mentioned, the Keeshond is a double-coated breed with a thick, downy undercoat and a harsher outer or guard coat. The Kees coat is also characterized by differing lengths of hair on various parts of the body. Coat texture, thickness, length and color will vary among individual dogs and throughout different bloodlines. Thus, slightly different grooming tools will be used on different types of coat. The most important thing to remember about your grooming equipment is that top-quality tools will make your job much easier. The initial cost may be a bit more, but you will definitely save in the long run. The tools you will need can usually be purchased at a well-stocked pet supply shop, at a local dog show or through a pet supply catalog.

The basic grooming tools you will need are:

- A pin brush — A wooden or plastic brush with polished metal pins set in a pliable rubber backing. Some groomers prefer a natural bristle brush with nylon pins set in a pliable rubber backing.
- A soft slicker brush — A brush that has very fine, slightly bent wire bristles set in a rectangular shaped flat backing with a wooden handle.
- A metal comb — A comb with moderately or widely spaced teeth. Some combs are really two in one, with moderately-spaced teeth at one end and widely-spaced ones at the other.
- A nail clipper — Either the scissors or guillotine type.
- Straight-edge scissors
- A spray bottle with adjustable sprayer top.

Optional equipment that you may wish to add to your grooming supplies might be:
- A "flea-comb" — A metal comb with very fine, closely-spaced teeth
- Thinning shears
- A dog nail file
- Tooth scaler
- An electric nail grinder
- Tack box — A carrying case for your growing supply of grooming equipment
- Grooming table — A portable table with collapsible metal legs and a non-slip surface

The grooming of your Keeshond should be done in a well-lighted area where there are few distractions. You should groom your dog on a stable surface with good footing. This could be a grooming table, picnic table or utility table covered with a rubber mat; even a carpeted floor will do.

With your dog standing, sitting or lying on the table, mist the coat lightly with a spray bottle containing water.

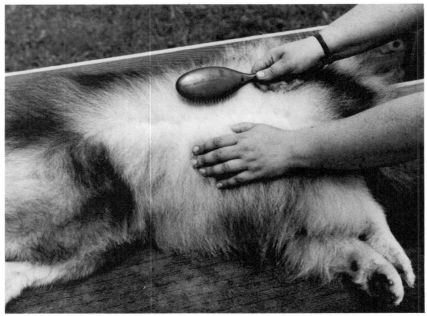

Starting on your dog's side, place your free hand on the dog's body, flattening a portion of the coat. With your pin or bristle brush, begin brushing the flattened coat upward and outward from the skin.

218

When working with a new puppy, take your time introducing him to the grooming process. Your puppy has probably already been exposed to some basic grooming before he left his breeder. Cutting those needle-sharp puppy nails is usually begun when the puppy is very young. A brief period of brushing with a soft brush provides the pup with some individual attention away from his littermates, as well as much needed human contact, stimulation and socialization.

Your puppy should be taught to sit quietly on the grooming table while you brush him; keep the grooming sessions brief initially. He should also learn to tolerate having his feet, legs, ears, teeth, face and tail touched and examined. If you prefer, he can also be taught to lay quietly on his side to be brushed and many groomers utilize this method. He should be exposed to the grooming tools and be taught not to interfere with their use. The same is true of a hair dryer. Proceed slowly and with patience.

Some groomers use a grooming arm with a noose for better control of the dog. A word of caution: Your puppy (or dog) must never be left unattended on the grooming table. It is too easy for him to slip, fall or jump from the table and he could very possibly injure hmself. This is especially true if you utilize the grooming arm; the dog could strangle on the noose.

You now have the basic ingredients to begin the grooming process. A good basic grooming routine should start with an overall inspection of your Keeshond. Take a good look at his teeth, eyes, nose, ears, foot pads, hair coat and skin. This is also a good time to make note of any changes in your dog's weight or amount of flesh. An increase or decrease may indicate a possible health problem or improper nutrition.

During this general inspection, you might keep in mind the following questions:

- Are the teeth white, clean and free from tartar?
- Are the eyes clear, bright and free of discharge?
- Is the nose slightly moist without being runny?
- Are the ears clean and free of foreign matter, excessive ear wax or odor?
- Are the pads of the feet free from cracks, cuts or sores?
- Is the coat shiny and fluffy, or is it dull, brittle and lifeless?
- Is the skin free from parasites (fleas and ticks), dandruff, rashes and sores?
- Are there any abnormal lumps or growths?

This brief examination of your Kees should yield valuable information as to his health and well being, since internal problems often manifest themselves externally. Certain abnormal conditions or symptoms may warrant veterinary consultation or attention.

For the next step in your grooming routine, you may wish to clean any foreign matter or discharge from the inside corners of your dog's eyes. A cotton ball moistened with water will serve well for this purpose.

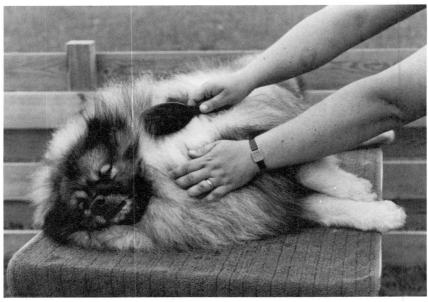

Continue flattening and brushing out the coat all over the dog.

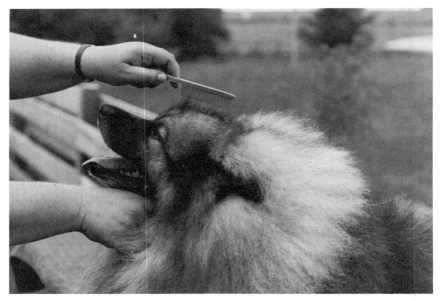

With a flea comb and/or soft slicker brush, comb/brush the short face and ear coat.

A cotton ball, this time moistened with a small amount of mineral oil, will also do for cleaning the inside of the ears.

Small amounts of tartar can be removed from the teeth by carefully using a scaler. Your veterinarian or a professional groomer can instruct you on its proper use. Another method is to use a toothbrush with either a paste of baking soda and water or a canine toothpaste; do *not* use toothpaste made for humans.

Toenails should be trimmed frequently, possibly as often as once a week. The tip of each toenail can be snipped off with the use of a scissor-type or guillotine-type nail clipper. Care should be taken to avoid cutting the quick, which contains a small blood vessel. If you accidentally cut the quick, the bleeding should stop within a short period of time. It is recommended that you have on hand styptic powder to speed up the clotting process.

At this point you may want to give your Kees some time out for a treat or a romp before proceeding to the next phase. Now that the preliminaries are done, it's time to begin brushing. The Keeshond coat generally does not mat, but there is one area in which you might find matting and that is in the soft, fine hair behind the ears. This requires daily inspection and combing to keep it free of matting. If a severe mat does occur, instead of trying to pull it out with a comb, take a pair of scissors and make one or two lengthwise cuts (from the tip of the hair to the skin) into the mat. Then carefully pull the mat apart with a wide-tooth comb.

With your Kees standing, sitting or lying quietly on the table or floor, mist the coat lightly with a spray bottle containing water. Some people prefer using distilled water or water mixed with a *small* amount of coat conditioner or coat dressing. Misting serves to reduce friction and the build-up of static electricity, thus reducing hair breakage.

Starting on your dog's side, place your free hand on the dog's body, flattening a portion of coat. With your pin or bristle brush, begin brushing the flattened coat upward and outward from the skin. Using a long, flowing motion, begin your brush stroke at the skin and continue just past the ends of the hair. Continue, slowly moving your free hand down and brushing the flattened hair up and out. You may want to lightly mist the coat several times during this process. Brush the entire body coat in this manner.

If necessary after brushing, *carefully* comb the coat to separate and remove any loose hair. Do not comb with too much vigor or you will pull out or break off healthy coat. If your Kees is shedding, remove any loose hair with your comb and brush. Different Kees shed in different ways and at different times of the year. A dog that has shed still needs grooming and regular brushing to promote and stimulate new hair growth.

Your grooming goal is for the coat to fluff out and away from the skin in a *forward* manner, framing the face and forming the silhouette that is an important part of the Keeshond's overall appearance.

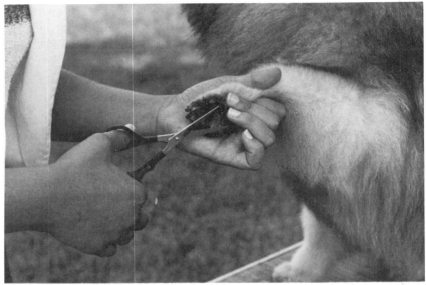

Using scissors, carefully trim the hair on the bottom of the foot so that it is flush with the pads.

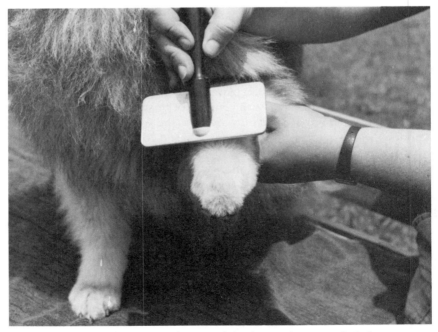

Now brush the hair up on the top of the foot with your soft slicker.

222

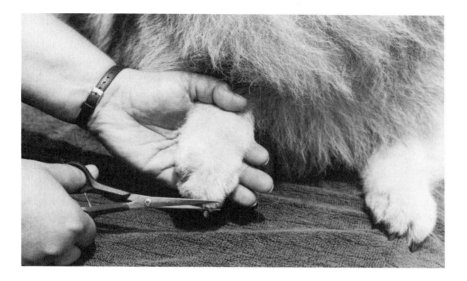

As shown in these photos, using your scissors, cut the hair on the top and sides of the foot, carefully removing small amounts with each cut. With this process, you are rounding and shaping the foot to resemble a cat's paw.

Next, give some attention to the face, ears, feet and legs. With a flea comb and/or a soft slicker brush, comb/brush the short face and ear coat. With your soft slicker, brush *up* all of the short hair on the legs.

Now you are ready to neaten up the short hair on the legs and feet by trimming. You want to give a rounded, proportioned look to the hocks (back of the rear legs) and a compact, cat-like appearance to the feet. Using scissors, carefully trim the hair on the bottom of the foot so that it is flush with the pads. Now brush the hair up on the top of the foot with your soft slicker. Using your scissors, cut the hair on the top and sides of the foot, carefully removing small amounts with each cut. With this process, you are rounding and shaping the foot.

Using your flea comb, comb the hair on the hocks outward from the skin. Using your scissors, trim away any stray hairs from the back of the hock. In order to give a rounded, proportionate appearance, remove only a small amount of hair with each cut.

Bathing

If thoroughly brushed once a week, a Keeshond's coat should not need frequent bathing. Of course there are always special circumstances that may warrant a bath or a partial bath for your dog. During shedding periods, a bath will help to loosen the coat so that it may be more easily removed. Your Keeshond should be bathed with a quality *dog* shampoo; we do not recommend using a shampoo designed for humans as the pH of dog hair is different from human's. A cream rinse or conditioner can be used on a dry, brittle or damaged coat. You should use tearless shampoo around the head and face.

Before you begin the bathing process, brush your dog's coat thoroughly and remove any mats. Place cotton balls in the ears to prevent water from running into the outer ear canal. Place the dog in the tub, using a rubber mat for good footing. Rinse your Kees with warm water and then add shampoo, working it well into the coat. Rinse the coat thoroughly with warm water, making sure that you remove all soap residue. Squeeze excessive water from the coat and blot the dog with towels.

Remove the dog from the tub and place him on the grooming table to begin the drying process. Use either a human hair dryer or a special dog dryer to accomplish this task. After the bath, be sure not to leave your Kees in a drafty or cool environment.

Grooming for the Show Ring

A clean, healthy, well-conditioned dog and coat are essential for your Kees' success in the show ring. Your Keeshond should be groomed and trimmed at home so that you need only do a final brush-up at the show. Each Keeshond owner has his or her own personal techniques and

224

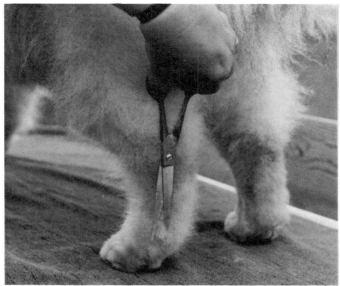

Using the flea comb, comb the hair on the hocks outward from the skin. Using your scissors, trim away any stray hairs from the back of the hock, removing only a small amount of hair with each cut.

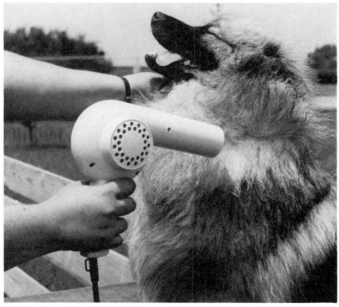

After squeezing excessive water from the coat and blotting the dog dry, put him on the grooming table to begin the drying process, using either a human hair dryer or a special dog dryer.

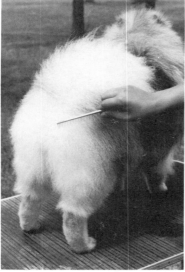

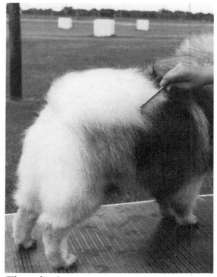

The pantaloons should be brushed to the side to form the character-istic "Dutchman's breeches." Radical trimming of the trousers and tail is strongly discouraged.

The finely groomed Keeshond will present a lovely silhouette with the tail blending in with the body and never appearing as an appendage.

For the sake of convenience, all grooming equipment can be transported to the show in a lightweight carrying case or tack box specifically designed for this purpose.

226

procedures for maintaining and trimming a show coat. Moderate trimming to enhance the dog's silhouette is sometimes done, but radical trimming, especially of the trousers and tail, is strongly discouraged. As an alternative, the coat can be fluffed and/or smoothed to improve the appearance of the dog's outline.

Trimming of the whiskers is optional. If you elect to trim the whiskers for the show ring, trim them very carefully with a small blunt-tipped scissors and only in a well-lighted area.

A no-rinse shampoo is handy for cleaning legs, feet, trousers, etc. After application, dry the hair with towels or a dryer. Some groomers use powder, chalk or cornstarch to dry, clean and fluff out leg hair and trousers. According to Chapter 14, Section 9.B of the AKC *Rules Applying to Registration and Dog Shows*, "such cleaning substances are to be removed before the dog enters the ring."

After slightly dampening and drying the legs, the powder can be applied with a short bristled brush; a fingernail brush works well for this. When completely dry, remove the powder by brushing with a bristle brush or soft slicker.

For the sake of convenience, all grooming equipment can be transported to the show in a lightweight carrying case. You may purchase a tack box specifically designed for this purpose or you can devise your own.

In the previous pages, we have attempted to touch upon all aspects of grooming your Keeshond. Your best resource for additional information and grooming techniques is a knowledgeable, skilled Keeshond breeder.

Ellen Crewe became involved in obedience in 1979. She quickly became hooked on the pleasures of training and showing. She began teaching classes in 1982 and the next year joined the staff of Keezette International as its obedience editor. She is also a member of the Dog Writers Association of America.

Her first Keeshond, Tigger, went on to win his American and Canadian Utility Dog titles and a Canadian championship; her second Kees, Blue (Car-Ron's Blue Moonshadow, Am. and Can. CD) currently holds American and Canadian Companion Dog titles, has points toward his championship in both countries, and is working on his Companion Dog Excellent title.

Ellen believes that obedience benefits both dog and owner. A trained dog is a happy dog, an easier dog with which to live whether at home or in the show ring.

12

How To Train Your Keeshond

by Ellen B. Crewe

EVERY BREED OF DOG has characteristics that typify the breed. The typical Keeshond's temperament is intelligent, sensitive and eager to please. These characteristics make him an ideal pet. But Keeshonds are a unique breed and, as such, should not be trained as a normal dog would be; a unique dog demands unique training methods.

Because of their high degree of responsiveness to praise and corrections, Keeshonds are quick to learn basic home behavior. It is easy to be lulled into thinking that your puppy will never need obedience lessons. However, when your youngster grows to adulthood, you may find it difficult to control him on visits to the veterinarian, vacations or just a walk around the block. An average-sized adult Keeshond will weigh between 30-45 pounds and can be quite a handful if he does not understand and obey a few basic rules of obedience.

It is easiest to begin basic training when your Keeshond is a puppy, but do not let age (yours or his) be a deterrent. It is never too late to start. My first Kees, Tigger (Can. Ch./OT Ch. Tigger's Moonshadow, Can. and Am. UD) was five years old and had no prior training when I signed up for a beginner's course at obedience school. I had been told he was "too old" to learn and would never earn an obedience title. Four years later he had earned all three of the titles in both the United States and Canada and has become only the third Keeshond in the history of the breed to do so. I believe the reason he accomplished so much, despite his lack of prior training and his age, is because he has the typical Keeshond desire to please.

The purpose of this chapter is to help you teach your Keeshond to be well behaved both at home and in public. If you wish to continue beyond the basic skills I have explained here, you should join a good obedience training school. I also suggest reading the other more in-depth publications identified in the Appendix.

The equipment you will need for basic training includes:

- A *properly fitted collar*. You should use a "rolled" leather buckle collar, rather than a choker, on a young puppy. A flat or strap-type collar will wear down your puppy's ruff. Get a collar that is slightly loose on his neck, but not so large that he can pull it off over his head. He probably won't like the collar at first so let him wear it for several days before training begins. For a teenaged puppy or adult Keeshond, a choke collar made of either metal links or round nylon cord will give you the best control. Measure around your dog's skull right in front of his ears and buy a choker no more than one or two inches longer than that measurement. Do not buy an adult-sized collar for your teenaged puppy to "grow into." If the collar is too long, the leash's snap will hit the dog's skull each time you make a correction and could terrify or injure your dog. NEVER leave a choke collar on your dog for all-day wear. There have been many cases where dogs have snagged the live ring on something and have literally choked to death. Use a choke collar *only* for training sessions or when walking your dog.

- A *six-foot leash*. Leather is the best of the three types of leashes on the market. The three-eighths inch width generally works best.

- *Rubber-soled, low-heeled shoes.* Sneakers are ideal as they provide secure footing.

- *Rewards for learning skills and obeying commands.* Treats or dog cookies should be used sparingly. If you only reward your Keeshond with food, you'll soon discover that he won't obey *unless* you have food. Learn to use your voice to express approval and your hands to give him a scratch behind the ears or a pat on the back. Cookies may taste good, but warm praise lasts longer and is a better training aid.

There are "Eight Commandments" to be followed for effective dog training, whether it be for the obedience ring or just everyday behavior.

- *Be patient.* Remember that dogs learn by repetition, rewards and corrections; they learn in a step-by-step process. Repeat each step until your Keeshond understands. Take as much time as is needed.

- *Stay calm.* If you let yourself become frustrated, you will gain nothing. Keeshonds are very sensitive and, if punished severely, may retain a life-long fear. If a new lesson is not going well, stop before you become impatient. Switch to a skill that your dog understands and performs well, praise him and end the session on a positive note.

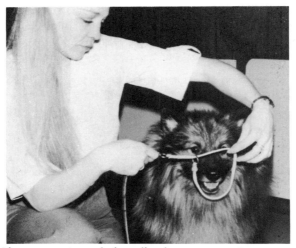

If you are using a choke collar, be sure to put it on your Kees so that the "live" ring is on the end of the collar that leads toward you across the *back* of the dog's neck.

To teach your puppy the "down," place your left hand firmly on his hips to hold his rear down. Holding a treat in your right hand, show it to him and then slowly sweep your right hand from his nose to the floor as you give the command.

To prevent your dog from jumping on people, as he is making a leap for you, shift your weight to one leg and quickly bump him in the chest wit the other knee as you say, "*off!*"

231

- *Be consistent.* Always correct your Keeshond when he makes a mistake or refuses to obey a command. You cannot correct once in awhile, overlook it another time and expect your dog to understand what you really want. A confused dog is neither a happy nor a reliable worker.

- *Praise him* every *time he does something on command.* Praise even if you had to correct him to get the desired response.

- *Talk to your dog.* Use a warm and happy tone of voice to keep his attention on you.

- *Give the command word only once.* If you get into the habit of repeating a command, then your Keeshond will learn that he doesn't have to respond to the first command. Say it once, give a correction with the leash to show him what you want, then praise him.

- *Gear your training sessions to your dog.* For a young puppy, an ideal lesson plan would be two or three five-minute sessions per day. An adult dog has a longer attention span and can be trained once or twice a day for up to 20 minutes.

- *Keep it fun!* End each session with play time. Throw a stick or ball, or get into a wrestling match with your dog. A perfect training period involves review of old skills, new lessons to work on and a time for play at the end.

There are two terms that need defining before you begin training your Keeshond. The first is a leash *pop* or correction. Your leash should always hang with a bit of slack because you cannot make an effective pop correction if the leash is tight to begin with. To make a good leash pop, you should jerk the leash briskly in the direction you want your dog to go; then *immediately loosen the leash to release the choker* and praise him. The firmness of the pop must be tailored to your particular dog. Watch your dog's reaction to the correction and proceed accordingly. Remember to immediately pile on the praise for a correct response.

The other term you should understand is *command*. A command is a single word, which, when taught with patience, praise and correction, tells your Kees what you want him to do. The proper tone of voice to use on a command is calm, firm but quiet. Do not *shout* out your commands. On any command where you want your dog to move, you should say your dog's name first in order to get his attention (i.e., "Bandit, *heel*").

COME

The first command that your Keeshond should understand is "come." A dog who will respond to a single call is a dog who can be trusted anywhere.

Put your dog's leash and collar on him and allow him to roam out to the end of the six-foot leash. When he is paying you no attention, call out in a firm but cheerful tone of voice, "Bandit, *come*." Immediately pop the leash to get him started toward you, then turn and run *away* from him. If you are running away from him while warmly praising, he will instinctively run to "catch" you.

Do several command-pop-run-and-praise exercises in each training session. Lots of praise and hugs (and a treat once in awhile) will soon have him coming at a run.

After a few days of this routine you'll notice that your Kees is coming before you get a chance to pop the leash. You're now ready to try him on a longer line. Get a twenty-foot length of lightweight nylon clothesline and a small snap. Tie the snap onto one end and knot a loop in the other end to use as a handle. Snap the long line onto your Keeshond's collar and allow him to explore to the end of the line. This time when you call, "Bandit, *come*," you may find he will not respond. Do *not* repeat the command. Immediately pop the long line and turn and run as before. Practice from varying distances, both indoors and out, several times a day. Make a game of calling him from around a corner or from one room to another in your home. Praise him warmly each time he comes.

If you are working with a young puppy, he might not be able to keep up with you on the running method. Buckle your puppy's collar on him and clip two leashes to it. Have two members of your family sit six feet away from each other on the floor and take turns calling the puppy. Since puppies are still getting accustomed to the collars, do *not* pop the leash as you would an adult. Instead, use a gentle tug on the leash to get the puppy's attention; then pat the floor in front of you or clap your hands, all the while praising and encouraging him to come to you. Do *not* drag the puppy. As soon as he's reached the first person and received his praise, the second can then call him.

Never call your dog to you in order to punish him for some misdeed. If you do, he will associate the scolding with the fact that he came to you and not with the deed for which he is being scolded. If you must scold him, go and take him to the scene of the crime. "Come" must always be associated with praise, hugs and happiness; that is the key to a fast and reliable response every time you call.

SIT

While your Keeshond is learning to come, you can also begin teaching him to sit. Place your dog at your left side and fold up his leash in your right hand so that there is only a foot or so between your hand and his collar. Firmly and cheerfully say, "Bandit, *sit*," pop up and back (diagonally toward your left shoulder) and at the same time you pop the leash with your right hand, slap him firmly on one of his hips with your left hand. You will note that I suggest using his name prior to the command to sit; although you want him to remain still (sit), he must *move* from a standing position in order to do so.

Do *not* attempt to get your dog to sit by pushing on his hips! He will lock his rear legs and resist the push; your continuing to push could injure him. A slap on the hips — just firm enough to startle him — is quicker and more humane.

A young puppy will probably respond better to a different method of teaching the sit. Kneel down next to your puppy. Bunch the leash up in your right hand and cup her rump in your left hand. Say, "Keesha, *sit*," tug the leash diagonally toward your left shoulder and at the same time apply pressure with your left hand on the backs of her legs. Just as you would be forced to sit if someone pushed a chair against the back of your knees, so will your puppy be forced to sit because of the pressure of your left hand. Praise her warmly, let her get up, then repeat the sequence.

Because of the Keeshond's intelligence and desire to please, you may find that your dog understands the sit command within a few days. Soon you won't need to use your hands to make a correction. However, if you give the command one day and he doesn't sit, do not repeat the command; go back to the hand corrections . . . and remember the praise.

DOWN

To teach the down, kneel next to your dog while he's sitting at your left side. Put your left arm over his shoulders and grasp his left elbow; then hold his right elbow with your right hand. Say, "Bandit, *down*," and lift his front paws off the floor, extend his forelegs and set his front end down. Praise; then allow him to get up.

He may try to resist by backing up, in which case you can practice against a wall. He may try to stand up with his rear end while you're trying to get his front end down. In this case, you'll notice that your left arm is lying across his back. Put pressure on his back with your arm to keep his rear down while you lower his front.

Another method that works well on puppies and adults is to utilize treats. Kneel next to your puppy, sit her in front of you and place your left hand firmly on her hips to hold her rear down. Holding a treat in your right hand, show it to her so that she knows you have food. Slowly sweep your right hand from her nose to the floor and out about six inches in front of her as you say, "Keesha, *down*." Her nose will naturally follow the treat as your hand moves down and away, and down comes the front end. As soon as her elbows hit the floor, praise her and give her the treat.

Praise your Keeshond for lying down on command while he is *in* the down position and not after he has gotten up. Within a short time you'll notice that your Kees will lie down on command with less and less physical assistance from you and soon will drop when you merely point at the floor and say, "Bandit, *down*."

234

STAND

It's a joy to have a dog who will calmly stand still while being examined by your veterinarian or patted by a stranger. Because Keeshonds are such people-lovers, they can be jumpers or wigglers when meeting both new and old friends. The stand is also useful when the dog has muddy feet after a romp outdoors. Teach him to maintain a stand while you pick up each foot to wipe off the mud. The little bit of time you spend teaching your dog to stand will be well worth the effort.

Gather your dog's leash in your right hand so that your hand is about a foot from the snap. Encourage him to come with you as you stroll along. Say, "*Stand.*" Pass your right hand over his head, just a few inches above his eyes, until you reach the end of the foot of leash and hold your hand steady while maintaining a *slight forward pull.* At the same time you are pulling forward on the leash with your right hand, use the *back* of your left hand to put backwards pressure on the front of his right rear leg. In this method you are actually gently stretching your Keeshond; he cannot sit down or lie down because you're holding him in a stand. As soon as he settles you can slowly release the pressure of both hands.

Two notes of caution: Do not use your palm to hold his rear leg because if he tries to sit or jump away, it is too easy to instinctively grab the leg and pinch it painfully. Also, be careful not to pop the leash while teaching the stand; use a gentle forward *pull* instead of a pop.

As with the sit and down, the instance your Kees is standing, praise him; let him move and repeat the sequence a few more times.

If your puppy (or adult) tries to jump away from your left hand on the previous method, here is an alternate method. As before, pass your right hand over her head as you say, "*Stand*" and at the same time stick your left forearm under her belly right in front of her rear legs. If she tries to jump or bounce away, just lift her hind feet an inch or so off the floor until she settles; then lower her rear as you quietly praise her.

As your training on the stand progresses, you'll need less and less of the hand corrections. Within a short time you may find that your Keeshond will stand with only a voice command or the hand-pass over his head.

STAY

This skill can literally save your sanity! Most Keeshonds love food, especially human food, and can be pests when you're trying to cook or eat a meal. Teach your dog to sit or down and stay put where he won't be underfoot.

Sit your Kees at your left side, praise him for the sit but instead of allowing him to hop to his feet as before, put your right hand — fingers spread wide — in front of his nose and firmly announce, "*Stay.*" Remain at his side and watch him closely. If he starts to get up, immediately repeat the

To teach your dog to stand, gather the dog's leash in your right hand and as you stroll along, give the command "Stand." Pass your right hand over his head until you reach the end of the leash and hold your hand steady while maintaining a slight forward pull. At the same time, use the back of your left hand to put backwards pressure on the front of his right rear leg.

Two moving as one. Notice the loose leash and Blue's attention on Ellen.

pop and slap corrections for a sit. Give him the hand signal in front of his nose again and be firmer with your command to "*stay*." His first stays should not be longer than five seconds. When he has remained sitting for the full five seconds praise him quietly, then let him know that he can get up by telling him, "Okay." Remember: Praise first, then release him from the stay.

As your Kees learns what the hand signal and stay command mean, you can gradually increase the length of time that he remains sitting at your side. When he'll stay for at least a minute, you can begin putting him on a stay, then taking *one* step out in front of him. (Turn to face him after taking the step so that you can watch him closely.) He'll probably try to come with you when you step away, so be ready to make the corrections. As you move away from him, step out on the *right* foot, indicating that you do not want him to accompany you; step out on your *left* foot when you want him to move with you.

As with the other commands, "*Stay*" should be spoken only once for each time you want him to do it. If your dog moves from his stay position before you release him, you must start over from the beginning and repeat the sit and stay commands. Once he is maintaining his position on a stay, do not repeat the commands.

When your Keeshond is steady on a sit-stay of one minute, gradually begin taking first two and then three steps away from him before you turn to face him. Gradually begin increasing the length of time he's on a stay before you return. Begin working on down-stays and stand-stays. If he breaks from a down, pop the leash down toward the floor. If your Kees moves while on a stand-stay, you must quickly return to him and put him back in the stand with the "stretched" technique: right hand across his head and left hand bracing the rear leg.

NOTE: You must never forget to release your Keeshond from a stay. As the training progresses, it is easy to get into bad habits. For instance, your dog may get excited when he realizes you are heading outside to run errands. Like most Kees, he loves car rides and will try to push his way out the door with you. You get an inspiration: Put him on a sit-stay. You do and are gone for two hours. You cannot expect him to remain on a sit-stay for this long. It is better to put him on a stay, step outside, pull the door almost shut and then tell him "Okay." That way he'll know that he's free to make himself comfortable while he awaits your return.

TWO MOVING AS ONE

Heeling is a fine art. It takes a lot of work and patience, but what rewards! It is a joy to be able to go for a walk with your beautiful Keeshond and not have to suffer the indignity of being dragged down the street. The concept of two moving as one explains what you're aiming for in heeling work: You will be free to go where *you* want to go and at the pace *you* want to move with no interference from your dog. Do you enjoy hiking? How about cross-country skiing or bicycling? Once your Kees understands heeling, you'll be able to enjoy a number of outdoor activities together.

Puppy Method

If your Kees is a young puppy you should not begin with formal heeling but try a "Siamese twin" approach. Imagine that the two of you are tied together by an invisible rope. Let your puppy wear her leash and collar but do not attempt to guide or correct her. Let her wander wherever she wants to, stopping here and sniffing there. While she's moving, keep step with her, always staying right next to her right shoulder, being careful not to step on her. If she stops, stop with her and wait until she's ready to move on. Over a period of several weeks, this method will accustom your puppy to having you at her right side.

NOTE: Puppies go through "fear imprint periods," typically at around eight weeks and four-and-one-half to five months of age. During these periods a normally well-adjusted, outgoing puppy may suddenly become shy or frightened of things she had previously taken in stride. You must handle the situation carefully to prevent a lifelong fear. For instance, she may suddenly become fearful of a trash can, and attempt to run away from it. Stand still; speak quietly to her but do not praise her. Cheerfully tell her that trash cans don't eat puppies and that everything is all right. If you are close enough to touch the object, put your hand on it and continue to speak calmly to your puppy. Eventually her curiosity will get the better of her and she'll take a step or two closer. Do not drag or pull her over to it. Let her investigate at her own speed. As she approaches the object, you should begin to praise her for her bravery. If she chooses not to fully approach the object, don't force the issue. Continue your walk and give her a break from the stressful situation. Take the time to help your puppy learn to cope with anything that frightens her as a youngster so that she'll grow up to be a well-adjusted, confident adult.

CONTROLLED WALKING

The next step toward formal heeling is called controlled walking. This method is also a good introduction to heeling for a previously untrained adult dog. Controlled walking means that you set the pace and direction of your walks rather than letting your Keeshond do the steering; in this way he learns to stay at your left side during halts, turns and changes of pace.

Do not use the command "heel" when you are starting out because controlled walking is not heeling. Instead, use another phrase such as "Let's go." Pop forward on the leash and step out with your left foot first. As long as your dog remains close to your left leg and stops moving when you halt, do not correct him. If, however, he suddenly dashes out ahead of you or starts lagging, then a quick, firm pop is called for.

As you move along, talk to your Keeshond. Lots of cheerful praise and chit-chat will go a long way toward keeping your dog's attention and will also bolster his enthusiasm.

The key points in controlled walking are to move briskly and speak cheerfully. The end result is a dog who enjoys moving smoothly with you. Keep your first lessons short as this is a whole new concept for your dog. If you start off with long walks filled with corrections, your dog will not enjoy kindergarten heeling and won't take readily to formal heeling.

HEEL

By now your Keeshond should understand controlled walking and be able to sit on command. Heeling puts these two lessons together so be certain that your dog is ready before beginning.

Remember to always step out with your *left* foot first after a halt. Because your dog is at your left side, he is very aware of your left leg and will quickly learn to regard that first left-footed step as a cue to begin moving.

"Heel position" means that no matter what you are doing (i.e., walking, running or standing still), your dog moves at the same rate of speed and the area between his nose and shoulders is even with your left hip and you are both facing in the same direction.

Use the *"heel"* command only once (each time you begin moving after a halt); then talk to your Kees as you walk to keep his attention on you. Keep the leash slack at all times except when a pop correction is necessary; then immediately loosen the leash again.

Command, "Bandit, *heel*," give a forward pop on the leash and step out with your left foot first. Walk at a brisk pace for a few feet and then halt. As soon as you have stopped, pop straight up on the leash as you say, "*Sit.*" Praise your dog; then start out again.

The short walks between halts will enable you to maintain control of your dog. He really won't be able to get too far out of line while moving and will quickly catch on to the idea that when you halt, he is expected to sit quickly at your side.

The key to keeping your Keeshond in heel position at the halts is the speed of your correction. As you slow down just prior to a halt, switch the leash to your right hand so that your left hand is free to give the rump slap. The instant that you halt, say "*Sit*" and make the correction.

Practice changing your pace from a brisk walk to a jog (leash pop forward) as you increase speed) and also to a slow walk (leash pop back). Work on making smooth turns at corners. The end result of all of your heeling work will be a dog that stays at your side no matter what speed you're moving and will calmly sit when you halt.

OFF

Dogs of all breeds — and especially Keeshonds — love to jump up on owners and friends to express affection. This behavior can be irritating if the dog has muddy feet or you're dressed for an evening on the town. Teach your Keeshond the meaning of the word "off" and you've solved the problem.

When your dog is making a leap for you or already has his paws on your waist, shift all your weight to one leg and quicky bump him in the chest with the other knee as you say *"off."* (Do *not* say "down" unless you want him to lie down.) After a few repetitions of the knee-bump, your Keeshond should learn that jumping on people is not acceptable behavior.

AUTOMOBILE BEHAVIOR

Keeshonds love to go for car rides and can be good companions on long and short drives. Here is a situation where obedience lessons really come in handy. Put your dog on a sit-stay until you have opened the back car door and are ready for him to jump in. Once he's in the vehicle, put him on a sit or down-stay so that he's not interfering with the driver. When you have arrived at your destination, your dog will probably try to leave the car with you. Teach him to "wait" or "stay" until you are ready for him to leave the car.

If you follow these simple training methods with your puppy or dog, both you and your dog will enjoy happier, less stressful lives together.

13

The Keeshond in Obedience

by Ellen B. Crewe

SHOWING A KEESHOND in obedience can be a lot of fun . . . if you have a sense of humor. First and foremost, be aware that Keeshonds will attract a lot of attention because they are not a commonly seen breed in the obedience ring. Then brace yourself the instant you enter the ring because your Keeshond's personality is bound to surface at some point. You see, Keeshonds are hams. They love people and applause. Sooner or later they're going to catch on to the fact that going to a dog show means a lot of attention from the adoring crowds.

I have suffered through more than a few shows where Tigger began to play to the audience for applause; then, getting the applause, he would continue to work but would punctuate his performance with barks. The audiences loved his enthusiasm and silliness; the judges enjoyed it too, but deducted points from Tigger's score because of his big mouth! At one show in Canada when he was eight and a half years old, he got a standing ovation from the judge and crowd, not because he had performed perfectly, but because they loved his enthusiasm and bounce. Most dogs that old do not bounce; Kees do.

Although considered an "unconventional" obedience breed, Keeshonds have what it takes to be star performers when given the proper education. Unlike many breeds, Kees do not flourish under heavy correction or pattern-oriented practice. Most Keeshonds are obedient because they *choose* to be, not because they are forced into it. To force a Kees is to destroy the sparkle and dash so welcomed in obedience work. It is not uncommon to see a Keeshond have the highest score in his class at an obedience trial and many Keeshonds have won Highest Scoring Dog in Trial honors at very competitive shows.

Competing in obedience trials is a wonderful hobby. If at all possible, join a training club in your area so that you can get help from experienced trainers in polishing both your and your dog's performances. Before you enter your first show, you would be wise to exhibit at matches. Obedience trial matches are run exactly like those at shows except that they are for practice only and do not count toward a title. The entry fees are much lower than at shows, so for a few dollars you can find out how well your dog will work in an unfamiliar place and around new people and dogs. Your training club should be able to tell you where and when the matches in your area are held.

There are three levels of competition in obedience. In both the United States and Canada, three "legs" or qualifying scores are required to earn each of the three titles. A qualifying score is at least 170 out of a possible 200 points, and the dog must earn at least half of the points available for each exercise.

The following describes the various exercises and points for each that are used in trials in the United States and Canada for the three titles:

NOVICE CLASSES
Title: Companion Dog (CD)

Exercise	U.S.	Can.
Heel on Leash and Figure 8	40	35

The judge will direct you on a heeling pattern that will include normal, fast and slow paces; right, left and about turns and halts. You will then also do a figure 8 pattern around two people. This exercise is to demonstrate how well your dog will heel while he is on leash.

Stand for Examination	30	30

You will stand your dog, tell him to stay, and then walk six feet away from him. The judge will approach your dog, touch him on the head, shoulders and back; then walk away. You return to your dog. This exercise is to show that the dog will remain in place and will let a stranger touch him. This is done on-leash in Canada but off-leash in the United States.

Heel Free	40	45

Same as the heel on leash, except that there is no figure 8 and the dog is being judged on how well he heels when you are not using a leash.

Exercise	U.S.	Can.

Recall — 30 — 30
You leave your Kees on a sit-stay at one end of the ring, walk to the other end and call him. He must remain in place until called, then must come at a brisk pace and sit in front of you. Then, on command, he must return to heel position at your left side.

Long Sit — 30 — 30
Up to 12 dogs at a time are placed on a sit-stay across one side of the judging ring. Their handlers walk to the othre side, remain there for one minute, then return to their dogs. The exercise is to demonstrate that the dog will remain in position when you leave him and walk several feet away.

Long Down — 30 — 30
Same as the long sit except that the dogs are left on a down-stay and must remain in place for three minutes.

200   200

OPEN CLASSES
Title: Companion Dog Excellent (CDX)

Exercise	U.S.	Can.

Heel Free and Figure 8 — 40 — 40
Same as the Novice heel free but now the figure 8 is also done off-leash.

Drop on Recall — 30 — 30
Same as the Novice recall, but in Open the dog must stop and lie down on command when he's about half way to you. Then, on another command, he must complete the recall and return to heel when directed. This exercise is to demonstrate that he will stay, come when called, stop when told to and then return to your side.

Retrieve on Flat — 20 — 25
Your dog must retrieve a wooden dumbbell, then sit in front of you holding it until you take it from him. This is to show his ability and willingness to retrieve an object you've thrown.

Retrieve Over High Jump — 30 — 35
Same as the retrieve on flat except that the dumbbell is thrown over a jump set at one-and-one-half times your dog's shoulder height. He must jump, pick up the dumbbell and jump again when returning to you.

Exercise	U.S.	Can.

Broad Jump — 20 — 20
The dog must jump a set of low hurdles, spaced to cover a distance three times his height at the shoulder, all in one jump, then return to you. He cannot walk on or between the hurdles. This is to demonstrate his willingness to jump a wide distance.

Long Sit — 30 — 25
Same as the Novice long sit, but in Open the dogs must remain sitting in place for three minutes while their handlers are out of the ring and out of the dogs' sight.

Long Down — 30 — 25
Like the Novice down, but for five minutes with the handlers out of sight.

200   200

UTILITY CLASSES
Title: Utility Dog (UD)

United States Exercises	Pts.	Canadian Exercises	Pts.
Signal Exercise	40	*Signal Exercise*	35

The dog must perform an off-leash heeling pattern, then stand, stay, down, sit and recall all on hand signals.

Canadian: Same as the U.S. signal exercise.

Scent Discrimination
| — Leather | 30 |
| — Metal | 30 |

Scent Discrimination (Canadian)
— Leather	20
— Metal	20
— Wood	20

Nine scent articles (similar to dumbbells) made of leather or metal are placed about 15 feet in front of the dog. One of the articles has your scent on it. The dog must trot to the articles and use his nose to find the article that you've handled and then return it to you. The exercise is performed twice: once with your scent on a leather article and once on a metal one.

Same as U.S. scent discrimination except that 12 unscented articles are used at once and the dog must find and retrieve the leather, metal and wooden article that has your scent on it.

244

Can. Ch. and Can. OT Ch. Tigger's Moonshadow, Can. and Am. UD, shows how to clear the Utility bar jump.

In Canadian Utility, a dog must use his nose to find articles made of leather, metal and wood that you have handled.

245

United States Exercises	Pts.	Canadian Exercises	Pts.

Directed Retrieve — 30

Three white cotton gloves are placed, evenly spaced, across the bakc of the ring. Your Kees must go out, pick up the correct glove (left, center or right, as you have designated) and return it to you.

Seek Back — 30

The dog must heel as in the Novice heel free, but during the heeling pattern, the judge will tell you to drop a glove you've been carrying. When you end the heeling pattern across the ring from the glove, you tell your Kees to find the dropped glove. Just like the other retrieves, he must locate the glove and return it to you.

Directed Jumping — 40

Two high jumps (a solid and a bar jump) are on either side and halfway between the front and back of the ring. Your dog must leave you, run to the opposite end of the ring and sit; then, at your direction, he must jump one of the jumps on his way back to you. He then repeats the sequence but must jump the other jump when returning.

Directed Jumping — 40

Same as the U.S. directed jumping.

Long Stand — 30

Up to 12 dogs at a time are left on a stand-stay; then their handlers walk six feet out in front of them. The dogs must remain standing for at leat three minutes, while the judge goes over each dog in turn like in the Novice stand for examination.

Long Stand — 35

Same as the U.S. long stand.

200   200

The American and Canadian Kennel Clubs also offer a title called Obedience Trial Champion, or OT Ch. In Canada this title is automatically conferred when a dog earns a Utility degree. In the United States it is more difficult to attain. The dog must first earn his UD, then he can win points toward the coveted OT Ch. only by earning the highest or second highest score in Open and Utility classes. One hundred points and at leat three first places are needed to earn an American OT Ch. The number of points awarded for each first or second place depends on how many dogs were

OT Ch. Whirlwind's Free Spirit, HOF, is the only Keeshond to have earned an American Obedience Trial Championshp. She is shown here with her proud owner/handler Teresa Turner of Georgia.

Brown's Little Jenny Sunshine, UD, HOF, is a multiple High in Trial winner. She is owned, trained and handled by Anne Brown Lyons of Kentucky.

defeated in that class. It is difficult to win an American Obedience Trial Championship, as the competition for points is very keen. Only one Keeshond to date has attained the title — OT Ch. Whirlwind's Free Spirit, HOF (story follows).

As you can see, the exercises in the Novice class are relatively easy; Open is somewhat harder and Utility quite difficult. With the proper training, most dogs can earn a CD. Perhaps half of these could go on to earn a CDX. In truth, very few CDX dogs have what it takes to earn a UD. But, don't let that stop you from dreaming. They told me that Tigger was too old to win a CD and four years later he became both an American *and* Canadian Utility Dog. If you and your Keeshond enjoy working and showing together, and your Kees is properly conditioned and trained, there is nothing to stop you from going all the way to that Obedience Trial Championship.

KEESHOND OBEDIENCE ACHIEVERS

by Carol and Ron Cash

What better way to chronicle some of the top achievers in the obedience field than to begin with the very best. As of this writing our breed boasts only one American Obedience Trial Champion, OT Ch. Whirlwind's Free Spirit, HOF. "Amity" finished the last of her 100 points on October 4, 1980, at the Chattanooga Kennel Club, where she finished with a first place in an Open B class of 23 dogs.

Amity finished her UD in November 1978 in just four shows, but was plagued during 1979 by a spastic colon. Thanks to the tender care of her owner/trainer Teresa Turner, Amity triumphed over her affliction. 1980 was a great year for Amity. She had two Highs in Trial, eight Combined, and was No. 1 Keeshond in the Keezette System and in the top ten Non-Sporting Dogs (Shuman System). The same year she finished her OT Ch. and was also a member of the T.N.T. Scent Hurdle Team. Teresa reports that Amity loves the scent hurdle work and barks continually until it is her turn.

Amity is an eager, willing and consistent obedience dog. She has always been a quick learner and easy to train. She is a happy worker, who, like a lot of Kees, has lost many points for barking! At ten years of age, Amity is now retired and happily living out her life as Teresa's pampered lap dog.

The Keeshond Club of America has instituted a system under which the accomplishments of Keeshonds in the show and obedience rings can be recognized. The Hall of Fame (HOF) for obedience achievers requires that a dog accumulate 100 points through placements in Utility and Open B classes in the United States. The award of an American OT Ch. would also automatically merit HOF status. Dogs must have their UD and one-half of the points must be earned at all breed shows (see Chapter 16 for a listing of HOF dogs).

Anne Brown Lyons acquired Brown's Little Jenny Sunshine, UD, HOF as a three-month-old puppy. Jenny was a natural in obedience from the start. Her obedience career spanned five years, during which she earned 61 qualifying scores ranging from 190½ to 199, averaging 196. Of these, 41 were placements, including 18 first and ten Highs in Trial.

Anne and Jenny proved that it is possible to show a dog in both obedience and conformation concurrently. In May 1978 Jenny won her Open A class and went on to win a run-off for her third High in Trial in between being groomed and rushed into the conformation ring to win WB and BOS.

In 1979 she was bred to Int. Ch. Ruttkay Echo Von Rhinegold, CDX, another top achiever in both show rings. Anne kept a bitch puppy and Ch. KentucKees Sarong, CDX, followed in the tradition of her sire and dam.

One of Anne's proudest moments occurred at the Keeshond Club of America Specialty in 1980. Jenny earned her first leg in Utility to give her a High-Combined of 397, a score that has not since been equaled at the national specialty. Now retired, she remains a much loved and treasured companion.

Another top achiever in both shows rings is Ch. Broadacre Aliesje V. Marjan, UD, HOF. When Jane Chambers first saw her at the age of two weeks, she was sure this was the puppy for her. Jane began training both herself and her new dog when Leesha was three months old.

At her first obedience trial, Leesha bounced her way to her first leg and a third place. She went on to earn her CD handily and in 1981 was rated No. 1 Obedience Keeshond (Delaney System) and No. 9 (Keezette System). All this followed just 12 weeks of training. In 1982 Jane and Leesha completed the CDX within six months with scores in the 190s. She ended 1982 as No. 2 Obedience Keeshond (Shuman System).

Leesha has always been a spirited and speedy worker. Jane tells of one show where Leesha came so fast on the drop on recall that when she commanded "Down," Leesha dropped so quickly that her body slid and rolled half-way down the mat. By the time she stopped rolling, she was at Jane's feet. The judge was amused but couldn't decide how to score the performance since there is nothing in the rule book about a dog that drops and slides!

Leesha was shown in 14 shows in 1983; she obtained her UD in six. Then Jane and Leesha turned their attention to the conformation ring. Handled by Carol Aubut, Leesha was WB/BOW at the 1984 Heritage Trail Keeshond Club Specialty. Back with Jane, she entered the obedience ring and walked away with High in Trial as well. She finished her championship in August 1984. In 1985 Leesha completed the requirements for her Hall of Fame designation. Jane is happy with Leesha's success and the joy she shows in her work.

Ch. Broadacre Aliesje V. Marjan, UD, HOF, owned by Jane Chambers, excels in both the conformation and obedience rings.

Tyler's Misty Joy, UD, HOF, and Ch. Casa Julday Ima Keesh Tou, CDX, both top obedience performers on the West Coast, are shown with their owner/handler Rondi Tyler.

Rondi Tyler came from a farm in Norway, so being around animals was a way of life for her. She and her husband, Carl, obtained their first Keeshond in 1977 and she went on to become Tyler's Misty Joy, UD, HOF. In 1977 she received her CD with placements of one first, one second and one fourth. In 1979 she received her CDX with two second placements and a third. Her UD was added on July 18, 1981, with a first and second placement. Misty had several Highs in Trial and was widely known for her performances. She received her Hall of Fame designation in 1982 when she as also honored as KCA Top Obedience Keeshond for 1981.

As of 1982, acording to Rondi's records, Misty held the record of defeating 119 dogs, the most for any Kees in one obedience trial.

In 1977 Carl and Rondi contacted breeder Julia Dayringer and purchased a bitch. Ch. Casa Julday Ima Keesh Tou, CDX, finished her championship in three months. Keesha proved that she had brains as well as beauty and finished her CDX in 1982 with five scores from 191 to 197, including two first places, two seconds and a fourth.

Showing two obedience dogs was a challenge for Rondi and it all came to a head at the Cabrillo Kennel Club Show in 1980. Both Misty and Keesha tied for High in Trial. A run-off proved difficult with two dogs and one handler, but Carl agreed to take Misty in. Both dogs did well, but Misty missed Rondi and Keesha took home the HIT.

David Boruff's association with Keeshonds began in 1980 when he came upon a photo of Ch. Ruttkay Roem. This led to his contacting Virginia Ruttkay and spending two days absorbing all that Virginia told him of the breed. At the end of the visit, Ruttkay-Valiant Neeko, Am. and Can. CDX, went home with David to Tennessee.

Surprisingly, upon leaving the Ruttkay kennel, all of Neeko's bravado left him. Despite David's efforts, he remained a shy and fearful puppy. Finally deciding that Neeko needed confidence, David began training him in obedience in 1982. In 1983 David won a week-long scholarship to the Volhard Training Camp; he returned home inspired and found an excellent trainer in Max Parris.

Neeko began obedience competition in 1983 and by year's end he was No. 8 under the Keezette System. In 1984, after finishing his CDX title with a Dog World Award, Neeko concluded his 12-show Open A career never failing to qualify or place.

During 1984, Neeko qualified 30 out of 39 times, 22 of which resulted in at least a class placement. He ended the year as Keezette's No. 1 American obedience dog and Canada's No. 2. He was also honored by the Canadian Kennel Club as the No. 7 ranked Non-Sporting obedience dog in Canada.

Neeko has always loved specialties and does some of his best work there. At the Golden Anniversary Specialty of the Keeshond Club of America in 1985, he earned a truly remarkable 199½ to become the Highest

Ruttkay-Valiant Neeko, Am. and Can. CDX, is owned and trained by David Boruff. This team took the HIT honors with a score of 199½ at the KCA Golden Anniversary Specialty in 1985.

Hi Struttin Banner Girl, CDX, is the winner of 15 Highs in Trial. She is owned and handled by Barbara Bagwell.

Scoring Keeshond of the Specialty. David says, "Neeko is not as consistent a worker as I would like but his tail-wagging enthusiasm, animation and showmanship make him an unforgettably eye-pleasing obedience dog." He takes a great deal of pride in his work, his devotion to David is readily apparent and his crowd-pleasing attitude lends glowing testimony to how well a dog can be trained with a minimum of force and a maximum of love.

Barbara Bagwell bought Hi Struttin Banner Girl, CDX, in 1974. Fanci was precocious right from the start and was already heeling on a show lead by the tender age of four months. She was shown in obedience for the first time at the age of eight months and won her first High in Match. In 1975 she received her CD and CDX in a matter of six months, receiving a Dog World Award in both Novice and Open.

Fanci was high Keeshond in the Delaney System for 1975 through 1979. She was No. 1 in the Keezette System in 1979 and 1982. In her career she scored 199½ twice, 199 five times and had 14 198½s to her credit. She won HIT 15 times, 14 of which were at all-breed trials. In 1979 Fanci went HIT at the large KCA National Specialty and retired the William G. Radell Memorial Trophy for top achievement in the obedience ring.

Fanci was trained for Utility but the development of a cataract ended her career. She is now enjoying her retirement as Barb's special friend.

One remarkable little puppy made a dream come true for her breeder, Julia Dayringer. Ch. Julday Wanderlust De Sylvia, UD, is one of the youngest Keeshonds ever to achieve a CD — at six months and 21 days of age, simultaneously winning a Dog World Award. She finished her CDX by the age of ten months and 19 days, and her Utility degree at 16 months and 27 days.

Lustie's show record for all her degrees averaged 197 for the 28 times she was shown. Out of Lustie's litter of seven (Ch. Ruttkay Go Man Go, CD, ex Ch. K.C.'s Holland Dutchess), three were to become Champion/Utility Dogs and still another obtained her CD.

But Lustie had beauty as well as brains and made her debut on April 15, 1962 in the breed ring. She went BOW and BOS; and then went into the Utility ring to take a 198. According to Mrs. Dayringer, "Lustie was always very anxious to go to a show . . . conformation and obedience worked great for us because she loved both."

Imagine a dog who at six months of age graduated first in her Novice obedience class, who at nine months of age had her Companion Dog degree. Within 18 months she could boast of a Utility degree as well as Mexican obedience and championship titles. This was Mex. Ch. Tasha Van Konig, Am. and Mex. UD, HOF, owned by Paul Salerno and Linda Salerno Weiss of California. Tasha accumulated all these distinctions in style. She received one perfect 200 score, numerous 199+ scores, and had countless placements in all her classes. She was awarded two specialty and one all-

Mex. Ch. Tasha Van Konig, Mex. and Am. UD, HOF, owned by Paul Salerno and Linda Salerno Weiss, received one perfect 200 and numerous 199+ scores in her very successful career.

Can. OT Ch. Milmar's Center of Attention, UD (sitting) and Jake's Mistake of Misazar, Am. and Can. CDX (lying down) are both high-scoring obedience performers. They are owned and shown by Joy Pool of Indiana. (Whitfield)

254

Misazar's Attention Seeker, UD, Can. CD, HOF, sails over the jump.
Bred owned and handled by Joy Pool, Mindy is a multiple HIT winner.

Can. OT Ch., U-CD Thumb-
elina of Tripl-Zee, Am. UD, to
our knowledge, is the first
Keeshond to earn a CD from the
United Kennel Club. Her proud
owners/trainers/handlers are
Bob and Zona Munro of Ohio.

255

breed Highs in Trial. For eight years, between 1975 and 1982, she was in the top ten Keeshonds in obedience, and she was ranked No. 1 for three years. In 1976 and 1977 she rated in the top 20 of all breeds in the United States, using the Shuman System. Because of these achievements, she was inducted into the Keeshond Hall of Fame.

Now you would expect a dog who has over 50 obedience placements to be well-behaved, but, according to Linda, Tasha has no manners at all. "She jumps out of motorhome windows upon arrival at dog shows, has stolen more food than most people eat in their lifetimes and no fence is too tall for her to climb nor too strong to eat through." Despite her delightful "bad manners," Paul and Linda remember with pride Tasha's ability to show everyone what a Kees could do in obedience.

Joy Willding Pool began training dogs in 1965 with her Toy Poodle. She became hooked and in 1973 bought her first Keeshond. Can. OT Ch. Milmar's Center of Attention, UD (Ch. Milmar's Flying Dutchman ex Ch. Car-Le-On's Precious Miss Priss, bred by Marilyn Miller) began her show career in 1975. That same year "Gretchen" received her CD with an average score of 196. In 1976 she received her CDX with an average score of 197½ and also her Canadian CD. She rounded off her Canadian experiences in 1977 with HIT and her CDX. In 1978 she earned her Utility Degree in the United States, with an average score of 192.

Gretchen was inducted into the Hall of Fame in 1981. She was officially retired that same year with 86 points toward her American OT Ch. She did make one further obedience appearance in 1982 and went home with first in her Veterans class with a score of 198.

In 1976 Gretchen was bred to Milmar's Matador of Karasar and Joy kept one of her puppies. Jake's Mistake of Misazar, Am. and Can. CDX, earned her Canadian CD in 1977. She earned her American CD in 1978 by qualifying each of the 11 times she was shown with an average score of 195.

"Misty" completed her American and Canadian CDXs in 1980. Shown only seven times, she received qualifying scores five times with an average of nearly 196. She also was awarded a Canadian HIT. Shown in Open in 1981, her average score was 195. She was No. 2 under the Shuman System and No. 1 in Keezette. She was retired at the end of 1981.

In 1980, Misty was bred to Ch. Graywyn's Hot Shot. Again, Joy kept a bitch puppy who did equally well in the obedience ring. Misazar's Attention Seeker, CDX, Can. CD received her American CD in 1982, qualifying every time, with an average Novice score of over 197½. In 1983 Mindy completed her Canadian CD and American CDX. Her average score in Open was 196; she earned two Highs in Trial and was rated No. 2 in the Keezette System.

Joy and Mindy are now training for the Utility ring. Misazar is justly proud of their three generations of obedience Keeshonds.

Pam's Keesha Dawn, UD, HOF, owned by Pam Flindt, was High Combined at the KCA National Specialty. This win was her fifth High Combined score in a very successful obedience career.

Although not receiving much attention, youngsters also excel in the obedience ring with their Keeshonds. Young Shad Hulick of Oregon is shown earning the final CD leg of Keeshof's Feathers of Hulick, and winning High Scoring Junior with a score of 193½.

TRACKING

Although not included at obedience trials, tracking is also an AKC licensed event. In addition to all the training, the actual degree involves two tests. The first test is a qualification test which you must pass before you can be certified for the degree-earning test.

The day before the test, two judges plot the track and place flags or markers at the turns. The day of the test, the track-layer walks the preplotted track and picks up all but the first two markers or flags. The dog is run on the track no sooner than a half an hour after the track-layer has laid the track, and no more than two hours after.

The dog and handler begin at the first flag. The dog must pick up the track-layer's scent and follow the track. The dog is worked on a harness and long lead and the handler must be no closer than 20 feet from his dog. The test ends when the dog either picks up or designates the glove at the end of the track. He can run the entire track successfully but if he fails to retrieve or indicate the glove, he has failed the test. You must pass the actual test only once to be awarded the degree. These tests are not given frequently and only ten dogs can compete in a given day.

Keeshonds are not generally known as "trackers" but several of the breed have attained the title of Tracking Dog (TD). As far as we know, there is only one Tracking Dog Excellent (TDX) Keeshond, and only two Utility Dog Tracking (UDT) Keeshonds. One of the UDT Keeshonds, and the only one still living, is Ch. Thomas' Tiki Puf of Van Florik, UDT, owned, trained and handled by Pat and Hank Thomas of Michigan

But Hank and Pat went one step further with their tracking. In March 1983 Pat and Ronson's Thomas' Tamara To Love, CD set out to achieve a real first: a Keeshond with a TDX degree. Tammie seemed to be a natural for tracking and easily earned her TD in 1981 at the age of only six months. For two years, Pat and Tammie trained for the coveted TDX in all kinds of weather and across all kinds of obstacles.

The day of their test was perfect: a fine, rainy mist with slightly warm temperatures, just what was needed to hold the scent to the ground. The test went well until they arrived at an old basement excavation that was about nine-feet deep. Tammie had no trouble with the pit; Pat was terrified. But Tammie had the situation well in hand; she braced herself so that Pat could literally pull herself out of the pit. It was a great example of the teamwork that earned them the coveted TDX — the first of the breed to do so.

As you have seen, there is no limit to the intelligence or ability of the Keeshond. Our obedience Keeshonds and their owners and trainers have done much to promote the breed and we encourage everyone to at least give obedience a try. You can *buy* a beautiful champion, but it takes special chemistry to create a beautifully working obedience Keeshond.

Although not included at obedience trials, tracking is also an AKC event. More and more Keeshonds and their owners are discovering the joy of tracking. Here Ch. Ronson's Thomas Hot Toddy, TD, is leaning well into his harness to track.

Ronson's Thomas' Tamara To Love, CD, TDX, owned by Pat and Hank Thomas of Michigan, is the breed's only TDX dog.

14

Breeding Your
Keeshond

WHEN YOU BRING your Keeshond puppy home, you
may have no plans for a litter of your own. But do not be surprised when
your enthusiasm and that of your friends makes you rethink the idea of
having a litter of puppies. The breed's history shows that the greatest
number of Keeshond breeders started out as pet owners. And it should be
noted that many of them also learned the hard way that breeding dogs is not
something to be undertaken lightly.

To raise Keeshond puppies can be a wonderful experience, but there is
far more involved than just having a boxful of puppies to admire and play
with. It is *not* all fun and games. There is the search for the stud dog, the
expense of the stud service and the travel problems associated with getting
your bitch there. Then there is the whelping process. If all goes well, it is a
joyful and miraculous event. But if something goes wrong, it can be a horror
that you will never forget — a horror that could kill your beloved pet.

After the puppies are born, there is the care — the feeding, weaning,
constant clean-up, worming, inoculations, veterinary bills and increased
feed bills. And let's not even talk about the heart-wrenching moment when
those adorable puppies go to their new homes! In short, breeding takes
much time, knowledge and expense and should not be done lightly and
without a great deal of thought and advice.

BREEDERS' RESPONSIBILITIES

There is only one acceptable motivation for breeding a litter of
Keeshond puppies: A desire to improve the breed. If you are planning to
breed your bitch because (1) it would be educational for the children, (2) it

would be good for the bitch, (3) all my friends want her puppies or (4) to make money — you are making a dreadful mistake . . . a mistake that can possibly hurt your dog and most definitely can hurt the breed as a whole.

Whelping puppies is a messy, sometimes terrifying, sometimes miraculous project. It is *not* something for a small child to witness. Things do not always go well in a whelping; puppies could be born dead or malformed. These are things that could frighten an adult, let alone a child!

So, if your rationale for breeding is to do something for your children, we suggest you find another educational outlet.

If you are planning to have a litter "for your bitch," we also recommend you rethink your position. Not all Keeshond bitches are perfect mothers. The dog we chose as our brood bitch was first a show dog. She absolutely loved the ring. When we decided to breed her, we thought she would take to the whelping box as well. She hated it. She was bred only once. The whelping altered her hormonal makeup and essentially ruined a very lovely show bitch. So, if you are doing the breeding for your bitch, think again.

Although the Keeshond is much admired, it is not a truly popular breed — and we like it that way! It always seems when we have puppies, no one wants one; when we don't, *everyone* wants one. If you breed a litter you must be prepared to keep every puppy if you are unable to find suitable homes for them. This can be a real shock if the litter turns out to be 12 or 13 adorable little fur-balls — fur-balls that grow up into dogs that can eat you out of house and home.

For some reason the uninitiated seem to think breeders make a lot of money breeding puppies. It just doesn't work that way. When you add up all the expenses required for proper care (let alone the man-hours involved), you barely recover what you have spent. If the litter happens to be small (one or two),you could end up losing a great deal — especially if your stud fee was a large one.

The word *breeder* technically applies to the owner or lessee of the dam of a litter at the time the mating took place. But the breeder is not the only one responsible for the litter. The owner of the stud dog shares equal responsibility for the production of puppies and should apply controls accordingly. Dogs of either sex that have improper temperament or are of poor quality should definitely *not* be bred; nor should owners of good-quality dogs allow them to be used at stud to inferior bitches. If you are in doubt about the quality of your dog or bitch, contact a local breeder and ask his or her opinion; do not rely on the well-intentioned but uninformed advice of your friends.

To get down off the soapbox, the real message is: Breed only if you are ready to accept the responsibilities and if you have the right motive. We do not need more unwanted Keeshonds. If you have no intention of breeding or showing your Keeshond, spay/neuter it and enjoy its companionship without fear of a mismating.

Good breeders have their puppies' interests at heart, limit production in relation to the potential opportunities to properly place Kees in their particular area and use only quality dogs for their breeding program. Every breeder of even one litter also has a responsibility to the breed as a whole. Whether the effects are good or bad depends to a great extent on the quality of the puppies and the breeders' understanding of ethical breeding practices and of their responsibility to make every effort to carry out those practices. The Keeshond Club of America's Breeders Code of Ethics at the end of this chapter provides guidelines and should be used as an addendum to any stud service contract or puppy sale contract.

PLANNING A LITTER

You have established your criteria, weighed the pros and cons and decided that you want to breed a litter. In order to achieve your goal of benefitting the breed, you must use only the best bitches and studs you can find and afford. For a reasonable expectation of quality, careful selection of both parents for a litter is a necessity. Decisions as to whether or not particular dogs and bitches should be mated to each other — or used at all for breeding — require a thorough study and understanding of the Breed Standard, genetics, pedigree research and the dogs contained therein. In this chapter we will attempt to give you some basics on the breeding of your dog; however, we strongly suggest that you read as much as you can on the subject and recommend the books identified in the Appendix of this book.

AGE OF THE BITCH AND STUD DOG

If you ask six different breeders at what age a bitch should be bred or a stud dog used, you will probably get six different answers. The feeling of the authors is that no bitch should be bred before she is at least 18 months of age, and preferably two years. Motherhood is a strain and a very young and inexperienced dam can encounter problems. As far as a stud dog is concerned, we don't recommend using one under the age of two. The rationale for this is that hips are not fully developed until that age and to receive an Orthopedic Foundation for Animals (OFA) rating against hip dysplasia, the dog must be two years of age.

From a strictly practical sense, the progeny of an accomplished show dog and show bitch will be more in demand than those of an unproven sire and dam. This timeframe allows for a show career before parenthood.

IMPORTANCE OF GENETIC KNOWLEDGE

When breeding dogs, we are dealing with nature's hereditary laws. In your quest to breed a better Keeshond, it is essential that you have at least a basic knowledge of genetics.

The apparent conclusions reached by geneticists are that only line breeding and/or inbreeding, combined with judicious outbreeding when advisable, can genetically "fix" as inheritable dominants the chromosomes and genes that transmit correct type and temperament to subsequent generations of animals. For the same reasons, however, close breeding also fixes faults as well as good points, and can bring out in the offspring either good or bad charcteristics carried as recessive by both parents. Therefore, to linebreed mediocre or worse members of a breed or to mate any that have the same obvious, major faults would be unwise, to say the least.

Most breeders engage in *line breeding*, which is breeding to dogs within a particular bloodline (such as Wistonia, Windrift, Candray, etc.) and between animals related to one another but less closely, such as first cousins, grandsire to granddaughter, uncle to niece, etc. *Inbreeding*, which should be done sparingly and only after careful research, is essentially breeding close family members, such as father to daughter, mother to son, brother to sister, etc. It must be done with extreme care and a complete knowledge of the bloodline. *Outbreeding* (breeding to another completely different bloodline) can be a constructive factor at times, but haphazard or continuous outcrossing accomplishes little or nothing of enduring value for breeders or the breed as it does not establish an actual line.

The subject of genetics is very interesting and much has been written on it. Space does not permit us to go into great detail on genetics but we do suggest you read further on the subject. Reference materials are included in the Appendix.

SELECTION OF THE STUD DOG

There are three considerations by which to evaluate the merits of a stud dog: his outstanding excellence as an individual, his pedigree and the family from which he derived, and the excellence or inferiority of the progeny he is known to have produced.

The possibility of fault offset is as important as the pedigrees on which you are breeding. If your bitch does not have particularly good color definition, it would be in your best interest to breed to a stud dog who not only displays clear color but whose ancestors (and, if he has them, progeny) carry the gene for correct color. His strengths may offset the bitch's faults. The same is true for a bitch with round, light eyes; she should be bred only to a dog who has and throws a true dark almond eye.

Not only is it essential to consider the fault offset in the parents, but also to have a knowledge of the faults and attributes of *their* parents and grandparents. If your bitch is large, she should be bred into a line that consistently produces standard-size progeny. Likewise, a lovely dog with strong, straight rear movement could probably compensate for a bitch who is narrow in the rear. You will not achieve total improvement in just one litter. Each litter is an experiment; hopefully, it is an experiment yielding better and better results.

You must begin your search for a stud dog quite early so that you have sufficient time to contact breeders and assimilate data. Once you have done your homework and reached a decision, it is time to contact the owner of the stud dog. Again, this must be done well in advance of your bitch's season in order to give the stud dog owner time to research your bitch's background. The stud dog owner should ask to see your bitch, if the stud you select is in your locale; if not, the stud dog owner may ask for photographs, pedigree, description and, quite possibly in today's electronic age, a videotape. You, in turn, should ask for the same things. In addition, both your bitch and the stud dog must have been x-rayed for hip dysplasia; OFA certification is advisable but not mandatory for most breeders. Prior to the breeding each dog should also be palpated for slipping stifles and have had a brucellosis blood test. Brucellosis is a virus that is transmitted by sexual contact, similar to venereal disease; there is no known cure and it can be fatal.

Stud service contracts vary from breeder to breeder and you can expect some of them to be very strict. Conscientious stud dog owners want to protect the good name of their dog and the purity of the breed as well. Our stud dog contract requires that all puppies be sold on a contract of sale that is acceptable to us, and that we be informed of buyers' names and addresses. Stud dog owners are also responsible for the birth of progeny and they should take their responsibility seriously.

Stud fees also vary widely, depending on the stud's record as a show dog and producer. Some stud dog owners prefer to reserve a puppy in lieu of a monetary fee. This works out quite well because you assume the puppy will be in a good home and you don't have a fee to worry about up front. One word of warning on stud contracts: Be sure that the contract is specific about rebreedings and one-puppy or no-puppy litters. If not specifically handled, this can cause problems later.

MATING

The owner of the stud dog should be informed as soon as the bitch comes into season, and arrangements must be made for shipping or delivering her to the stud dog. If you have chosen a stud dog out of your general area, you are faced with the trauma of shipping your beloved pet. Take the same precautions you used when you prepared for her arrival: proper crate, travel arrangements made in advance, etc. A card detailing the bitch's condition should be attached to her crate so that airline personnel take special precautions for her security.

The only time the bitch may become pregnant is during her period of oestruation, what we refer to as her "heat" or "season." A bitch's first season usually occurs when she is between six and nine months of age, with the average age being eight months. In rare instances it may come as early as five months or as late as 13 months of age. After the first season, oestrus usually recurs at intervals of approximately six months. The bitch's cycle may be influenced by factors such as change of climate or environment.

Bitches have been known to come in season, be shipped to the stud dog and immediately go out of season again. Needless to say, this is frustrating to all concerned.

Usually a bitch's season will last approximately three weeks. Prior to the beginning of her season, the bitch may become more restless, affectionate or sexually aggressive. The bitches in our household begin riding each other *and* the males! Often there is increased frequency of urination and the bitch may be inclined to lick herself more frequently. Watch for these signs and the first tell-tale spot of blood since the bitch must be confined and protected from this point on.

The first physical sign of oestrus is a bloody discharge of watery consistency. The vulva becomes congested, enlarged and reddened and the external parts become puffy and swollen. The color of the discharge gradually deepens to a rich red color, then gradually lightens so that by the tenth to twelfth day it is only slightly reddish or straw-colored. During the next day or so it becomes almost clear. During the this same period, the swelling and hardness of the external parts subside and by the tenth or twelfth day they are softened and spongy. It is at this time that ovulation takes place and the bitch can be bred.

If you do not plan to breed your bitch at this time, you must take exceptional care during these few days to make sure that she doesn't escape and get bred by another of your dogs or some vagrant in the neighborhood. Bitches are terrible flirts and are at their best (or worst!) during these few days. If there are other males in your neighborhood, you might find them outside your door, so be extremely careful until you are certain her season is over. Some bitches have been successfully bred on days 20 to 25 of their season, so extreme caution is the byword.

If you plan to breed your bitch, great care must also be exercised in determining when to introduce your bitch to her new mate. A wise breeder will keep a daily record of the changes in the bitch's condition and will arrange to introduce the two dogs when the discharge has lightened and the external parts are softened. A quick trip to the veterinarian for a vaginal smear is definitely recommended. By looking at the blood cells microscopically, a good veterinarian can tell you almost to the minute when your bitch will be ready to be bred.

If you are the stud dog owner, you need to take extreme care when the bitch arrives for breeding. If you have other dogs, you must ensure that she is kept away from them. You are now responsible for her care and protection. Remember as well that she is someone's pet, that she is away from her owners perhaps for the first time and is frightened, so treat her as you would your own dogs.

When the signs are correct for introducing the two dogs, it is vitally important that you be there. Do not just throw the dog and bitch into a room and ignore them. Both dogs are emotionally upset and, instead of a mating, you could have a fight on your hands. Encourage them to get acquainted. Bitches usually will flirt with their new mates and a good stud dog is very gentle and solicitous of her advances. If the bitch refuses the advances of the dog, or the dog is not interested in her, it is preferable to separate the two, wait a day and then permit the dog to approach the bitch. Patience is important.

When we supervise a mating, once the dog has mounted the bitch, one of us holds the bitch's head so that she will not turn and bite the male when penetrated. Some bitches require muzzling and we use a soft elastic bandage if this is necessary. The other of us positions himself at the stud dog's rear to assist in turning him, if required. Some stud dogs will not allow anyone to touch them; others are thankful for the help.

Male dogs have a bulb on the penis that swells after penetration of the vulva. The restricting band of the vulva "ties" the two animals together. On penetration, be prepared! Every bitch we have bred has been a screamer. This can go on for minutes or through the entire tie. If you have close neighbors, it is a good idea to warn them so they don't think you are committing murder or worse. After penetration, the male usually will turn himself over the bitch's back so that the two are now tied back to back. The tie may last for a few minutes — or as much as an hour or more. It is important that someone be there to soothe the dogs, offer them water and ensure that they do not try to separate. Forced separation can cause physical harm to both dogs. The involuntary action of the muscles in the bitch's vulva maintains the tie; when she relaxes, the tie will break.

After the tie is broken, the bitch should be crated for a half hour or so and not be allowed to relieve herself. The dog should be kept separate from other males for a period of time since he will have a distinct odor and will also be feeling more than a little macho!

It is generally recommended that a bitch be bred twice, skipping a day in between the matings. After breeding, the bitch should be confined for a week to ten days to avoid mismating with another dog.

ARTIFICIAL INSEMINATION AND FROZEN SEMEN

Should a natural mating not be possible, insemination can be accomplished artificially. Both stud dog and bitch should be taken to a veterinarian at the appropriate time for mating. The veterinarian will collect semen from the stud dog and insert it by a tube into the lower vagina of the bitch. This type of mating is usually repeated again on the third day.

Recently the American Kennel Club has recognized breedings accomplished through the use of frozen semen. AKC-licensed clinics have now been established in various areas of the United States to provide for the collection and storage of frozen semen. Semen is collected from the stud dog at any time and is stored in plastic "straws" or in pellet form. The advantage of this system is two fold: The semen of a stud dog can be used long after his death to carry on a bloodline, and it does not require the

A lovely mother an contented litter of two-week-old puppies. The independent one grew up to become Can. Ch. Paladin's My-Oh-My Passionella, owned by Jack and Madeleine Nugent.

Puppies cluster together for companionship and warmth. Don't be concerned when they twitch; it is all part of the growing process.

shipment of your bitch to the stud dog. In this case, the semen is shipped to your veterinarian and the insemination occurs locally. This is a very new practice and few clinics have been established to collect and store frozen semen. To date, while many Keeshonds have been collected, no Keeshond litters have been born as a result of frozen semen. As the technology spreds, it should become normal practice in the future.

PERIOD OF GESTATION

Now comes the hard part: the waiting. The period of gestation of the bitch (duration of pregnancy) is usually estimated at 63 days. Some puppies can be born as early as 57 days but if the puppies have not arrived by day 64, your veterinarian should definitely be consulted.

For the first five to six weeks of her pregnancy, the bitch requires no more than normal good care and unrestricted exercise. At about day 24, a good veterinarian should be able to carefully feel walnut-sized lumps on the uterus. If he can, you at least know you have been successful. If he cannot, don't be discouraged; this examination is definitely not foolproof. Do not do this palpation yourself; you could unknowingly cause injury to your bitch or her whelps.

After the fifth to sixth week, you should increase her food and limit her exercise. She should not be permitted to jump about in her latter weeks of pregnancy.

If you plan to do the whelping yourself, now is the time for you to begin gathering the birthing equipment. You will need a whelping box big enough to accommodate the bitch and her puppies. It should be high enough to keep the puppies from crawling out and have a hinged door so that she can come and go as needed. Do not force her to jump over the box because she will be heavy with milk and could seriously injure herself. You can make a whelping box or you could perhaps borrow one from another breeder. If you build one yourself, ask other breeders for instructions and suggestions. If you paint the whelping box, be sure to use a child-proof paint. Some people use a child's formed plastic swimming pool. It is easy to clean and the sloping sides prevent the dam from lying on the puppies.

The other things you should have on hand for the delivery include:

- A dozen white washcloths. These are invaluable to clean up the whelping box, massage the puppies, give them warmth, etc. After the cloths have been bleached and washed, they can be used to clean up milky mouths and dirty bottoms. Remember, puppies are messy!

- A pair of scissors (preferably blunt tip).

- Some *waxed* dental floss to tie off the umbilical cords.

- A small cardboard box with a heating pad on which to place the puppies while another is being born.

268

- A scale to weigh the puppies at birth and later on a daily basis. We use a kitchen food scale that is broken into ounces and goes up to about five pounds.

- A large supply of paper towels and newspapers.

- A trash can or bag.

You will be constantly cleaning up during the whelping process. Be careful not to use a disinfectant spray because it could be too strong for the newborn puppies; clean with plain soap and water.

Whatever you choose for your whelping box, prepare it several weeks in advance, put it in a secluded place away form other animals and children, and introduce your bitch to it. Our whelping box is placed beside our bed (since puppies always seem to come at night!) and our bitches take to it immediately.

The subject of prenatal x-raying is very controversial among breeders. We are proponents of x-raying and have done so with our litters. The x-raying must be done *after* the 55th day so as not to threaten the puppies. Although the Keeshond is generally a normal whelper, complications can arise. Our reason for x-raying the bitch is to determine the number of puppies, their position in the birth canal and the possibility of any overly large whelps necessitating a C-section. Again, this is controversial and many breeders (and veterinarians) do not recommend it.

Several days before she is due, your bitch will begin arranging the bedding in the whelping box to suit herself, tearing blankets or newspaper and nosing the parts into the corners. This is your first sign that whelping is near. At about day 60 we begin taking the bitch's temperature in the morning and in the evening. Her normal temperature should be about 101°F. When you see a drop to 98°F or so, whelping should occur within 24 hours. Constant supervision is necessary at this time. If you work, plan on taking some vacation time. Your help may be required, especially with an inexperienced dam.

During the whelping process,, an inexperienced breeder can be confronted with situations that he or she is unable to handle. When we had our first litter, we had an experienced breeder at our sides through it all. Although not a Keeshond breeder, her knowledge, experience and reassurance were invaluable.

Prior to the actual whelping, the bitch's water will break. This may be in the form of an evacuation of water or it may actually be a sack. Shortly thereafter, she will begin having contractions. These contractions should not go on for a long period of time without giving birth. Your veterinarian's phone number should be at hand and he should be alerted in case you need help. If the contractions continue for an hour with no whelp, you should immediately contact him as she may be in trouble and require a Caesarian.

The birth of the first puppy may terrify an inexperienced bitch so be prepared to step in and help her. As the puppy arrives, the enveloping membrane must be removed as quickly as possible so that the puppy does not suffocate. Some bitches are quite adept at doing this and at severing the umbilical cord, but ours never have been. If the bitch does not immediately do so, you must tear the membrane, tie a length of dental floss very close to the puppy's belly, and then tear or cut the umbilical cord three or four inches from the puppy's belly. If the bitch severs the cord, watch to make sure she does not get it too close or keep pulling on it as this could cause a hernia on the puppy. If the bitch severs the cord, immediately pick up the puppy and tie off the cord with the dental floss.

At this point, the bitch may be more interested in eating the afterbirth than in the birth of her puppy. If she is adamant about it, allow her to eat one or two of the afterbirths. (This is not a pleasant sight so make sure anyone present has a strong stomach.) If she has a large litter and is allowed to eat all the afterbirths, she could get severe diarrhea. Between whelpings, clean the box with soap and water and put down fresh newspapers.

After the cord has been tied on the puppy, you need to ensure that all fluid is out of the lungs. In human babies, the doctor smacks the baby smartly on the bottom, which induces the baby to cry and expels the fluid from its lungs. In puppies it is much the same. You can very carefully cup the puppy in your hands and shake downward in front of you to expel the fluid. The method we use may sound cruel but is very effective. We pinch the puppy just over the shoulder blades until it yelps and fluid is expelled. This is less dangerous than swinging the puppy downward and achieves the same effect.

At this point we do our record keeping. We record the weight of the puppy, the time and circumstances of the birth (in or out of the sack, cord cut, etc.). Then we mark the puppy so we will know which one is which. Breeders have different ways of doing this. Some will use different colored pieces of yarn around the puppies' necks. This has always worried us so we paint their toenails! The first male, for instance, will have no nail polish; the second will have polish on one toenail of his front foot; the first bitch, polish on one rear toenail, etc. All these markings are written in the record book. The only drawback is that you have to keep painting the toenails until the puppies develop true distinguishing characteristics.

When you have recorded all necessary information, if the dam is not again having contractions, give the puppy back to her. A *word of caution:* When you are taking and returning the puppies to the dam, be extremely careful. She will be very worried about the puppy and can excitedly reach up and grab at it. There have been horror stories about new mothers accidentally biting off tiny limbs.

When the contractions begin again, it is wise to remove the puppies, placing them in the cardboard box on the heating pad, which you have

At about three to four weeks it is time to begin weaning the puppies. Generally, this results in more food *on* the puppies than *in* the puppies.

As the puppies grow and get steadier on their feet, we find it easier to feed from a community bowl than from individual ones.

preset on *warm* (not hot). After each birth, return at least the last puppy to her to ease her anxiety.

The puppies will arrive at intervals of a few minutes to an hour until all are delivered. It is wise to call your veterinarian if the interval is greater than an hour and you know there are more puppies or if the dam is having contractions or seems overly anxious. Often puppies will be in distress or born nearly dead. Quick action is required. Call your veterinarian immediately. One of our last litter had excess fluid in her lungs, and we worked on her for several hours before she was out of danger.

After the last puppy has been born, the dam has been cleaned up and the whelping box washed, it is a good idea to place in the box a piece of carpet big enough to fill it so that the puppies will have some traction for their nursing. We buy a section of carpet and cut several pieces since it will become soiled and is easier to replace than to clean. *Note:* Some carpeting, especially the indoor/outdoor variety, has been chemically treated. Be sure that anything you use near the puppies has not been treated since chemicals can interact with the puppies' urine and cause chemical burns.

Return the puppies to the dam and encourage each one to suckle. You might try giving the bitch some water or milk mixed with egg yolk and honey. She may even be interested in food. If so, she definitely should be fed.

After things have settled down, it is time to take a closer look at your puppies. Hopefully, all has gone well and there are no defects or abnormalities. If, however, a puppy is badly deformed (limbs missing, cleft palate, etc.) it should be put down as quickly and with as little fuss as possible. Sometimes puppies are stillborn; early disposal is recommended.

And now you and the proud mother can sit back and admire a lovely new litter of puppies. Take advantage of the peace and quiet; it won't last long! The day following the whelping, you should bundle up the bitch and all the puppies for a trip to the veterinarian. He or she will give the dam an injection that will clean out the uterus and assist in returning it to its normal size. The veterinarian will also check the puppies to ensure that there are no cleft palates, heart defects, or other major problems that you might have overlooked and that all are healthy. Most American breeders have the dewclaws removed about two or three days after birth. This is done mostly for cosmetic reasons but safety is also a concern. Only two of our dogs have dewclaws and they are forever snagging them on shrubbery, clothing, etc.; they serve no useful function in the modern Keeshond. We suggest leaving the dam at home during this trip to the veterinarian. The cries of her babies may unnecessarily upset her. With the application of ointment, the puppies will heal in two or three days. It is a procedure we recommend.

POST-NATAL CARE

If you think your work is now done and you can just sit back and relax, you are in for a shock. True, the next couple of weeks will be relatively easy.

The puppies are very dependent on their mother and, hopefully she will be very devoted to them. If she is, all you need worry about is keeping their whelping box or pen clean, the dam well fed and cared for and the puppies weighed twice a day to ensure they are growing.

If your bitch is not a good dam or if she has a problem nursing (eclampsia, insufficient milk for a large litter, etc.), you may be required to tube-feed. Your veterinarian will guide you.

This is a miraculous time for breeders as each day you see the puppies change and grow. Don't be concerned about the puppies' twitching spasmodically. It is perfectly normal and all part of the growth process. Their little legs get sturdier, the coats begin to bloom, shoulder stripes and spectacles appear. During these first days and weeks, we handle our puppies frequently; however, we do not allow strangers or other dogs near the box as this could upset the dam. Although the puppies cannot see or hear, they do respond to touch and gain socialization and reassurance from your carresses.

At about ten-to-14 days the eyes begin to open; the ears open at about 21 days. Suddenly they are real puppies. Now the fun begins. They learn to recognize you and come waddling over, tails awag, at your approach. Keeshond puppies are definitely not quiet; I think ours were born barking! Believe me, you won't get a full night's sleep until you move them into another room.

We begin weaning our puppies at about three to four weeks of age. Every breeder has a special diet and we suggest you check with your veterinarian and other breeders for their suggestions. As a supplement to nursing, we begin weaning on raw hamburger combined with Esbilac and mixed into a thick soup. The puppies must have acquired the ability to "lap" or they will choke on their food. The first couple of feedings usually result in more food *on* the puppies than *in* them! At this point, a camera is a necessity because you can never relive these precious moments. They should still be encouraged to nurse; however, four- to five-week-old puppies have *teeth* — very sharp teeth — and the dam soon tires of being used as a pin cushion and begins to discourage their nursing.

The manner in which you feed Kees puppies also differs among breeders. We have tried separate bowls (as the puppies get a bit older and capable of eating unassisted) and we have tried a large pan that they all share. The latter seems to result in more food on their feet than in their mouths. Glady and Don Gates of Seawind Kennels in Nova Scotia may have the perfect setup. Don has made a wooden platform about five or six inches high with a hole cut in the middle. Into the hole, Glady places a pie pan so that the rim fits over the mouth of the hole. In this way, the puppies eat at shoulder height and seem to get more into their tummies and definitely less on their feet.

As the puppies mature, they quickly outgrow the whelping box and need more and more space to exercise and play. At about three to four

273

weeks we move them into an exercise pen with a hard floor. A word of caution: Do not use linoleum as it could contain poisonous chemicals and the puppies might ingest it. At one end we place newspaper; their food goes at the other end. It is amazing how quickly they learn to waddle to the newspaper to relieve themselves. We also string toys across the exercise pen just above their heads, and we tie socks to the bars of the pen. This gives them something to do and stimulates both intelligence and coordination.

EVALUATION OF POTENTIAL PUPPY BUYERS

The puppies will grow rapidly and suddenly the time will come for them to leave the nest and go to new homes and new lives. Hopefully, you will have wonderful homes ready and waiting for them (all those friends who insisted they wanted one), but if not, you will have to do some advertising. Ads in breed and all-breed publications are helpful, as are those in the local newspaper. You will need to develop a plan for evaluating potential buyers of your beautiful babies.

It is obviously best to personally meet prospective buyers. In this way you can see how they react to the puppies and let your own feelings be your guide. If this is impossible, we strongly suggest that you at least talk with them by phone. You should have a prepared list of questions for each prospective buyer. If they use another person as a reference, check it out. Let's face it; they aren't just buying a puppy. They are adopting a member of your family, one that you brought into this world and raised as your own. Not just anyone will get these puppies.

You should ask:

- "Why do you want a Keeshond?"

- "Have you seen an adult or just photos in a book or a puppy in a pet shop?" (We ask this question because all too often people fall in love with an adorable little puppy only to get disenchanted with a full grown dog with a full coat of hair.)

- "How many family members are there?" (If the people have children, we want to know their ages and who will be caring for the dog.)

- "Will the dog be left alone all day; and, if so, what arrangements will be made for the dog's exercise and comfort?"

- "Do you have a fenced-in yard? If not, how do you plan to exercise the dog?"

- "What are your specific plans for this dog?"

If they request a bitch, we would want to know why. Are they planning on breeding? If so, why? If they request a male, we ask if they are planning to use it at stud and, if so, why? We reiterate the responsibilities and expenses that go along with breeding and urge that a purely pet dog or bitch be

We string toys across the puppy pen just about head level. This gives the puppies something to occupy their time and stimulates both intelligence and coordination.

There is nothing cuter than a 7½-week-old Keeshond puppy. As a breeder, you have spent weeks loving and nurturing the puppies and only the very best homes are good enough for them. *(Marcelli)*

275

neutered or spayed. Some breeders even require this by contract.

You must be careful that the prospective buyers are not searching for puppies to begin or add to a puppy mill, or that they will not be sold to a pet shop. The use of a very strict contract of sale, with the promise that you intend to enforce it, should deter this type of individual. Inclusion of the Code of Ethics adopted by the Keeshond Club of America should be mandatory for all puppy sale contracts. We also include a clause that states that the dog cannot be sold, transferred, given or leased to another individual without prior approval of its breeder. In this way, we protect the dog (and our bloodline) from falling into irresponsible hands.

LEAVING THE NEST

According to Clarence Pfaffenberger, noted canine behaviorist, seven to eight weeks is the ideal time for a new owner to take his puppy home. However, the Breeders Code of Ethics states that no puppy may leave the breeder until it reaches the age of eight weeks. There is definite proof that puppies need their dam until they are at least seven weeks old, and the last two weeks on a part-time basis only. If there is a time when they need her more than any other, it is the fourth week, from the 21st to 28th days. To remove him from his mother for any great length of time during this week may be very bad for the puppy. By the eighth week gentle discipline can be enforced and for this reason many obedience trainers prefer to take their puppies home between seven and eight weeks of age.

According to Mr. Pfaffenberger, the period of 21 to 28 days is so strange to the puppy that at no other time in a puppy's life can he become so emotionally upset, nor could such an upset have such a lasting effect upon his social attitudes. By the 28th day, the learning stage has become established and the puppy is emotionally stabilized to where he can be taught simple things. If a puppy is taken away from its mother and littermates before the end of seven weeks, it can miss some of their canine socialization and show less interest in dog activities than if it is left for the full seven weeks. Mr. Pfaffenenberger has found that some dogs taken away from their dam and littermates before seven weeks were impossible to breed because they did not relate to dogs. Knowledge of the developmental stages of dogs is important and we recommend that new breeders (and owners) read *The New Knowledge of Dog Behavior* by Clarence Pfaffenberger (Howell Book House).

The future of the Keeshond is in the hands of every breeder of every litter; it is an awesome responsibility.

276

THE KEESHOND CLUB OF AMERICA CODE OF ETHICS
A Guide for Breeders and Owners of Keeshonden

This Code of Ethics is presented as an informative guide for breeders and potential breeders of Keeshonden, whose foremost aims are the welfare and improvement of the Breed. The By-Laws of The Keeshond Club of America, Inc. state that the Club "shall do all in its power to protect and advance the interests of the Breed." In 1962 a Resolution was adopted "strongly disapproving the practice of selling Keeshonden to pet shops and/or other commercial dog dealers." In applying for membership, applicants "agree to further the Club's objectives and to conduct all their activities in connection with the Breed in an ethical manner."

An ethical breeder conducts his activities as follows:

Breeding: He conscientiously plans each litter based on the parents' appropriate temperament and qualities in relation to the Breed's AKC-approved official Standard, and before deciding to produce a litter, considers the possibilities of properly placing puppies he cannot keep himself.

He only uses for breeding adults which are of sound temperament; are free from congenital defects such as hereditary orchidism (i.e., males whose testicles are not both normally descended), blindness, deafness, etc. and those whose hips have been x-rayed with proper positioning and pronounced normal by a veterinarian personally qualified in the field of hip dysplasia.

He only breeds healthy mature bitches (preferably after one year old and after the first season); allows proper spacing between litters; urges bitch purchasers to spay those which for any reason will not be used for breeding, and to properly safeguard unspayed bitches from unplanned matings.

Health: All his stock is kept under sanitary conditions; is given maximum health protection through worming and inoculations.

Registration: He registers his breeding stock with the American Kennel Cub, and keeps accurate records of matings and pedigrees.

Sales: He does *not* sell or consign puppies or adults to pet shops or other commercial dealers.

He sells Keeshonden, permits stud service, and leases studs or bitches *only* to individuals who give satisfactory evidence they will give them proper care and attention, and are in accord with this Code of Ethics. He makes available to the novice the benefit of his advice and experience.

All stock leaving his possession is at least eight weeks old. He provides buyers with written details on feeding; general care; date of worming and inoculations against distemper, hepatitis, leptospirosis, etc.; and the Keeshond's four-generation pedigree. He provides and requires written agreements signed by all parties to all sales and other transactions, and accordingly completes and delivers the forms necessary for registration. *NOTE:* Under American Kennel Club rules (Chapter 3,

Section 6) — *all* such forms *must be completed and supplied* by all parties to transactions, unless they have agreed otherwise in *written, signed agreements.*

All his advertising is factual. It does not offer Keeshonden at less than the minimum price, nor is it so worded so as to attract undesirable buyers, or to encourage raising Keeshonden merely as a money-making scheme.

He does not supply Keeshonden for raffles, "give-away" prizes or other such projects.

Price: By setting a reasonable price for his young puppies, the breeder upholds the value of the Breed and of his own stock. He gives his adults and puppies first-class care and cannot afford to sell at a low price.

When confronted by a situation not covered by this Code of Ethics he conducts himself as he would like to be treated under similar circumstances.

15

Showing Your Keeshond

W E HAVE RECOMMENDED that you purchase the best Keeshond possible, even if only for your family pet. As your young dog begins to mature, he draws admiring glances and maybe some comments about his "show potential." *You* feel he is the perfect dog; should you consider showing him? Before you make that decision, you should know a little about the sport of showing dogs.

The underlying purpose of exhibiting your dog at a dog show is to receive the opinions of knowledgeable judges as to the dog's quality for breeding potential. Conformation means how closely your dog conforms to the Standard for the breed. But there is much more to it than that. Showing your dog at matches and shows can open up a whole new world of pleasure, gain you many new friends and establish a closer relationship between you and your Keeshond. As you gain knowledge you should be able to recognize the good points in other people's dogs and the faults in your own. You must learn to be a graceful winner and a cheerful loser because you will definitely lose more than you win.

Let's talk basics for a moment. What *is* a dog show? There are several different types of dog shows and even categories within a show. The sport of dogs is generally broken down into four main categories: conformation, obedience, field trials and tracking.

Most exhibitors (and puppies) gain their experience in conformation and obedience by attending matches. These are held by all-breed and specialty (single breed) clubs and provide excellent training grounds for novice handlers and their dogs. Generally, puppies must be at least two months old, but adult dogs of any age can be shown. These matches are

Ch. Curaçao Chimichanga, owned by John D. Van Kleeck and Jimmy Kranz, is a Best in Show Dog.

Ch. Cedarcrest's Quarterback, bred by Carolyn Reinders and Debbie Dorony-Lynch, was BIS at the Kokomo Kennel Club Show on May 10, 1986. He is owned by Carolyn Reinders of Ohio.

open to the general public and can be entered the day of the show. Match shows are informal affairs where the ring and judging procedures are similar to those at regular AKC all-breed point shows. However, no points are offered toward a championship title. Matches offer an excellent opportunity to observe all breeds of dogs, meet breeders (matches are also an excellent source of contact when looking for a new puppy since many breeders bring their litters with them to show) and determine if the sport of dogs is for you. Most matches offer classes for both conformation and obedience.

Point shows are those at which championship points are awarded. To compete in them entries must be made several weeks in advance on official AKC entry forms. Dogs must be at least six months of age; to compete in conformation classes, dogs must not have been neutered or spayed. Altered dogs are permitted to be shown in obedience. A bitch that is is season is not permitted to be shown in obedience; she can be shown in conformation, but common courtesy requires that she be kept away from other dogs until it is time to enter the ring.

Field trials are also AKC-regulated events. Since Keeshonds are not sporting dogs, we have never heard of one competing in this type of event. The setters, retrievers and spaniels excel in field work.

Tracking is an extension of obedience work but tracking tests are not conducted at regular AKC shows; rather, there are special tracking events held periodically to test the tracking skills of dogs — including Keeshonds. (See Chapter 13 for further details on tracking Keeshonds.)

CHAMPIONSHIP TITLES

To become a Champion of Record, the American Kennel Club requires that a dog or bitch win a total of 15 points under at least three different judges, and those points must include wins of three points or more in at least two shows (called "major" wins) under different judges.

Championship points are awarded only to the Winners Dog (WD) and Winners Bitch (WB). In other words, the dog and bitch judged best of the nonchampions in its breed wins the points at each show. The number of ponts acquired depends on the number of entries present over which the dog and bitch win their respective Winners Class, which is comprised of the first-place winners from each of the five or six classes for each sex. These classes are: Puppy (sometimes split into two classes by age), Novice, Bred by Exhibitor, American-Bred and Open. A balancing of points can be achieved when one of the two dogs is chosen Best of Winners. In other words, if there are two points in males and three points in bitches, and the male is chosen Best of Winners (BOW), he will receive the three points since he defeated the Winners Bitch. Still other points can be won by winning Best of Breed or Best of Opposite Sex over dogs already titled as champions.

Just to confuse things even more, Reserve Winners Dog and Reserve Winners Bitch are also chosen. These are the runners-up. In the United States and Canada, there are no points associated with RWD or RWB. However, should the dog awarded Winners be disqualified for some reason, the points would then go to his or her runner-up. This very rarely happens and at bigger shows the RWD and RWB is more of an honorary award.

No more than five points can be won at any one show. The requirements for one- through five-point wins vary in different breeds and geographical areas in the country. Those point schedules are annually established by the AKC and are printed in the front of all dog show catalogs.

After the WD and WB are chosen, they re-enter the ring along with the dogs and bitches who have already attained their championship (called "Specials"). From these dogs are chosen a Best of Breed (BOB), Best of Opposite Sex (BOS) to Best of Breed and a Best of Winners (best between the WD and WB). The BOB and BOS need *not* be a champion and many times a young WD or WB has triumphed over the Specials.

All during the day this activity goes on in many rings and in each breed. After all Bests of Breed are chosen, these winners go on to compete in their respective Group — Hound, Sporting, Working, Toys, Terriers, Non-Sporting (in which Keeshonds compete) and Herding. In each of these Groups, four dogs are chosen. The first place winner in each of the seven Groups then goes on to compete for the top dog of the day, the Best in Show.

At the same time all this activity is underway, obedience trials are being conducted in still other rings. (See Chapter 13 for details on these activities.)

Conduct at all obedience and conformation shows is established by the American Kennel Club under its *Rules and Regulations Applying to Registration and Dog Shows.* We recommend that you contact the AKC at 51 Madison Avenue, New York, NY 10010 for a copy.

SPECIALTY SHOWS

Specialty shows are point shows devoted to one breed only; they may or may not include an obedience trial with their conformation classes. The show is run the same through the classes; however, since there are no other breeds with which to compete, there are no Group or Best in Show competitions. However, specialty shows do offer some additional classes which are of great interest. The Keeshond Club of America conducts a Futurity Stakes at its national specialty each year. Regional specialty clubs hold sweepstakes. Other classes are offered for Stud Dog, Brood Bitch and Brace competition.

Ch. Chalice's Silver Horizon is shown taking BIS at the Kennel Club of Buffalo in July 1983. He is owned by Cindy Nary.

Junior Handler Jennifer Marx is shown with her dog after winning Best Junior Handler at the KCA National Specialty in 1985.

WHAT TO DO AND WHAT TO BUY

So you have decided that you would like to give conformation showing a try. What do you need to do? The first thing we would suggest is that both you and your dog attend conformation handling classes. Such classes usually meet once a week and are sponsored by a local all-breed club. If you are unfamiliar with all-breed clubs in your area, the American Kennel Club can give you the name of the club's secretary. We recommend these classes as they will teach you the basics and give you pointers for fine-tuning your handling performance.

Once you are familiar with ring procedures, it is time to enter your first show. At least three weeks prior to the scheduled show you need to complete the official AKC entry form and send it off (with your check) to the show superintendent. These entry forms are contained in a premium list which is sent out by the various show superintendents. To get on their mailing list can be difficult; the best way is to talk to breeders/exhibitors in your area and ask them for copies of the various premium lists. Once you determine you will be entering other shows, write to the superintendents and request that you be added to their mailing lists.

Another excellent source of advance show information is *Pure-bred Dogs — American Kennel Gazette*. Published monthly by the AKC, this magazine lists judging information, entry fees and show superintendents. It is available by subscription only from the American Kennel Club and contains not only judging information, but also articles and breed information. It is a must for all dog lovers whether they are interested in showing or not. A second magazine — *The American Kennel Club Show, Obedience and Field Trial Awards* — is a compilation of results from shows previously held by the AKC. You should order both magazines if you are seriously interested in showing your dog in conformation or obedience; to the novice dog owner, the second issue is unnecessary.

About a week before the show in which you have entered your Keeshond, you will receive from the show superintendent an identification card with your armband number, together with the judging program listing the ring number, time Kees will be judged and the breakdown of the dogs entered. The first number in the breakdown is the number of class (nonchampion) dogs; the second is the number of class bitches; and the last two numbers represent the champions, with the number of dogs first and bitches second. You need not be present at ringside until the scheduled hour to be judged, but we suggest that you spend some time before judging watching the events in the ring.

The equipment you will need to take with you should be sufficient to groom your dog and see to his needs. This will include the appropriate brushes, combs, sprays, etc. (see Chapter 11). If you are showing in conformation, you will need a show lead. In general show leads are of two types: Resco, which is a noose-type leather lead; or Martingale, which is a combination choke collar and noose. The Martingale is a good choice for a novice handler or dog because it gives a bit more control and there is less likelihood the dog will slip out of it. These can be obtained at pet supply stores or at the show.

You will also need bits of cooked liver or other tidbits to keep your dog's attention in the ring. The Keeshond is a "baited" breed and we utilize liver, squeaker toys or whatever to keep that lovely alert expression. A plastic dish and water bottle are also essential. Most shows do not provide chairs at ringside if you wish to watch the judging, so, at least for outdoor shows, it is a good idea to include a folding chair. Outside shows can also be very hot so be certain that you bring something to provide shade for your dog in his crate, exercise pen or at ringside.

AT THE SHOW

When you arrive at the show, find a parking place and purchase a catalog, the first thing we would recommend is that you locate the ring in which you will be showing. If it is reasonably near your judging time, you can pick up your armband from the steward in the ring; otherwise, you can get it just prior to judging. Exercise your dog and see to his need for water, etc. NEVER leave your dog in an unattended vehicle in warm weather, and never leave a Keeshond in the hot sun. Make sure he has plenty of shade and water.

In plenty of time prior to Keeshond judging, groom or touch up the grooming you have already done. Plan to arrive at ringside in sufficient time to watch some of the judging prior to your being called into the ring.

When your number is called, follow the steward's instructions. Listen to the judge; if you do not understand what he asks of you, do not hesitate to request clarification. Some of the judges have been doing this for so many years that they tend to forget there are novices in the ring. Basically, in the conformation ring you will be required to pose your dog for the judge's inspection. The judge will walk up to your dog, either examine the bite of the teeth himself or ask you to show it to him, run his hands over your dog and, if the dog is a male, check to ensure that both testicles are descended. He may also lift one or two of the dog's feet. Knowing this, you should begin practicing these procedures when your puppy is very young. Puppies do not like to have anyone look in their mouths, especially if they are teething. Getting a dog to accept this takes practice and patience. Remember that the judge should always have a clear view of your dog so when the judge approaches to go over your dog, move to the side so as not to inhibit the judge's examination. However, keep control of your dog and if he attempts to turn around as the judge is examining him, gently hold your dog's head.

The Keeshond is a free-stacking, baiting breed. This means that you should not have to pose your dog; he should naturally come to a stop and stand with all four feet perfectly square. Now, this takes practice so begin

After retiring from a successful Junior career, Tracee Buethner of North Dakota continued her winning in the professional ring. Tracee and her mother write the Junior column for *Keezette*.

Another very professional Junior Handler is Jamie Jacobs of California. She excels in both Junior and professional rings and is shown here with Ch. Windrift's High Society, HOF ("Snootie"),a BIS winner and 1986 KCA National Specialty BOB winner.

when he is a young puppy by showing him what you want him to do. By the time he enters the professional ring, he will be a natural showman. Gait your Kees at the judge's direction — usually in a triangle pattern. The best speed at which to gait a Keeshond is a brisk walk or slow trot. Keeshonds are not working dogs and should *not* be run around the ring. Keep one eye on the judge and the other on where you are going. Unless the judge tells you to relax your dog (which they will sometimes do in a large class or on a very hot day), do your best to keep your dog animated and posed. Generally, when you are in the ring and working your dog, you should stand directly in front of him and keep his attention with the bait, squeaker toy or whatever held about at waist or pocket level. One word of caution: Some judges do not approve of the use of bait in the ring so we suggest you train your dog to watch your hand or pocket in the anticipation of bait. With our dogs, anyone whose hand goes anywhere near his pocket is fair game. The object is to keep your dog's ears up, his expression alert and his neck arched so that he presents a pleasing picture to the judge.

If your dog wins first or second in his class, be sure to stay at ringside to go back in again when his number is called for Winners or Reserve Winners judging.

JUNIOR SHOWMANSHIP

Junior Showmanship competition is the training ground for the handlers of tomorrow. In this competition, the youngsters (instead of the dogs) are judged on their knowledge and ability to handle their dogs. Classes are generally broken down into Novice and Open classes, and further broken down by age (10-13 and 13-17) within each class. Novice classes are for those youngsters who have not won three first-place ribbons in Junior Showmanship competition. Open is for the more experienced junior.

Junior Showmanship teaches ring courtesy, handling and sportsmanship, and improves the knowledge of the sport of dogs. It is very competitive (sometimes *too* competitive) and its top handlers often go on to careers as professional handlers or judges.

Because Keeshonds are natural showdogs and do not require a lot of handling (such as removing the collar, holding up the head or tail), Keeshond handlers often have a more difficult time getting the judge's attention. But this should not discourage you; we have many successful juniors in our breed who have gone on to win the coveted Best Junior in Show award.

If your children are interested in showing, we strongly recommend that they begin with Junior Showmanship, or they might find an outlet for their interests in your local 4-H club. They will learn the fine art of handling — how to gait in various patterns, how to accentuate the dog's good qualities and overcome his bad, how to be a good sport — and they form a tight bond

287

with their dog. Most matches offer Junior Showmanship and this is the place to start. For more information on Junior Showmanship, we suggest you read *The New Complete Junior Showmanship Handbook* by Brown and Mason (Howell Book House).

Whatever type of activity you enter, keep in mind that dog shows are supposed to be fun — fun for you and fun for your dog. At the end of the day, win or lose, your dog is still your best friend. No ribbon or trophy — or the lack thereof — can change that. Tomorrow's show will have a different judge, with different opinions and probably a different outcome. Keep on trying — and enjoy!

16

Keeshond Clubs in the United States

THE KEESHOND CLUB of America (KCA), the parent club for the breed in the United States, was founded in 1935, in Chestnut Hill, Pennsylvania. An official Standard for the breed was submitted by the club and approved by the American Kennel Club in that same year; it was slightly amended in 1949 and still stands today.

The Keeshond Club of America held its first specialty in 1937 at the Ladies Kennel Association of America all-breed show in Long Island, New York. The total entry was 17.

Starting in 1962 the parent club inaugurated many programs to serve its members and the breed as a whole. A breeders Code of Ethics was created, as well as a Puppy Futurity Stakes to be held in conjunction with the national specialty each year, national trophies, etc. Over the years these activities have continued and been expanded. Members earning a championship or obedience degree on their dogs are awarded a special commemorative medal. The trophy fund has been expanded so that awards are presented each year for top achievements in the show rings and in breeding programs.

The first Futurity Stakes were held in 1965 at the Ladies Kennel Association Show with 20 entires. The Futurity Stakes are open only to KCA members or members of affiliated clubs. Litters are nominated before they are born and puppies are kept nominated until the national specialty where they are judged by a breeder/judge selected by the membership. It is a very exciting and highly competitive contest since many of the Futurity winners have gone on to become top achievers in their adult years.

During the early 1980s, the KCA instituted Select Awards to be given at the national specialty each year. The winners of Select Awards (up to ten dogs) are Keeshonds of exceptional merit that are chosen by the Best of Breed judge from the competitors in that class. The winners are announced at the KCA banquet that evening. The breeders of these dogs then become eligible to serve as Futurity judge at the national specialty two years hence. The final judge selection is decided by vote of the KCA membership.

In recent years, the KCA has held independent specialtes (not in conjunction with an all-breed show). These specialties are generally hosted by local breed clubs and are spread around the country from year to year. One of the larger KCA national specialties was held in Cleveland, Ohio, in 1979. These authors were show chairman and show secretary and we are proud to say the specialty was a huge success with an entry of over 400 Keeshonds, including 50 in obedience.

This record entry was broken in 1985 when the Buckeye Keeshond Club and Southeast Michigan Keeshond Club hosted the 50th Anniversary of the Keeshond Club of America. Held at the Holiday Inn in Westlake, Ohio, the festivities went on for four days and drew hundreds of exhibitors and spectators. Judging began with an A-OA match sponsored by the Buckeye Keeshond Club; the entry at this match topped most specialty shows. The judging continued the next day with the KCA national specialty which drew a total entry of 646 comprised of 437 dogs. The obedience trial alone drew 121 Keeshonds, the largest obedience entry in the history of the breed. The Futurity Stakes were made up of 49 dogs and 47 bitches, and the Veterans Sweepstakes (a first in the breed) contained 14 dogs and 13 bitches between the ages of eight and 11 years.

Show chairman for this gala event was John Sawicki of Michigan, show secretary was Carol Cash and obedience chairman was Bette Poto of Ohio. The two clubs worked hand-in-hnd to give the attendees a show that will be difficult to equal. Futurity Stakes were judged by Mrs. Jan Wilhite (Charmac Keeshonden), Veteran Sweepstakes by Mr. Christian Fedder of South Africa, dog classes by Mr. Melbourne T. L. Downing, and bitch classes, Best of Breed and the nonregular classes by Mr. Frank Oberstar. Best in Futurity was won by Yan-Kee Fantasia, bred and owned by Peter and Holly Colcord of New Hampshire; Best of Opposite Sex in Futurity went to Ashbrook's Johnny Reb, bred by Linda Moss and owned by Linda and Christy Schwartz. Best in Veterans Sweepstakes went to eight-year-old Ch. Ronson's Benji Boy of Cascadia, bred by Judy Daugherty and owned by Ronald Fulton. Best of Opposite Veteran was won by Ch. Candray Cotillion, ten years young, bred and owned by George Wanamaker. The highlight of the day came when the Veterans Sweepstakes trophy was presented by Mrs. Eloise Geiger of Mar-I-Ben Keeshonden. A real veteran of the show ring herself, Eloise had been felled by a stroke and her presence at the show was cause for added celebration.

Ch. Ruttkay Commander, HOF, owned by Mrs. Thomas J. Hancock of Ohio and handled by Jeanne Buente-Young, is shown taking BOB at the 1980 Heart of America Keeshond Club Specialty.

Joanne Reed proudly displays the Keezette trophy for breeder of the BOB dog at the 1982 KCA National Specialty. BOB winner was Am. and Can. Ch. Windrift's Gambler, CD, HOF, ROM.

The Winners Dog, who triumphed over 101 competitors, was Ledwell Alexander, owned by Betty Olafson of Ontario, Canada, and handled by Nancy Latthitham. Reserve Winners Dog went to Ashbrook's Hurricane, TD, bred by Linda Moss and owned by David Boruff and Linda Moss.

Winners Bitch came from the 6-9 month puppy class. Kameo's First Impression, bred and owned by Kaylene Vasquez, triumphed over 109 bitch competitors and then went on to Best of Winners.

But the big story of the day was the Best of Breed competition and this was won by Ch. Dal-Kees Mighty Samson, bred by Ann Lowell and Carol Aubut and owned and handled by Jan Wanamaker. Best of Opposite Sex went to the lovely Ch. Yan-Kee Starkist, bred, owned and handled by Peter Colcord. This was the second time this dynamic duo had taken the top honors; they were also BOB and BOS at the KCA National in 1984.

The huge obedience trial, judged by Miss Irma Dixon and Ms. Virginia Powell, included a new category for the breed: team competition. Four teams, representing Colorado, Ohio, Oklahoma and Pennsylvania, competed. The Colorado team, resplendent in their Dutch Boy costumes, took home the trophy. But the big winner of the day was the High in Trial dog. David Boruff's Ruttkay-Valiant Neeko, CDX, triumphed with a nearly flawless score of 199½ from the Open B class. Mutual love and devotion were apparent in the performance of this pair.

The Golden Anniversary show also featured Junior Showmanship, which was judged by Mrs. Peggy Rettig. Winner of this competition was Jennifer Marx.

The following list identifies the winners of Best of Breed (BOB), Best of Opposite Sex (BOS), Best of Winners (BOW), Winners Dog (WD), Winners Bitch (WB), Best in Futurity (BIF) Best of Opposite Sex in Futurity (BOSIF) and High in Trial (HIT) at KCA National Specialties from 1974 through 1986:

1974
BOB — Ch. Star-Kees Dingbat
BOS — Ch. LeJean's Utsi
WD/BOW — Star-Kees Caped Crusader
WB — Winsome's Silver Dawn
BIF — Star-Kees Ego Trip
BOSIF — Grayfalls Meisje
HIT — Mister Bojangles

1975
BOB — Ch. Maverick Son of Ilka
BOS — Ch. Jomito Krossandra
WD/BOW — Crispy Schultz of Holloridge
WB — Julday Honeycomb Junee
BIF — Shady Hill's Facile Feller
BOSIF — Cai-Lin Royal Imp V. Candray

Ch. Yan-Kee Starkist, HOF, is shown with her breeder/owner/handler Peter Colcord winning BOB at the 1985 HTKC Specialty. The judge is Dr. Samuel Draper; presenter is Lucy Buckley.

Sweepstakes Judge Ron Cash is shown presenting BOS in Sweepstakes to Traveler's Fairville Kameo, owned by Jean and Tom Toombs, at the 1985 KCDV Specialty. Presenter is Barbara Eng.

1976
BOB — Ch. Windrift's Midnite Love
BOS — Ch. Kee Note's By Birdie of Dankee
WD — Odin of Fairville
WB/BOW — Shadowood's Xaviera V. Jee Jac
BIF — Kee Note's the Entertainer
BOSIF — Rokerig's Raquelsey

1977
BOB — Ch. Star-Kees Dingbat
BOS — Ch. Traveler's Swirling Silver
WD/BOW — Coincidence of Cari-On
WB — Wistonia Wyndixie
BIF — Winsome's Tigger Too
BOSIF — Windrift's Cover Girl
HIT — Lobo of the Villa's

1978
BOB — Ch. Rich-Bob's Stormy Weather
BOS — Ch. Shamrock Peg O'My Heart
WD/BOW — Traveler's Inherit the Wind
WB — Russ-mar Fancy Pants
BIF — Fearless Filibuster
BOSIF — Keli-Kees Kandi
HIT — Ch. Charann Christmas Holli

1979
BOB — Am. and Can. Ch. LeJean's Ramrod
BOS — Ch. Zeeland's Ad Lib
WD/BOW — Paladin's Shady Hill Joshua
WB — Ann-Kees Mindy of Car-Le-On
BIF — Wysperwynd What the Dickens
BOSIF — Holland Hond's Moonflower
HIT — Hi Struttin' Banner Girl, CDX

1980
BOB — Ch. Foxfire's Artful Dodger
BOS — Ch. Traveler's Swirling Silver
WD/BOW — Charmac Scatman to Star-Kees
WB — Merith's Shady Lady
BIF — Charmac's Scatman to Star-Kees
BOSIF — Ashbrook's Kenarae Seawitch
HIT — Brown's Little Jenny Sunshine, CDX

1981
BOB — Ch. Foxfair's Persuasive Friend
BOS — Ch. Windrift's Honey Bear
WD/BOW — KeeXote's Kinderbat
WB — Cari-On Pepermint Paddy
BIF — Zureeg A.W.O.L.
BOSIF — Nordic's Viking of KeeNote
HIT·— Tyler's Misty Joy, CDX

1982

BOB — Ch. Windrift's Gambler, CD
BOS — Ch. Windrift's Love Unlimited, HOF
WD/BOW — Chalice's Silver Horizon
WB — Charmac's Fortunate Happening
BIF — Windrift's High Society
BOSIF — Cook's Pass the Buck to Bucaroo
HIT — Tyler's Misty Joy, UD
Jr. Handler — Kirstie Lytwynec

1983

BOB — Ch. Ashbrook's Sea Nymph
BOS — Ch. Jaze Shadow Dancer
WD/BOW — Yan-Kee Superstar
WB — Candray Minuet
BIF — Windrift's Spark of Wyldfyr
BOSIF — Karolina Kommander
HIT — Ruttkay Valiant Neeko

1984

BOB — Ch. Dal-Kees Mighty Samson
BOS — Ch. Yan-Kee Starkist
WD — Klompen's Tommy Tittlemouse
WB/BOW — Woffee Wild Imagination
BIF — Tanglewood Whirling Dervish
BOSIF — Cedarcrest's Quarterback
HIT — Storm Cloud's Silver Lining, CD

1985

BOB — Ch. Dalkees Mighty Samson
BOS — Ch. Yan-Kee Starkist
WD — Ledwell Alexander
WB/BOW — Kameo's First Impression
BIF — Yan-Kee Fantasia
BOSIF — Ashbrook's Johnny Reb
HIT — Ruttkay Valiant Neeko, CDX
Jr. Handler — Jennifer Marx

1986

BOB — Ch. Windrift's High Society
BOS — Ch. KeesLund's Kameo Kaper
WD/BOW — Jo-Lyn Hot Persuit O'Bonnyvale
WB — Wyndspell California Caper
BIF — Yan-Kee Neiman Marcus
BOSIF — Winsome's I've Got a Dream
HIT — Steeldust Wind Kist

The Keeshond Club of America has also instituted a system for recognizing outstanding sires and dams. When originally begun, to qualify for a Register of Merit (ROM), sires must have produced 12 or more American champions and dams five or more American champions. To

BOS at the 1985 KCA National went to Ch. Yan-Kee Starkist, HOF, and her breeder/owner/handler Peter Colcord. Also shown are, left to right: Judge Frank Oberstar, KCA President Jim Davis, Show Secretary Carol Cash and Show Chairman John Sawicki. BOB at this show was Ch. Dal-Kees Mighty Samson, owned and shown by Jan Wanamaker.

A new feature at the KCA Golden Anniversary Specialty held in Westlake, Ohio, was the introduction of obedience team competition. Here the Colorado team, puts their dogs through their paces at the direction of Judge Irma Dixon.

296

qualify for a Register of Merit Excellent (ROMX), sires must have produced 20 or more American champions and dams eight or more. Effective January 1, 1984, the requirements were revised to 12 Champions for ROM sires and seven for ROM dams, and 25 champions for ROMX sires and ten for ROMX dams.

Following is an alphabetical listing of these exceptional producers through the awards presentation at the 1986 KCA specialty:

REGISTER OF MERIT

Sires

Ch. Candray Ghost of Wintergreen (Wanamaker)
Ch. Cornelius Wrocky Selznick, HOF (Flakkee)
Ch. Damarkee The Party Crasher (Springer)
Ch. Dirdon's Fancy Dan (Cummings)
Ch. Emissory of Evenlode (Worley)
Ch. Flakkee Sweepstakes, HOF (Flakkee)
Ch. Foxfair's Persuasive Friend, HOF (Marcelli)
Ch. Graywyn's Hot Shot (Gray)
Ch. Holland Hond's Landmark (Aubut & Cinkosky)
Ch. Karel of Altnavanog (Ruttkay)
Ch. Mar-I-Ben Lamp Lighter (Geiger)
Ch. Nederlan Herman V. Mack, HOF (Hempstead)
Ch. Nether-Lair's Banner De Gyselaer (Peterson)
Ch. Ruttkay Bold Venture (Ruttkay)
Ch. Ruttkay Go Man Go, CD (Matthews)
Ch. Smokywood Outlaw of Carleon (Hellie)
Ch. Tom Tit of Evenlode (Fitzpatrick)
Ch. Waakzaam Winkel, CD (Dayringer)
Ch. Whiplash of Wistonia (Wistonia)
Ch. Wil-Los Jamie Boy (McNamara)
Ch. Windrift's Gambler, CD, HOF (Sinclair)
Ch. Windrift's Willy Weaver (LeHouillier)
Ch. Wrocky of Wistonia (Flakkee)
Ch. Wylco of Wistonia (Flakkee)

Dams

Ch. Ajkeer Magic Sparkle (Kaurman)
Ch. Amanda of Evenlode (Koehne)
Ch. Ashbrook's Kenarae Seawitch (Moss & Bosch)
Ch. Boone's Lady Velvet (Sullivan)
Ch. Candray All That Glitters (Wanamaker)
Ch. Cascadia Dawn Treader (Daugherty)
Confyt Claver Van Klompen
Ch. Conquest's Contessa (Beeman)
Ch. Conquest Penny Pitter Patter (Fulton)
Coughlin's Piipchen Doll (Coughlin)
Ch. Countess Nan-Le-Dar (Hartegan)

Damarkee's Zilver Bairn (Davis & Taylor)
Donlyn's Gizma Gidget (Mooney)
Ch. Fearless Fortune Cookie, CD (Wilhite)
Flakkee Baccarat (Flakkee)
Flakkee Sensation (Flakkee)
Ch. Gae-Kees' Never On Sunday (Gamache)
Ch. Grayfalls Melody of Lo-Mar, CDX (Gray & White)
Ch. Gregory's Pittance of Tryon (Magliozzi)
Ch. Honeycomb's Klementyne (Baxter)
Japar Adelia (Parshall)
Jee Jac's Sparkling Silver (Howard)
Ch. Jomito Zephyr (Kluding)
Katrinka II (Schoenherr)
Ch. Keedox Mischief's Bit A Honey (Brewer)
Ch. Keedox's Koka Kola (Thornton-Rucker)
Ch. Keedox's Mischief (Brewer)
Ch. Keenote's Free Bird (Hartegan)
Ch. Keeszar Mint Julep V. Kenarae (Springer)
Ch. Keli-Kees Cotton Tail (Kelley)
Ch. Keli-Kees Erin O'Mist (Kelley)
Ch. Lorelei Van Ruttkay (Ruttkay)
Ch. Merrikee Sunny Debutante (White)
Ch. Rhapsody of Westcrest (Goebel)
Ron-By's Kandle of Will O'Louise
Ruttkay Jezro's Gay Nathalia (Ruttkay)
Ruttkay Tricia of Kathrdon (Ruttkay & Hellie)
Ruttkay Zilver Frost Van Roem (Scharff)
Silver Tiara of Milmar (Miller)
Ch. Somerville Chelsea Morning (Kelly)
Sonja Sobaka of Holloridge (Katomski-Beck)
Ch. Tassel of Artel (Vincent)
Ch. Traveler's Fly-By-Nite (Schoenfelder)
Ch. Traveler's Zeedrift Carioca (Reed)
Tryon's Dividend (Malet)
Tryon's Instant Mischief (Haberman & Boylan)
Tryon's Ms. Got Wrocks (Daugherty)
Ch. Tryon's Pound Sterling, CD (Haberman & Ellis)
Ch. Vaaker's Mary Poppins (Dorony-Lynch)
Ch. Vandina of Vanellin (Fitzpatrick)
Ch. Van On's Firecracker (Cummings)
Ch. Van On's Fussy Hussy (Worley)
Ch. Virginia of Vorden (LaFore)
Ch. Von Storm's Electra (Nickerson)
Ch. Von Storm's Katydid, CD (Daughty)
Ch. Whimsy of Wistonia (Flakkee)
Windrift's Lovelace (Reed)
Windrift's Midnite Miss (Arnds)
Windrift's Wonder Woman (Hardie & Reed)
Ch. Wynstraat's Delft (Vincent)

High in Trial winner at the 1985 KCA National Specialty was Ruttkay-Valiant Neeko, CDX, shown with owner/handler David Boruff. The judge was Irma Dixon; presenter is Obedience Chairman Bette Poto.

In 1986 tradition was broken for the second time when a bitch was awarded BOB at the KCA National Specialty. Ch. Windrift's High Society, HOF, is shown here with her owner/handler Rita Jacobs. The judge is Nancy Riley; the presenter is Joanne Brown.

REGISTER OF MERIT EXCELLENT (ROMX)

Sires

Ch. Dalbaro Beachcomber (Parshall)
Ch. Flakkee Jackpot, HOF (Flakkee)
Ch. Kee Note's Sterling Silver (Hartegan)
Ch. Rich-Bob's Stormy Weather (Cuneo)
Ch. Racassius of Rhinevale (Olafson)
Ch. Ruttkay Roem (Ruttkay)
Ch. Sinterklaas Brave Nimrod (Kelley)
Ch. Star-Kees' Batman (Stark)
Ch. Star-Kees' Dingbat, CD, HOF (Reed)
Ch. Tryon's Beorn, HOF (Wymore)
Ch. Wistonia Wylie (Wistonia)
Ch. Wynstraat's Kerk (Vincent)

Dams

Ch. Flakkee Winsome Miss, CD (White)
Ch. Keli-Kees Kandi (Johnson)
Ch. Keli-Kees Melody of Killarney (Kelley)
Kenmerk O'Pretty Puss (Worley)
Mil-Elm Majorette (Coci)
Moisje V. Fitz (Fitzpatrick)
Ch. Picvale's Miss Vixon of Banks (Smith & Croken)
Ch. Ruttkay Little Miss Napua (Foster)
Ch. Tryon's Fearless Fruhling (Cuneo)
Ch. Van Fitz Hocage (Cummings)
Ch. Wallbridge's Best Bet (Riley)
Ch. Whincindy of Wistonia (Wistonia)
Ch. Wil-Los Zoet Zang (Bender)
Ch. Wistonia's Sal of Wayward (Coughlin)

The Keeshond Club of America also established a system to recognize top show dogs in both the conformation and obedience rings. To qualify for the conformation Hall of Fame (HOF), a dog must first be a champion. A male must earn 100 HOF points in the United States by winning BOB or BOS at Keeshond specialties, BIS and Group placements at all-breed shows, plus 1,000 Phillips points (number of dogs defeated). To gain the conformation HOF, a bitch must earn 20 HOF points and 200 Phillips points. To qualify for the obedience HOF, a dog must accumulate 100 points through placements in Utility and Open B competition in the United States. The attainment of an OT Ch. would automatically qualify a dog for entry into the HOF.

HALL OF FAME

Ch. Baronwood's Calculated Risk (Smith)
Ch. Baronwood's Flip Wilson (Smith)
Ch. Baronwood's Sling Shot (Smith)
Brown's Little Jenny Sunshine, UD (Brown)
Ch. Charmac's Fortunate Happening (Brown)
Ch. Coincidence of Cari-On (LeHouillier)
Ch. Cornelius Wrocky Selznick (Flakkee)
Ch. DeVignon's Ducomo (Vinion)
Ch. Fearless Flavor for KeesLund (Pomato & Cuneo)
Ch. Flakkee Hijack (Flakkee)
Ch. Flakkee Instamatic (Flakkee)
Ch. Flakkee Instant Replay (Flakkee)
Ch. Flakkee Jackpot, ROMX (Flakkee)
Ch. Flakkee Keeboom Diamond Lil (Witt)
Ch. Flakkee Main Event (Flakkee)
Ch. Flakkee Snapshot (Flakkee)
Ch. Flakkee Sweepstakes, ROM (Flakkee)
Ch. Fritz Van Voornaam, UD (Wray)
Ch. Holland Hond's Landmark (Aubut & Cinkosky)
Ch. Japar Ace In The Hole (Gibson)
Ch. Jul Day Snoodark (Fitzpatrick)
Ch. Jul Day Wunderlust De Sylvia, UD (Dayringer)
Ch. Karolina Ashbrook Contender (Stroud)
Ch. Keedox Bibbidi Bobbidi Boo (Thornton-Rucker)
Ch. Marcy's Teddy Bear, CDX (Zingler)
Ch. Mar-I-Ben Licorice Twist (Bender & Geiger)
Ch. Markwright's Square Rigger (Hudson)
Mefrouw Anneke, UD (Christen)
Milmar's Center of Attention, UD (Willding)
Ch. Nederlan Herman V. Mack, ROM (Hempstead)
Ch. Pandora of Redding, UDT (Brown)
Park Cliffe Cindy Van Pelt, UD (Menninger)
Prins Keesy Van Adrian, UD (Scott)
Ch. Rovic's Chimney Blaze, UD (Rovic)
Ch. Royal J's Duke of Crinklewood (Sullivan)
Ch. Ruttkay Clyde's Cubby (Ruttkay)
Ch. Ruttkay Commander (Hancock)
Ch. Ruttkay Dutch Boy (Brandeau)
Ch. Ruttkay Sirius (Ginsberg)
Ch. Star-Kees' Dingbat, CD, ROM (Reed)
Ch. Tasha Van Konig, UD (Salerno)
Ch. Traveler's Swirling Silver (Smith & Krueger)
Ch. Tryon's Beorn, ROMX (Wymore)
Tuf Feo of Donmina, UD (Whitmore)
Van Bie Ponderosa Koningen, UD (Ballen)
Van Gyzt Hans, UD (Blachnik)

Ch. Vangabang of Vorden (Fitzpatrick)
Ch. Van Mell's Pot of Gold (Van der Meulen)
Ch. Von Storm's Emaria (Riley)
Ch. Von Storm's Emerson Prince Piet (Hempstead)
Ch. Waakzaam Wollenhoven (LaFore & Duncan)
Ch. Wallbridge's Best Bet, ROMX (Riley)
Ch. Wallbridge's Velasko Smokey (Shoudy)
Ch. Walloon's Christmas Holly (Kerns)
OT Ch. Whirlwind's Free Spirit, UD (Turner)
Ch. Windrift's Gambler, CD (Sinclair)
Ch. Windrift's Love Unlimited (Arnds)
Ch. Windrift's Midnight Love (Reed)
Ch. Windrift's Producer (Reed)
Ch. Woffee Brazen Detonation (Doescher & O'Connor)
Ch. Yan-kee Starkist (Colcord)
Ch. Zeedrift Kwikzilver (Sims)

The Kultz Trophy was presented to the KCA by Mrs. Doreen Anderson of Scotland in 1964 as a challenge award to the member-breeder of the most champions recorded during the year. It had to be won three times for permanent possession. Its first winner was Marilyn Bender with four champions finishing in 1964. During the 20-year existence of the trophy, 14 breeders have earned one leg and seven of those 14 have earned two legs. The winners have accounted for 102 American champions. Finally, in its 20th year, the trophy was retired by Helen Cuneo. It is fitting that her "Cookie Monster" — Ch. Tryon's Fearless Fruhling, ROMX — has reached the top of the Dams of American Champions list.

Regional and local Keeshond clubs provide the opportunity to participate with breeders and fanciers in your locale. The following provides a listing of Keeshond clubs and their areas of representation. Those clubs indicated with an * are licensed to hold specialty shows.

* Buckeye Keeshond Club — *northern Ohio*
* Capital Keeshond Club — *Virginia, Maryland, Washington D.C.*
  Friends of Keeshonden — *Houston and southern Texas*
  Greater Charlotte Keeshond Fanciers — *Charlotte, North Carolina area*
  Greater St. Louis Keeshond Club
  Greater Twin Cities Keeshond Club — *Minnesota*
* Heart of America Keeshond Club — *Kansas, Missouri, Nebraska*
* Heritage Trail Keeshond Club — *New England*
  Keeshond Club of Central Florida
* Keeshond Club of Dallas — *northern Texas*
* Keeshond Club of Delaware Valley — *eastern Pennsylvania*
  Keeshond Club of Greater Oklahoma City
  Keeshond Club of North Georgia — *Atlanta and northern Georgia*
  Keeshond Club of Northern New Jersey

* Keeshond Club of Southern California
* Keeshond Fanciers of Central States — *Illinois, Indiana*
* Nor-Cal Keeshond Club — *northern California*
  Ohio Valley Keeshond Club — *southern Ohio*
  Pacific Crest Keeshond Club — *Oregon and Washington*
* Sahuaro Keeshond Club — *Arizona*
  SE Michigan Keeshond Club — *Detroit and southern Michigan*
  SE Wisconsin Keeshond Club
  Twin Peaks Keeshond Club — *Denver, Colorado area*

In addition to the Keeshond Club of America, the parent club of our breed in this country, there is another nation-wide club for Keeshond fanciers. The American Keeshond Society (TAKS) was formed in 1977. Their focus is on education, rescue work and communication. They are not licensed to hold dog shows, but at their annual meeting each year they conduct a Standard Evaluation Clinic. At this clinic, two licensed Keeshond judges and a qualified breeder evaluate eight Keeshonds in accordance with the Standard. It is an excellent learning experience for everyone.

If you are interested in joining any of these local or national organizations, we suggest you contact the American Kennel Club, 51 Madison Avenue, New York, New York 10010 for the name and address of the appropriate club secretary.

BIBLIOGRAPHY

ALL OWNERS of pure-bred dogs will benefit themselves and their dogs by enriching their knowledge of breeds and of canine care, training, breeding, psychology and other important aspects of dog management. The following list of books covers further reading recommended by judges, veterinarians, breeders, trainers and other authorities. Books may be obtained at the finer book stores and pet shops, or through Howell Book House Inc., publishers, New York.

BREED BOOKS

AFGHAN HOUND. Complete	Miller & Gilbert
AIREDALE. New Complete	Edwards
AKITA. Complete	Linderman & Funk
ALASKAN MALAMUTE, Complete	Riddle & Seeley
BASSET HOUND. New Complete	Braun
BLOODHOUND. Complete	Brey & Reed
BOXER. Complete	Denlinger
BRITTANY SPANIEL. Complete	Riddle
BULLDOG. New Complete	Hanes
BULL TERRIER, New Complete	Eberhard
CAIRN TERRIER. New Complete	Marvin
CHESAPEAKE BAY RETRIEVER, Complete	Cherry
CHIHUAHUA. Complete	Noted Authorities
COCKER SPANIEL. New	Kraeuchi
COLLIE, New	Official Publication of the Collie Club of America
DACHSHUND. The New	Meistrell
DALMATIAN. The	Treen
DOBERMAN PINSCHER, New	Walker
ENGLISH SETTER. New Complete	Tuck, Howell & Graef
ENGLISH SPRINGER SPANIEL, New	Goodall & Gasow
FOX TERRIER. New	Nedell
GERMAN SHEPHERD DOG, New Complete	Bennett
GERMAN SHORTHAIRED POINTER, New	Maxwell
GOLDEN RETRIEVER. New Complete	Fischer
GORDON SETTER. Complete	Look
GREAT DANE, New Complete	Noted Authorities
GREAT DANE. The—Dogdom's Apollo	Draper
GREAT PYRENEES. Complete	Strang & Giffin
IRISH SETTER. New Complete	Eldredge & Vanacore
IRISH WOLFHOUND. Complete	Starbuck
JACK RUSSELL TERRIER, Complete	Plummer
KEESHOND. New Complete	Cash
LABRADOR RETRIEVER, New Complete	Warwick
LHASA APSO. Complete	Herbel
MALTESE. Complete	Cutillo
MASTIFF, History and Management of the	Baxter & Hoffman
MINIATURE SCHNAUZER, New	Kiedrowski
NEWFOUNDLAND. New Complete	Chern
NORWEGIAN ELKHOUND. New Complete	Wallo
OLD ENGLISH SHEEPDOG, Complete	Mandeville
PEKINGESE, Quigley Book of	Quigley
PEMBROKE WELSH CORGI, Complete	Sargent & Harper
POODLE, New	Irick
POODLE CLIPPING AND GROOMING BOOK, Complete	Kalstone
PORTUGUESE WATER DOG, Complete	Braund & Miller
ROTTWEILER. Complete	Freeman
SAMOYED, New Complete	Ward
SCOTTISH TERRIER. New Complete	Marvin
SHETLAND SHEEPDOG. The New	Riddle
SHIH TZU, Joy of Owning	Seranne
SHIH TZU, The (English)	Dadds
SIBERIAN HUSKY. Complete	Demidoff
TERRIERS, The Book of All	Marvin
WEIMARANER. Guide to the	Burgoin
WEST HIGHLAND WHITE TERRIER, Complete	Marvin
WHIPPET, Complete	Pegram
YORKSHIRE TERRIER. Complete	Gordon & Bennett

BREEDING

ART OF BREEDING BETTER DOGS, New	Onstott
BREEDING YOUR OWN SHOW DOG	Seranne
HOW TO BREED DOGS	Whitney
HOW PUPPIES ARE BORN	Prine
INHERITANCE OF COAT COLOR IN DOGS	Little

CARE AND TRAINING

BEYOND BASIC DOG TRAINING	Bauman
COUNSELING DOG OWNERS, Evans Guide for	Evans
DOG OBEDIENCE. Complete Book of	Saunders
NOVICE. OPEN AND UTILITY COURSES	Saunders
DOG CARE AND TRAINING FOR BOYS AND GIRLS	Saunders
DOG NUTRITION, Collins Guide to	Collins
DOG TRAINING FOR KIDS	Benjamin
DOG TRAINING, Koehler Method of	Koehler
DOG TRAINING Made Easy	Tucker
GO FIND! Training Your Dog to Track	Davis
GROOMING DOGS FOR PROFIT	Gold
GUARD DOG TRAINING. Koehler Method of	Koehler
MOTHER KNOWS BEST—The Natural Way to Train Your Dog	Benjamin
OPEN OBEDIENCE FOR RING. HOME AND FIELD, Koehler Method of	Koehler
STONE GUIDE TO DOG GROOMING FOR ALL BREEDS	Stone
SUCCESSFUL DOG TRAINING, The Pearsall Guide to	Pearsall
TEACHING DOG OBEDIENCE CLASSES—Manual for Instructors	Volhard & Fisher
TOY DOGS, Kalstone Guide to Grooming All	Kalstone
TRAINING THE RETRIEVER	Kersley
TRAINING TRACKING DOGS, Koehler Method of	Koehler
TRAINING YOUR DOG—Step by Step Manual	Volhard & Fisher
TRAINING YOUR DOG TO WIN OBEDIENCE TITLES	Morsell
TRAIN YOUR OWN GUN DOG, How to	Goodall
UTILITY DOG TRAINING. Koehler Method of	Koehler
VETERINARY HANDBOOK, Dog Owner's Home	Carlson & Giffin

GENERAL

A DOG'S LIFE	Burton & Allaby
AMERICAN KENNEL CLUB 1884-1984—A Source Book	American Kennel Club
CANINE TERMINOLOGY	Spira
COMPLETE DOG BOOK, The	Official Publication of American Kennel Club
DOG IN ACTION, The	Lyon
DOG BEHAVIOR, New Knowledge of	Pfaffenberger
DOG JUDGE'S HANDBOOK	Tietjen
DOG PSYCHOLOGY	Whitney
DOGSTEPS, The New	Elliott
DOG TRICKS	Haggerty & Benjamin
EYES THAT LEAD—Story of Guide Dogs for the Blind	Tucker
FRIEND TO FRIEND—Dogs That Help Mankind	Schwartz
FROM RICHES TO BITCHES	Shattuck
HAPPY DOG/HAPPY OWNER	Siegal
IN STITCHES OVER BITCHES	Shattuck
JUNIOR SHOWMANSHIP HANDBOOK	Brown & Mason
OUR PUPPY'S BABY BOOK (blue or pink)	
SUCCESSFUL DOG SHOWING, Forsyth Guide to	Forsyth
WHY DOES YOUR DOG DO THAT?	Bergman
WILD DOGS in Life and Legend	Riddle
WORLD OF SLED DOGS. From Siberia to Sport Racing	Coppinger